Praise for **After the Affair**

"*After the Affair* is a superb book. This is one of the best self-help books we have read, and it demonstrates that it is possible to share our science and experience with the public in a meaningful way."
—*Behavior Therapist*

"This book is extraordinary in the insight it offers into why an affair occurs, how an affair affects both people in a marriage, and most important, how the healing process can lead a couple to levels of intimacy they have never experienced."
—Kelly D. Brownell, Ph.D., director of clinical training, department of psychology, Yale University

"A hopeful and sensitive guide to healing."
—John Gray, Ph.D., author of *Men Are from Mars, Women Are from Venus*

"For married or cohabiting couples who want to rebuild their relationship after one partner has had an affair, this tough-minded, insightful manual will be eminently practical. . . . This wise book fills a gap on the self-help shelf."
—*Publishers Weekly*

"While partners in [damaged] relationships may see only pain, mistrust and the ashes of their love, clinical psychologist Janis Abrahms Spring offers another vision: the spark of a deeper, stronger relationship."
—*Plain Dealer* (Cleveland)

"*After the Affair* is filled with critical insights, practical advice, and exercises for dealing with anger and rebuilding trust. As a practicing therapist, Dr. Spring recognizes the importance of offering help to both partners as they re-create themselves and their relationship after the affair."
—Dana Crowley Jack, Ed.D., author of *Silencing the Self: Women and Depression*

"Dr. Spring possesses a remarkable combination of clarity, wisdom, spirit, and heart. This is an extremely helpful and healing book—a gift to us all."

—Harriet Lerner, Ph.D.,
author of *The Dance of Anger*

"An outstanding book for couples dealing with the aftermath of an affair. Dr. Spring wisely gives equal consideration to the emotions, doubts, and concerns of both the hurt partner and unfaithful partner."

—Jeffrey Young, Ph.D., author of
Reinventing Your Life

"Dr. Spring provides specific exercises for rebuilding trust, and outlines with a wonderful straightforward delicacy, the steps to begin to feel comfortable with one another affectionately and sexually again. The writing is clear and easy to understand. This is not a formula self-help book, but one that allows for the diverse richness and confusions of our intricate personal relationships."

—*Woman*

"This is a very wise book and I recommend it to clients who are trying to recover from an affair as well as to those who are contemplating starting one!"

—Ellen F. Wachtel, Ph.D., author of
*Treating Troubled Children and Their
Families*

"Done in a sensitive, compassionate style that clearly talks to the reader. I definitely recommend *After the Affair* as a valuable resource for clients and mediators."

—*Mediation News*, Academy of Family
Mediators

"If you do the work Dr. Spring suggests, you'll end up having a better marital relationship than you ever imagined."

—Constance Ahrons, Ph.D., author of
The Good Divorce

AFTER THE AFFAIR

ALSO BY JANIS ABRAHMS SPRING, Ph.D.,
WITH MICHAEL SPRING

How Can I Forgive You?:
The Courage to Forgive, the Freedom Not To (Harper, 2004)

Life with Pop:
Lessons on Caring for an Aging Parent (Avery, 2009)

AFTER THE AFFAIR

*Healing the Pain
and Rebuilding Trust
When a Partner Has
Been Unfaithful*

Completely Updated Second Edition

JANIS ABRAHMS SPRING, PH.D.
WITH MICHAEL SPRING

WILLIAM MORROW
An Imprint of HarperCollinsPublishers

Grateful acknowledgment is made for permission to reprint portions of the following copyrighted material:

Drawing by Bruce Eric Kaplan. Copyright © 1993 *The New Yorker* Magazine, Inc. All rights reserved.

Grown-Ups by Cheryl Mercer. Copyright © 1988 by Cheryl Mercer. Reprinted by permission of the Putnam Publishing Group.

"The Hug" from *The Man with Night Sweats* by Thom Gunn. Copyright © 1992 by Thom Gunn. Reprinted by permission of Farrar, Straus & Giroux, Inc.

Private Lies: Infidelity and the Betrayal of Intimacy by Frank Pittman. Copyright © 1989 by Frank Pittman. Reprinted by permission of W. W. Norton & Company, Inc.

Silencing the Self by Dana Crowley Jack. Copyright © 1991 by Dana Crowley Jack. Reprinted by permission of Harvard University Press.

The Technique of Marriage by Mary Borden. Reprinted by permission of Doubleday, a division of Bantam Doubleday Dell Publishing Group, Inc.

Women Who Run with the Wolves by Clarissa Pinkola Estés, Ph.D. Copyright © 1992, 1995 by Clarissa Pinkola Estés, Ph.D. Reprinted by permission of the author and Ballantine Books, a division of Random House, Inc.

FIRST EDITION

Designed by Caitlin Daniels

Library of Congress Cataloguing-in-Publication has been applied for.

ISBN 978-0-06-212270-4

16   DIX/RRD   20   19   18   17   16   15   14   13   12   11

To my best buddies,
Aaron, Max, and Michael

CONTENTS

Contents

ACKNOWLEDGMENTS

When I first started giving workshops in couples therapy, I'd leave fifteen minutes at the end to discuss the treatment of infidelity. Gradually, as it became clear that virtually nothing had been written on how to help couples who were trying to recover from an affair, I decided to focus my talks and private practice on this topic, and to write this book.

At first, I got mixed reactions. Patients and therapists said, "Great. When can I get a copy?" Friends said, "How exciting. Let's have a party." Acquaintances said, "Thank God this has nothing to do with me." Publishers and editors said, "Yes, there's definitely a need for such a book, but will anyone be brave enough to pick it up and bring it to the cashier?" While I was looking for an editor, I found that more than one was afraid to touch it for fear that it would stir up problems in their relationships. "I have a good marriage," one editor told me. "I'm afraid this material will infect us." Fortunately, once HarperCollins bought the book, and my husband, Michael, agreed to help me write it, everyone seemed to stand behind it.

I never knew what it meant, or took, to write a book. Now I know. And now, every time I walk into a bookstore or library, I am in awe of the incredible expenditure of time and energy so many people make just to put their ideas into print.

I went into this project thinking I was an expert, but the

more I interviewed and treated couples, the more I learned. As Anna says in *The King and I*, "By your pupils you are taught." By listening to my patients and others who have endured a betrayal or who have had affairs themselves, I came to understand how individuals cope with and resolve—or fail to resolve—their infidelity crises. Their candor and self-scrutiny made it possible for me to recognize patterns in what people experience and what they need to heal.

There are many people I'd like to thank for helping me bring this book to completion, including those mentors and colleagues who trained me. When I was just out of graduate school, Dr. Aaron T. Beck, founder of cognitive therapy, let me sit by his side and observe him supervising students at the Center for Cognitive Therapy. He taught me when to intervene and when to remain silent, when to critique a belief and when to leave it alone. He provided a model of therapy and a career for me that has helped me become an effective therapist. I also was fortunate to be supervised by Dr. David D. Burns, who taught me with humor and ingenuity many strategies to help people change. I extend deep appreciation to Dr. Jeffrey Young, who integrated cognitive therapy with other established models and significantly expanded its effectiveness in dealing with more intractable clinical problems. He combed through sections of this manuscript, offering detailed comments about how our childhood affects who we are today. My thanks to Dr. Richard Stuart, Dr. Neil Jacobson, Dr. Norman Epstein, Dr. Don Baucom, Dr. Chris Padesky, and Dr. David Bricker—all of whom have furthered my application of cognitive-behavioral principles to the treatment of distressed couples. I'm also indebted to Dr. Kathryn E. Hertlein and Dr. Kimberly Young for providing current references on cybersex affairs and addiction.

Claire Quigley at the Westport Public Library and Kristina Coop of the University of North Carolina provided much needed library and research assistance.

When everyone else was still debating the salability of this book, my agent, Chris Tomasino, stood by me and encouraged me. She also read every word of the manuscript and offered astute editorial suggestions. Her assistant, Jonathan Diamond, was always available to help me.

I thank Peternelle van Arsdale and Janet Goldstein, my editors at HarperCollins, for shepherding me through this process. My gratitude also to Clio Manuelian, my publicist, for her contagious enthusiasm; Kristen Auclair for managing countless editorial details; Guy Kettelhack for his help in preparing the proposal; and Scott Gould of RLR, my agent, for this second edition.

A special thanks to Gail Winston, my friend and editor for both editions. Thanks also to her assistant, Maya Ziv, and Diane Burrows for their invaluable support.

Also, I thank with all my heart:

My parents, Dolly and Louis Lieff, for years of sacrifice to give me a great education, and for encouraging me to develop my own separate voice.

My brother, Joel, for being a kind soul and always looking out for me.

My stepchildren, Declan and Evan, for their wisdom, and for all the good times we've shared together, away from the computer.

My children, Max and Aaron, who have brought laughter and meaning to my life. I'm so lucky to have lived these years with them by my side.

And my husband, Michael: Is there any activity more intimate than writing a book with someone? I respect (and envy) his perfectionistic eye and extraordinarily clear mind. I'll miss those hours sitting elbow to elbow with him at the computer, fighting fiercely over a word or concept. I thank him for the ton of time he gave this manuscript, and for his wonderful good nature, which kept us going.

INTRODUCTION

Can a Couple Survive Infidelity?

As a clinical psychologist who has been treating distressed couples for thirty-five years, I answer yes—provided that each of you is willing to look honestly at yourself and at your partner, and acquire the skills you need to see yourself through this shattering crisis.

It may help to remind yourself that you're not alone. Statistics vary widely, but according to one of the most recent and reputable studies, as many as 37 percent of married men and 20 percent of married women have been unfaithful.[1] No one knows the exact percentages; I'm sure that someone who lies to a spouse might also lie to a researcher. But even by the most conservative estimate, we can say with some confidence that, in the United States, 1 in every 2.7 couples—more than 21 million—is touched by infidelity.[2]

WHAT CONSTITUTES AN AFFAIR?
Must an affair be coital? What about a kiss? What about lunch?[3]

I don't try to answer these questions because, in the end,

what matters is what matters to you. A breach of trust depends entirely on what you agreed to—or thought you agreed to. Virtually all of you would feel betrayed by a partner who had intercourse with a third person, whether during a one-night stand or as part of a long-term emotional entanglement. But many of you would also feel betrayed, and certainly threatened, by other intimate behaviors—a hug, say, or the sending of a dozen white roses. Five years ago a patient of mine named Sharon took her blouse off and showed her breasts to her best friend's husband. They never went further, but the two couples have been struggling with this violation ever since.

In this second edition, I've added a chapter on the "new" infidelity: the electronic or e-affair. Chapter 10 will help you determine what constitutes an affair in cyberspace and give you the tools you need to negotiate your differences.

THREE JUDGMENTS I DON'T MAKE

1. *I don't make blanket judgments about whether affairs are, in themselves, good or bad.* What may be enhancing for one of you may devastate the other, and destroy the relationship. I have found, however, that a continuing affair, without the consent of both partners, perpetuates the dysfunction in a relationship and makes the forging of an intimate attachment virtually impossible. If you're an unfaithful partner who is serious about reconnecting, you must, I believe, give up your lover.

2. *I don't separate the two of you into victim and victimizer, betrayed and betrayer.* Each of you must accept an appropriate share of responsibility for what went wrong. Rather than assign blame, I encourage each of you to confront those parts of yourself that led to the affair, and to change in ways that rebuild trust and intimacy. That doesn't mean I hold you equally accountable for the affair—no one can make another person stray. But I do ask you both to be accountable for whatever space you created that made room for another person to come between you.

3. *I don't suggest that you should stay together no matter*

what, or bolt just because you feel unhappy. Instead, I invite each of you to explore with me your unique reasons for having or giving up a lover, for choosing or refusing to recommit. Your decision should be deliberate and well-considered, not based on feelings alone. Your feelings, in fact, may betray you.

A WORD ABOUT THE CHOICE OF TERMS

Throughout the text I refer to partners as *hurt* or *unfaithful*. The hurt partner is the person in the primary relationship whose assumption of monogamy has been violated. The unfaithful partner is the one who had the affair. It was difficult choosing labels for these people. Certainly the unfaithful partner may feel equally hurt at times. In general, however, it's the one whose partner strays who experiences the greater sense of devastation. I don't categorize partners as *betrayed* or *betrayer* because these words convey a certain moral righteousness or condemnation, and put the burden of responsibility on one partner alone, which is almost never the case. I refer to the person with whom you or your partner had the affair as the *lover* or the *affair-person*. As a rule, I use the term *lover* when I'm speaking to the unfaithful partner and the affair is still alive. I use the term *affair-person* when I'm speaking to either partner and want to remove the romantic connotations of the word *lover* and protect the feelings of the hurt partner.

The quotes and case studies I refer to throughout the text are drawn from my practice over the years, but I've masked all identities so that I don't violate any confidences.

WHO IS THIS BOOK FOR?

I wrote *After the Affair* primarily for any two people who want to explore the possibility of rebuilding their relationship after one or both of them have been unfaithful. This includes married and cohabiting couples, heterosexuals and same-sex couples. I try to address hurt and unfaithful partners with equal weight.

My book is also for:

- people whose relationship ended as a result of infidelity, who are having a difficult time moving beyond the experience, and who want to understand why the relationship didn't survive and what they should accept as an appropriate share of responsibility for what went wrong;
- people who want to make better sense of the infidelity they experienced in their own families when they were growing up, in order to avoid similar patterns of behavior in their own relationships;
- professionals and spiritual leaders who treat individuals and couples affected by infidelity;[4]
- partners who are thinking of having an affair and who want to understand their feelings better before taking any irreversible steps;
- partners who want to think through the advantages and disadvantages of revealing a terminated affair;
- partners who have no intention of disclosing a terminated affair, but who still want to rebuild their relationship and learn about themselves;
- partners who suspect their mates of infidelity but have never confronted them;
- couples who are struggling with secrets, lies, and trust issues other than infidelity;
- couples who want to learn how to cope with the inevitable disenchantments of conjugal life, before turning elsewhere.

THREE STAGES OF HEALING

The book guides you through three identifiable stages—some would call them minefields—as you react to, grapple with, and recover from the affair.

The First Stage: Normalizing Your Feelings

Once the affair is revealed, both of you are likely to get swept up in an emotional whirlwind, the hurt partner overcome by a profound sense of loss, the unfaithful partner overcome by conflicting choices and emotions. By giving a language to your feelings, I hope to reassure you that you're not crazy or unstable, that others have experienced the same pain and confusion, that you're not alone.[5]

The Second Stage: Deciding Whether to Recommit or Quit

Before your emotions can settle down, you need to confront your ambivalence about whether to stay or leave. By exploring your options, you'll be able to make a thoughtful decision based on your circumstances and needs. "What can I expect from love?" "Should I trust my feelings?" "How can I tell if my partner is right for me?"—these are the types of questions I'll help you answer.

The Third Stage: Rebuilding Your Relationship

If you decide to recommit, you're likely to spend months, perhaps years, working to restore trust and intimacy. By reviewing strategies with you, I hope to give you the tools to:

- decipher the meaning of the affair, and accept an appropriate share of responsibility for it;
- say goodbye to the lover;
- earn back trust (if you're the unfaithful partner), or communicate what you need to trust again (if you're the hurt partner);
- talk in ways that allow your partner to hear you and understand your pain, and listen in ways that encourage your partner to be open and vulnerable with you;
- recognize how you may have been damaged by early life experiences, and how you can keep these experiences from contaminating your relationship today;
- manage your differences and dissatisfactions, so that you can stay attached even when you don't feel particularly loved or loving;
- become sexually intimate again;
- forgive your partner, and yourself.

I assume throughout the book that the secret is known, but in some cases it won't be. In the Epilogue, I help you, the unfaithful partner, weigh the pros and cons of telling. Whatever you decide, you and your partner can still work to renew your life together.

A DEATH KNELL OR A WAKE-UP CALL?

Some of you may not want to risk starting over and exposing yourself to further hurt or disappointment. Turning your back on a damaged relationship may be the simplest or most sensible solution, one that frees you from the tyranny of hope. But it may also be a way to escape growing up, facing some bitter truths about life, love, and yourself, and assuming the terrible burden of responsibility for making your relationship work.

This book reaches out to those of you who are deeply wounded by an affair but are conflicted enough or courageous enough to admit that you may still want to stay together, confront how you each contributed to the infidelity, and work to rebuild trust and intimacy. If you choose to recommit to each other, you may in time come to see the affair not merely as a regrettable trauma but as an alarm, a wake-up call. You may eventually discover that you needed a nuclear explosion like an affair to blow your previous construction apart and allow a healthier, more conscious and mature version to take its place. Given how battered you both feel, you may not have many chances to test the strength of your relationship. I encourage you to enter the process, to challenge the hurt, and to see what you're capable of producing together. In essence, on the count of three, I invite the two of you to step into the center of the ring, remove your boxing gloves, and join hands.

STAGE ONE

Reacting to the Affair:
"Is What I'm Feeling Normal?"

ONE

The Hurt Partner's Response:
Buried in an Avalanche of Losses

"When I was fifteen, I was raped. That was
nothing compared to your affair. The rapist was a
stranger; you, I thought, were my best friend."

"When I first uncovered your secret, I stopped
feeling special to you. But on a deeper level,
I lost trust in the world and in myself."

These comments only begin to suggest the profound and
sweeping losses you're likely to experience when you first learn
that your partner has been unfaithful. There's no way to prepare yourself for this crushing revelation. Your view of your
life and the world you live in may be ripped apart. Whatever
self-assurance and security you felt in the past may now seem
naive or false. "Where have I been?" you ask yourself. "Do I live
on this planet?"

Your mind and body are likely to be in shock. Gone is your fundamental sense of order and justice in the world. Gone, too, are your sense of control over your life, your self-respect, your very concept of who you are. You may feel abandoned by everyone—family, friends, God. A stranger to yourself, you may swing wildly from one extreme to another, determined and confident one moment, humiliated and needy the next. Battered by feelings so intense, you may start to wonder, "Am I going crazy?"

I want to assure you that you're not—that, in fact, what you're experiencing is a normal and appropriate response to an acutely traumatizing experience. You're reeling not only from the loss of the integrity of your relationship but also from the loss of an illusion—that you're special to your partner, and that the intimacy you thought you shared with that person would last forever. In the face of such shattering news, it would be strange if you didn't feel lost.

It took Marsha, a forty-year-old social worker and mother, more than a decade to find her feet again:

After thirteen years of marriage, Larry announced he was trading me in for the babysitter, a girl fourteen years his junior. My first reaction was, "This couldn't possibly be happening to us, we're the perfect couple. The baby-sitter's almost a daughter to me, how could she betray my trust?" When Larry moved in with her, I went to bed for a month. Overnight, I went from a person who was capable, independent, full of zest, to a total zombie— paralyzed by a depression I had known only from an academic distance. One night I was lying in bed comparing the silence in the house with the terror and confusion in my head, when I heard the garage door rattle open. "He's come back," I thought. "He wants to work it out." I raced downstairs in my pajamas—first looking in the mirror to check how I looked—only to realize that the garage door had never budged. I had imagined the whole thing.

It suddenly occurred to me: "I've not only lost my spouse, I've lost my mind." My confidence continued to plummet. I saw myself as a fraud, a hollow shell, too empty to practice therapy, parent a child, or deserve a decent partner. Life belonged to others, not to me. I was still struggling with my depression three years later—long after my husband and I were back together—when I learned in a workshop on Post-Traumatic Stress Disorder[1] that someone under extreme emotional stress is likely to withdraw from life and lose touch with themselves, even experience delusions. My mind clicked: So that was it. My depression had a name. I wasn't cracking up; what I was going through was normal. If only I had known earlier, I would have felt less alone and perhaps opened myself up sooner to the possibility of a future. If only someone had helped me understand what happens, that would have been an act of supreme kindness.

This is where this chapter begins, in preparing you for the losses virtually all hurt partners are bound to experience in the crucible of infidelity. Once you realize how universal your responses are, you're likely to feel less gutted by the betrayal, less rocked by your own fierce emotions. Once you can anticipate your reaction and give it a name, it should become more tolerable to you. The healing process begins when you bear witness to your feelings and make sense of your pain. What's critical to remember is this: The greatest threat to recovery is the loss of hope itself.

THE PHYSIOLOGICAL IMPACT OF THE AFFAIR

It's likely at this moment that you're undergoing physiological changes in both your nervous system and your cognitive functioning. As adrenaline and other stress-related hormones pour into your sympathetic nervous system, you experience a heightened state of arousal. You're constantly on the lookout for signs that your partner is straying again. Chronically anxious and agitated, you take longer to fall asleep, awaken frequently during the night, and are more sensitive to noise. You become exhausted from sleeping too little and thinking entirely too much.

Your mind is punctured by vivid and upsetting memories, sensations, images. When you are asleep, the quality of your dreaming becomes more violent and alarming. When you are awake, you find yourself suddenly lost or otherwise disoriented.

What happened to Gloria, a thirty-year-old journalist, is typical. "The day after my husband admitted he was having an affair, I got lost going to work," she told me. "I was terrified that I was going crazy. I mean, this was a route I had followed daily for five years."

Pam, a thirty-seven-year-old real estate agent, tells a similar story: "When Jeff admitted that he was in love with another woman, I made him pack his bags and move out. The next weekend I went to visit friends on Block Island to avoid facing my loneliness. On my way I stopped at a golf tournament and walked the course. So far, so good. But when it came time to return to my car, I couldn't remember where it was. I finally found it after an hour of searching, but I was so shaken, I drove home crying all the way. I canned the weekend and stayed home in bed instead. It wasn't my spaciness that upset me so much, it was the meaning I gave to it, that I was losing my mind."

Because of alterations to your nervous system, your intense emotions may overwhelm you with a sense of terror and helplessness. "The whole apparatus for concerted, coordinated and purposeful activity is smashed,"[2] writes Abram Kardiner, describing the neurophysiological effects of trauma.

Another, very different physiological change takes place with the release of endogenous opioids, similar to morphine, into your nervous system. This dulls your perception of pain and shields you from extreme emotional stress. In other words, your body constricts, goes into hibernation, shuts down. Your range of feelings and sensations narrows, and you lose interest in relationships and activities that only weeks before gave you pleasure and purpose. As you struggle to pull yourself together, you find yourself barely functioning. Your mind wanders. You have trouble concentrating. At work, you shuffle papers across your desk; at home, you sit staring off into space. Having lost confidence in your ability to interact with the world, you shrink back into yourself, into isolation. You feel oddly numb and detached.

"It's like going through the motions of living, aware that a part of you has died," explained Stephanie, a forty-two-year-old special education teacher. "I once felt like John and I were connected by a golden thread. I'd glance across the room and feel the energy drawing us to each other. Now the best I can say is, I'm managing. We're still together, but inside I'm dead."

In his novel *Separation*, author Dan Franck describes the hurt partner's emotions as the reality of his wife's affair sinks in: "He has been living in terror; but it now gives way to smooth, dull shores of sadness. Terror is mobile; sadness stagnant. Like water in a vase."[3]

THE PSYCHOLOGICAL IMPACT OF THE AFFAIR

There are nine different types of losses that you, the hurt partner, are likely to experience. All are variations on one very basic loss, one that goes beyond the loss of your partner: the loss of self. It may be hard for you to recognize this loss in any of its forms, because none of them is tangible. But though you look the same to others, inside you're likely to be hemorrhaging. Suddenly you feel you've lost your:

1. Identity
2. Sense of specialness
3. Self-respect for debasing yourself and forfeiting your basic values to win your partner back
4. Self-respect for failing to acknowledge that you were wronged
5. Control over your thoughts and actions
6. Fundamental sense of order and justice in the world

7. Religious faith
8. Connection with others
9. Sense of purpose—even the will to live

Loss of Identity: "I no longer know who I am."
The discovery of your partner's affair forces you to redefine yourself in the most fundamental way. "If you, my life partner, are not the person I thought you were, and our marriage is a lie, then who am I?" you ask. Suddenly you see yourself as fractured, disfigured, different from how you've ever known yourself before.

In the past, you may have described yourself as capable, independent, funny, bold, friendly, warm, stable, loving, generous, attractive. No more. Now you experience yourself in a hundred negative ways—as jealous, enraged, vengeful, out of control, petty, diminished, bitter, frightened, lonely, physically ill, defiled, ugly, mistrustful, socially disgraced. Blinded by your partner's deception, you lose sight of your familiar self and doubt your goodness, your desirability, your basic ability to negotiate with the world.

" 'Vibrant, athletic, plucky'—that's what they called me in my college yearbook," reminisced Jane, a thirty-one-year-old accountant married five years. "Now, after John's affair, I don't seem to have the energy, or inclination, to even go outside. I feel too exposed."

Roberta, married fourteen years, also grappled with her sudden loss of identity. "I used to like myself. I used to think of myself as a nice person, as a loving, lovable human being. That's gone. I can't stop thinking that the reason Don cheated on me is because I'm too sweet, too ordinary. Maybe I'm alone for a reason. Maybe no one worth knowing would want to be in a relationship with me."

If you're as depressed as Roberta, you're likely to magnify your defects and accept excessive blame for your partner's adulterous behavior. Whatever you loathed about yourself now defines you. You alone, you assume, have caused this terrible thing to happen. "If only I remodel myself, I can win my partner back," you think, deceiving yourself into believing that the fate of your relationship is in your hands. Later on, you should be able to look at yourself more objectively, and assign blame more equitably. Right now, though, you're unlikely to have the distance or perspective to be fair to anyone, least of all yourself.

The loss of your basic sense of self is an injury that cuts much deeper than the infidelity itself. What could be more distressing than the experience of being stuck in skin that feels alien to you, disconnected from that core self you always counted on to tell you who you are?

Loss of Your Sense of Specialness: "I thought I meant something to you. Now I realize I'm disposable."

Swept away with your sense of self is your conviction that you and your partner were meant for each other, that no one could make your partner happier, that together you formed a primal and irreducible union that could not be shared or severed. The affair marks the passing of two innocent illusions—that your marriage is exceptional, and that you are unique or prized.

By the time Miriam reached her teens, she had been raped by her stepfather and abandoned by her mother, who refused to believe her allegations. Miriam came to view herself as damaged goods and found herself drawn to men who treated her as shoddily as her parents had. After putting herself through secretarial school, she got a job as a receptionist at a law firm. There she met Ed. At first she distrusted his interest in her— why would anyone be drawn to her for herself? she wondered. Gradually, however, she came to rely on his generosity and protection. After living with him for three months, she agreed to marry him. She wasn't passionately in love with him, but he was the first man who made her feel decent, valued, clean. When she discovered, a year later, that he was sleeping with his secretary, she lost her newly found self-esteem. "You were the most special person in the world to me," she told him, "my best friend, the first person I could totally trust. I felt completely safe with you and could tell you anything. But what mattered even more was that you allowed me to believe in me—that I was okay, that what had happened to me as a child wasn't my fault, wasn't because I was bad. For the first time in my life I felt special and loved for who I was. Now I realize that I'm disposable, garbage."

When you, like Miriam, are willfully discarded by someone who once made you feel irreplaceable, you may devalue yourself not only as a partner but also as a parent. Demoralized by the destruction of your nuclear family, you may write off your importance to your children, and believe that you have little to give to anyone, even those who love and need you the most.

"I thought seriously about getting a one-way ticket out of here, leaving everyone and everything behind," confessed Nancy, the mother of a nine-month-old girl. "I felt I couldn't compete with Jim's girlfriend—she seemed so young and alive compared to me. Why would my child want to be with me, the loser? What could I possibly offer her? I lost my sense of myself as a nurturing, significant, worthy human being. Thank God I came to see this was just my depression talking and stayed put. Maybe I wasn't special to Jim anymore, but I was still my daughter's only mother."

When you, like Nancy, lose your sense of specialness and feel like a ghost of the person you once were, it's important to realize that your perception of yourself, filtered as it is through your partner's infidelity, shouldn't be trusted. Your ability to see yourself clearly right now is likely to be at an all-time low.

Loss of Self-Respect for Debasing Yourself and Forfeiting Your Basic Values to Win Your Partner Back: "I'll do anything to keep this relationship together."
Nothing may seem more unforgivable to you than the way you prostrate yourself to win your partner back once the affair is revealed. Your desperate acts, you realize, violate your core values and principles. Not only has your partner abandoned you, *you've* abandoned you.

Jane's story is a poignant example of the extremes to which you may go to wrest your partner back—extremes that later fill you with shame and rage.

"A year before I learned about my husband's affair, I developed breast cancer," she told me. "The radical mastectomy and silicone implant seemed to restore order to my life. But when Dave told me he was involved with another woman, I got so depressed I couldn't eat and quickly lost ten pounds—leaving my healthy breast looking flat compared to my artificially puffed up one. So I decided to have that breast inflated as well. I can't believe I was stupid enough to think this would matter. The plastic surgeon I consulted never questioned my motives or informed me of the hazards. A mammography expert cautioned me against manipulating the healthy breast tissue—it might make it harder to inspect it in the future, he said—but I chose not to listen to him and went ahead with the surgery. What seemed everything to me was my appearance, my ability to compete physically with my husband's lover. Of course what eventually happened was I gained back the weight, and now my healthy breast is fuller than the removed one."

Jane's husband returned to the marriage, but she continued to flagellate herself. "I'm left facing myself, wondering, 'Where was I? Where was my head? How could I have been so out of touch with myself? How could my priorities have been so screwed up?' I'm left looking at myself in the mirror, trying to piece together what happened."

Ruth, a forty-seven-year-old accountant, offers another example of how hurt partners sacrifice their dignity and self-respect to keep their relationships alive. "I couldn't help feeling competitive, actually inferior, to Jerry's young lover," she told me, "so I spent—I should say wasted—hours, as well as a fortune, trying on skimpy underwear in the Bloomingdale's lingerie department when I should have been visiting my mother, who was in the hospital recuperating from the removal of a cancerous tumor. It's so depressing, I feel sick just telling you about it. I'm humiliated by what I've done—by what I've become."

Jed, a thirty-three-year-old editor in one of New York's major book publishing houses, struggled with the same issues:

My wife, Julie, promised me maybe a hundred times she'd break up with her boyfriend, and each time I believed her. Once she asked my permission to go off for the weekend with him so they could test their love, and I was crazy enough to agree. Of course she kept right on seeing him. Then she asked me to move into our beach cottage for a few days so the two of them could have a final fling in our New York apartment. Can you believe that I went along? I felt like someone forced into exile, like an accomplice to a crime.

At the time, I guess I felt I had no choice. I had a lousy salary and couldn't afford to just walk out. But by agreeing to something so clearly unagreeable, I changed inside. I felt violated by Julie, but worse, I felt violated by *me*. We're back together again, but I'm still struggling to regain my self-respect. I mean, I gave her no ultimatum. I hardly fought back. I went numb, like an animal in captivity. I figured she'd come back to me, the way she always did, and I was right. But I never asked myself, "What's in this for me? And at what price?"

For anyone who feels like Jed or Jane or Ruth, it's important to understand that your basic values haven't changed, but that this emotional maelstrom has temporarily shattered your ability to make thoughtful decisions in defense of your best self. In time you'll develop a clearer and more compassionate picture of what you're going through and why you're acting the way you are. If you feel you've lost yourself, be assured that you're not alone, and that your response is exactly appropriate to your injury. The emotional shock makes virtually everyone behave in ways that engender self-hatred and regret. If you can accept how deeply the infidelity has altered you, both physiologically and psychologically, perhaps you can learn not to judge yourself so harshly.

Loss of Self-Respect for Failing to Acknowledge That You Were Wronged: "Why didn't I draw the line?"

Your self-respect may crumble when you look back at those days before the secret was revealed and realize how you hid from your suspicions, or kept them to yourself. "How could I have accepted my partner's denials so meekly?" you wonder. "How could I have been so stupid and cowardly that I didn't confront my partner with the truth?"

Obviously, not all suspicions are justified; some people mistrust obsessively and imagine what isn't true. Often, however, the clues are unmistakable.

After his wife's affair, Tom recoiled in disbelief at how he had intuited what was going on for months but had stuffed it away in a corner of his mind: "My wife sells computer software and travels a lot. Once, when she flew back from London, I thought I'd surprise her and pick her up at the airport. I saw her and her boss walking out together through the customs area, and from the way he touched her waist, I knew instantly they were lovers. But what did I do? I left without her ever knowing I was there, and sent her flowers with a note that said, 'I'm afraid I'm losing you.' When she read it, she scoffed at me for feeling insecure, and you know what? I needed to hear this so badly, I made myself believe it. I began to doubt what I had seen. Inside, though, I knew."

Betty, a psychologist married eleven years, was equally mystified by the magic she performed in her head to dispose of disturbing information: "When I got back from a behavior therapy convention—it was out of town—I asked my husband, Jim, how he'd spent his Saturday night. He told me he had felt exhausted and gone to bed right after dinner. Well, for some reason I also asked the babysitter what she had done that night. She told me she had stayed up late talking to Jim about his career—at the kitchen table. I knew the stories clashed, but I couldn't deal with the implications. The idea of striking out on my own was more than I could handle. I said nothing. But the truth was so obvious, it's embarrassing."

Dave, married four years, told me how he handled a similar deceit: "One day I found an unopened condom in my wife's car. It was a different brand than we normally used, so I asked her about it. She tossed off some excuse—that it was a sample that came in the mail—a story not even the biggest moron would have swallowed. I look back now and wonder why I didn't confront her, why I didn't draw the line."

Dave, Betty, Tom—all of them muzzled their voices and stopped trusting what they knew at some level to be true. To preserve their illusions, they denied the legitimacy of their suspicions. Their failure to process or protest what was happening compromised their greatest asset—their authentic selves. "The loss of self coincides with a loss of voice in relationship," Dana Crowley Jack points out in *Silencing the Self*. "Voice is an indicator of self."[4]

Once the affair is out in the open, you can expect to swing to the other extreme of hypervigilance. Your suspicions are likely to be so visceral, so relentless, that whatever your partner says or does, you can no longer distinguish truth from fiction. Not only can't you trust your partner, you're also unable to trust your own perceptions. "What's my partner hiding from me," you wonder, "and what am I hiding from myself?"

On some level, this transformation from blindness to watchfulness is adaptive; the mind retains the memory of the injury to protect you from future harm. Should you and your partner split up, your mistrust is likely to follow you into other relationships. Should you stay together, it may lessen if your partner proves to be dependable, but it's unlikely ever to completely disappear.

Loss of Control Over Mind and Body: "How do I turn my head off? How do I stop myself?"

As you try to unscramble what has happened to you, both your thoughts and actions may spin out of control. You're likely to become more obsessional, dwelling on your partner's lies, the details of the affair, the events that led to it. You may also become more compulsive at work and play, pushing harder and more frenetically to diffuse your anxiety. None of these responses, however, will give you the relief you seek. Let's look at a few of them and see why.

Obsessive Thoughts: "How do I turn my head off?"
The mind has a mind of its own and, at times like these, refuses to be controlled. Your obsessions take over, and you find yourself staring off into space as images of your spouse and the affair-person bombard your consciousness, interrupting your sleep or concentration.

From the day Lynn learned about Mark's affair, she became fixated on it. "I keep thinking the same thoughts—like a broken record, like a broken head," she told me. "I have endless, imaginary conversations with him: 'I was always there for you, Mark,' I tell him; 'I was always there.' I wake up at three A.M., dreaming of him and this woman in bed together, wondering how she touched him, how he thrilled her. I keep playing it through my head, trying to make better sense of it, but all I do is make myself sick."

Another hurt partner, Steve, spent every free moment piecing together the clues to his wife's deception. Alone or with her, he kept playing the same mental tape: "You mean when you said you were off on a business trip on our anniversary last May, you were really with *him*?" "When I walked in on you, talking on the phone, you were talking to *him*—in our bedroom?"

"As much as I hate being cheated on," Steve told me, "what really gets to me is how my mind's been contaminated. I never used to think like this."

Don't be surprised if you find yourself conjuring up scenes of violent revenge against your partner or the affair-person. The viciousness of these images may alarm you—they're so uncharacteristic of the way you normally think—but under the circumstances they're not abnormal.

"I used to consider myself fairly laid back," a hurt partner told me. "Now I'm consumed with hate. I hear myself hurling insults at my wife and her boyfriend, wanting them to suffer, too. Yesterday, when I saw him crossing the street, I thought of running him over. In the end, it's *me*, of course, who suffers. They couldn't care less how crazy I've become."

If your ruminations are seriously compromising your ability to function, you can turn ahead to Chapter 8 for suggestions on how to short-circuit them. You can also consult a physician for medication to calm you down and help you sleep at night. At the same time, try to accept what's happening within you as an appropriate reaction to the shock of the revelation. The most you may be able to do right now is to step back and observe your obsessions with compassion. Though they lead nowhere fruitful, they're your mind's way of imposing order and justice on your world and giving yourself a sense of control.

Compulsive Behavior: "How do I stop myself?"
Your mistrust will cause you to behave compulsively, reflexively—without reason or restraint.

"It's been six months since I found out what was going on with his assistant," Marge told me, "but I can't stop myself from picking through his jacket pockets, desk drawers, you name it. When he's asleep, I scroll through his messages. I walk by restaurants and hotels where he used to take his girlfriend; I learned how to track his whereabouts on his iPhone. I call him at the office to see if he's there, and if he's not, I use his password to listen to his voice mail. I occasionally hire a private investigator to see if he's where he says he is. I even count his Viagra pills to see if he's been with someone else. I watch, I check, I set traps. And I waste an unbelievable amount of time and money. I know I'm out of control, but I can't seem to help myself. Who made me a detective?"

You, like Marge, are no doubt determined never to be made a fool of again. If your partner pledges fidelity, a certain amount of checking can provide a dose of concrete reassurance. Your constant vigilance, however, is likely to exhaust you physically and mentally, and further undermine your self-respect. It certainly won't bring back the trust or closeness you're hoping to restore.

Checking up on your partner is only one form of excessive behavior. Smoking, drinking, shopping, redecorating—these are all ways of trying to reduce your anxiety, dull your pain, and reward yourself in the few ways you have available to you.

You may also find yourself becoming more sexual, sometimes in irresponsible or inappropriate ways. A patient named Gail is typical: "The night I found out about Tom's affair, I went out to a bar, got drunk, and had unprotected sex with a stranger. I didn't even know the guy's name. The next day I went to a wedding and found myself flirting with my college roommate's husband. I was so crazed, I even tried to pick up some guy sitting next to me on the subway. The whole thing is mortifying, the way I flaunted and cheapened myself. It's not that my behavior was unjustified or immoral; it was stupid and self-destructive. It was as if, because I was hurt, I had to let the world know that nothing mattered. It was as if, because I was made to feel like a nobody, I had to treat everyone else that way, too. I was so bitter, I wanted to wipe out everything good or decent—including myself."

Another common form of compulsive behavior is excessive exercise and dieting—activities that, you hope, will give you more control over your life, make you more attractive to your partner, and restore your self-esteem. While there are some short-term benefits to these activities—you may improve your health, become more physically fit, and release pent-up tensions—you should realize that, in your hypercritical and depressed state, you're in no shape to evaluate your physical attractiveness, and you risk subjecting yourself to a regimen that's punishing, depriving, and extreme. Go ahead and pump iron or live on salads if that makes you feel better, but understand that no Cybex workout or Mediterranean diet will get at the root problems—your fear of abandonment and your shattered sense of self.

Another type of compulsive behavior is seeking out people who have influence over your partner and exhorting them to help you get your partner back. If nothing else, this keeps your hopes afloat and, like excessive exercise, gives you the illusion of power over, or at least some say in, the fate of your relationship. It's hard to sit passively and watch your life fall apart.

"I was frantic to get Glenn back so I spent hours micromanaging relationships with anyone he might listen to," recalled Abbey. "I contacted both of his parents and several of his best friends and pleaded with them, please, to talk to him. I called his brothers and their wives—even the priest. I threatened to take the kids out of state if the marriage broke up—not that I'd ever go, but I wanted to get to his parents, who couldn't bear losing their grandchildren and would pressure him to stay with me. I was swinging in the dark, but I refused to just wait around and pray for his return."

Some of you are likely to find yourselves moving compulsively between extremes, determined to save your relationship one minute, and end it the next. "My mood keeps changing," a hurt partner named Tina explained. "I wake up wanting to have nothing to do with my husband, and stay as far away as I can. An hour later, I love him to death and want to spend every minute with him. I'm constantly asking myself, 'Is he really worth fighting for?' When I answer yes, I act as sweet as possible, work on looking great, and cook him his favorite dinners. I'm not going to make it easy for him to leave me. But then I wonder, 'Do I really want this guy; he's hideous,' and I make an appointment with the attorney and arm myself to fight for my rights. It's not that I can't make decisions, I can't *stop* making them."

To divert yourself and ward off loneliness, you may make too many plans with too many people who mean nothing to you. Like other forms of compulsive behavior, these distractions serve as a temporary antidote to feelings of anxiety or emptiness. But if you want to put yourself back together, you need to slow down, confront your pain, figure out why the affair happened, and decide what you want to do about it.

It's scary to feel that you've lost control over your mind and body, that your mind wields so little influence over the way you conduct your life. Rest assured, however, that though you're experiencing yourself in odd ways, your behavior is not odd.

Loss of Your Fundamental Sense of Order and Justice in the Universe: "The world no longer makes sense."

You may have thought that you understood how the world works and that, through this understanding, you could exert some control over your life. "What goes around comes around," "As ye sow so shall ye reap"—these and other maxims you once lived by may have seemed unassailable. When you learn of your partner's affair, however, your belief in the order and justice of the world gets blown apart, and with it, your assumption that you are good, and that the world is fundamentally safe and meaningfully ordered.

When you suffer a personal violation of this magnitude, you're forced to confront your basic ideas about what's fair and just in every aspect of life, including love and marriage. You may never have articulated these assumptions, but once they're contradicted, you'll be struck by how much you depended on them. Your belief that if you did X, Y would follow—that you could anticipate and then do what was needed to be loved—made you feel effective and secure, and gave your world a structure you could count on. Now you realize how little control you have over your own happiness, and how little you can depend on being treated fairly by anyone, even the people you love.

When Sam learned that his wife, Jane, was sleeping with a twenty-three-year-old carpenter, his whole world came unglued: "I had thought of myself as a basically decent husband who earned his wife's love," he told me. "I was completely committed to her and tried to be there for her—helping around the house, working with her on her graduate school papers. I tried to be even-tempered and considerate, even when she wasn't. My mother used to say, 'Treat your wife like a queen and she'll make you her king.' What a joke. Maybe I failed her in some major way, but she never let on or gave me a chance to change. Now I feel misled and cheated. I see you don't win any prizes for being decent; in fact, you can get kicked in the face. I hate her for what she's done to me. I've become cynical and selfish, and I doubt I'll ever see people as good, or love as good, again."

Before the emotional anarchy of the affair, you, like Sam, probably held certain common assumptions about how relationships work:

- "I have some say over how my marriage goes."
- "If I'm basically a good and loving person, I'll be loved in return."
- "If I'm a decent partner, my marriage will be safe."
- "I know what to do to make my partner happy."
- "I can trust my best friend."

These ideas, once so self-evident, now may strike you as terribly naive. Rather than give them up, however, you may question your goodness, your decency, your judgment. In an effort to make sense of it all, you may start believing that you got what you deserved.

Depressed, confused, you may assume either that the world doesn't work according to the principles you once took for granted (a condition that leads to outer chaos), or that *you* don't measure up (an idea that leads to inner chaos). Not now perhaps, but later on, you'll see that both of these perspectives are exaggerated and overgeneralized. You really don't have to crucify yourself, or the world. Life is not so random, nor you so foul.

Loss of Religious Faith: "Why has God forsaken me?"

Some of you, trying to explain your suffering, may feel punished or abandoned by your God. As Rabbi Harold Kushner points out in *When Bad Things Happen to Good People*, when people are struck by misfortune, the question they most frequently ask is: "If God existed, if He was minimally fair, let alone loving and forgiving, how could He do this to me?"[5]

However you see it—a cruel God betrayed you, an indifferent God deserted you, a just God found you unworthy and gave you what you deserved—you're likely to be robbed of the solace you once found in religion or religious ritual, and to feel more alone and needy than ever before.

Your faith may be further eroded by what you see as the insensitivity or aloofness of your religious mentors, and the loss of the spiritual family from which you derived both a sense of social identity and emotional support. At a time when you're looking to community leaders for psychic renewal, reinforcement of traditional family values, or basic comfort, you may feel terribly let down.

Some members of the clergy will spoon out the old religious platitudes, telling you, for instance, that if you forgive, you shall be forgiven. Others, concerned about contributions and church attendance, won't want to take sides. Many will be sensitive and supportive, of course, but, given how wretched you're feeling, it's possible that no one can console you right now.

Though it was Rachel's husband who had the affair, it was she who felt shunned by her rabbi:

My religious faith always mattered a great deal to me. I was president of the local Jewish family services when my husband, the great, respected Jewish leader of the community, moved in with a non-Jewish girl. I don't know if I went into hiding or if people shied away from me, but I felt rejected by everyone in the community, even the rabbi. Once, when I saw him putting his arm around my husband, I thought, "This is the man who batmitzvahed me, married me, and brissed both of my kids. Someday he will bury my parents." Somehow I thought that he, if anyone, would come through for me, but whenever I caught his eye after services, he turned away. When he continued to say nothing—no advice, no words of commiseration—I decided, "This is it; I don't want to be Jewish." To rid myself of my pain, I renounced my religion.

I needed to separate myself, to find a different identity, even if it was an anti-identity. My husband returned eventually, but it took eight years before I could feel comfortable observing the Jewish rituals again. One day I went to see the rabbi and confronted him with my rage. He seemed to have had no idea, all those years, how hurt and alone I had been. Now that he knew, he told me he felt hurt *I hadn't come to him* earlier for direction.

There's no way to know for sure, but my guess is that he was too timid, too political, to get involved. My husband, after all, was influential. As far as I was concerned, here was one more man who didn't have the courage or humanity to extend himself beyond his own self-interests and who expected me to make him feel important. Go fuck yourself, is how I felt. I discarded a lot of dead wood in those months and began to find other ways to embrace my spiritual needs.

For you, as for Rachel, being let down by religious leaders can turn your faith into a mockery and your God into a detached and powerless figurehead. Whether your disillusionment is with a member of the clergy or with God Himself, you're likely to feel abandoned by one of your most familiar and profound sources of affirmation and spiritual sustenance. Try to keep in mind that such feelings are normal at this stage and do not necessarily presage a permanent loss of faith.

Loss of Connection with Others: "Who can I confide in? Who's there for me?"

Your sense of shame and inferiority may make you think that everyone's talking about you and avoiding you like the plague—why else have they stopped calling to say hello or invite you out?

While one part of you wants to reach out and tell the world how you've been violated, another part wants to remain silent and alone. One moment you're craving confirmation that you're a likable human being, and clinging to anyone who will listen to your story and acknowledge that you've been harmed. The next, you're withdrawing into isolation, driven by a sense of pride, a fear of ridicule, and a perverse sense of responsibility for protecting the very person who deceived you.

Mary, the daughter of a well-established investment banker, was raised to keep family secrets and to solve problems for herself. When she found out about her husband's affair, she badly needed to connect with family and friends, but sealed herself off instead. "After what that bastard did to me, it's unbelievable that I saw it as my sacred job to protect his name," she told me, looking back. But when he continued to play around, she allowed herself to seek the support of allies. "Let him worry about his own reputation," she said.

If your parents are alive, you're likely to agonize about telling them. Whatever you decide to do involves substantial risk and leaves you asking yourself: "Will their knowing make future family gatherings unbearable? Will turning them against my partner make it more difficult for my partner to stay? Do I really want my parents to know my relationship is in trouble? Do I want to be dependent on them—to be cradled by them—again? Can I deal with their pity, their disapproval, their condemnation? Do I want to share with them the messy, humiliating details of the affair? Once I've become their child again, how will I break away?"

If you're a parent, you're bound to agonize about telling your kids. "Is it wise to burden them with the ugly truth?" you ask. "Are they too young to understand?" You long for their compassion, but worry about turning them against their other parent. One side of you says, "Yes, I'd love to poison their relationship with the person who destroyed me. I'd love to get even. I want the kids to love me more." But another side—the one that knows that each parent is an irreplaceable role model, and that children learn what it means to be an adult from both parents—reels at the idea of forcing them to split loyalties. "Do I want them to grow up with an incomplete or warped sense of self?" you ask. "What will the truth do to their ideas about themselves? Will they be more likely to have affairs when they grow up? Will they be afraid to commit to intimate relationships of their own? Will they blame themselves for what happened? Perhaps if I can put the marriage back together quickly, they'll never have to know."

You also worry about unburdening yourself to friends. "Can I trust them to keep my secret?" you wonder. "Will I end up making a public spectacle of myself? No one likes socializing with an unhappy couple, so will we find ourselves sitting at home alone every Saturday night? Friends I confide in will probably say insulting things about my partner, either because they're genuinely outraged or because they want to make me feel better, so won't it be awkward getting back together as a group again? Worst of all, what if someone sympathizes with my partner?"

It's important to realize that some people treat adultery as a contagious disease that might infect their own relationships if they get too close to you. Since for these people the subject of infidelity is taboo, try not to expect too much from them or to take their coldness personally. It's likely that they're threatened by what they don't understand, or that their own relationships are more fragile than they know or want to admit.

Most of your friends will want to help and comfort you, but simply don't know what to say or how to begin. Even a funeral has established rituals for expressing condolences, with well-wishers coming forward with prescribed words of support; but at the news of a partner's infidelity, even your closest friends may have no idea how to help you grieve. Unsure of what to say or do, they may avoid you or cut you off. It's important to realize that they may be looking for cues from you that you want company, that you don't want to be alone. Often their staying away is motivated by respect for what they believe is your wish for privacy. You may need to invite them back into your life.

Some of you may think of talking to a therapist, someone anonymous and neutral who listens and tries to help. This may seem the most logical recourse, but you may feel conflicted about it. "It took me months to call you for an appointment," one betrayed wife told me. "I thought you'd be shocked at my secrets." When this woman finally did come to see me, she told me all about her husband's current affair but said nothing about the many one-night stands that preceded it. "As crazy as it sounds, I was afraid you'd encourage me to leave him, and I wasn't sure I wanted to," she admitted. Her assumption was that if she got into therapy she'd be forced to decide whether she wanted to end her marriage when all she really wanted was to explore her ambivalence (something I'll help you to do in Chapters 3 and 4). At the end of her first appointment, she stood up and said, "I now realize why I'm here. I need to talk out loud and sort out my feelings about what's happened to me. I don't have to know where it's all going to lead. I'm here for me, to bring me back to life."

Opening yourself to others is fraught with danger. Parents, children, friends, therapists—all may help you at this difficult time, but all may also fuel your sense of alienation. It's hard to know whom to trust, and how much to say. There are no rules, no rights and wrongs. All you can do is think through the consequences of revealing the secret; no one can weigh your risks against your needs but you.

Whatever you decide to do, beware of isolating yourself and overdeveloping your solitary life. If you assume that your closest friends don't want you around, or that you always must be buoyant and entertaining when you socialize, you'll make yourself even lonelier and deny yourself the consolation you so sorely need. If there's a network of people who give wholeness and meaning to your life, reach out and reengage yourself with them, even if you're uncomfortable and self-conscious at first.

Loss of a Sense of Purpose—Even the Will to Live: "Sometimes when I'm driving home at night I think it would be easier to swerve off the road and end this agony."
When you can't imagine ever loving or being loved again, when you lose your ability to value yourself or your life, when living feels more painful than not living, it's not surprising that your thoughts turn to suicide. This is the most tragic response to your partner's affair: the loss of the will to live.

Paula, the mother of a mentally retarded daughter, was pregnant with her second child when she learned that her husband was sleeping with her best friend, Sybil. "One day I lost it," she told me. "I couldn't come up with any reason to live. I felt like a complete failure. Sybil was sophisticated and sexy. The people I thought were my two best friends had betrayed me. My unborn child deserved more than I could give, or the world could give, I thought, so I shut the garage door, sat my daughter down next to me in the car, and turned on the motor. Was I out of my mind? I think I was—with grief, with hatred. I was saved by the realization that this was a crazy thing to do, that I had an obligation to be there for my children, and that perhaps my husband had acted crazily as well. On some level I understood that his fling was an attempt to escape responsibility for our daughter and deal with his anxiety over the health of our next child. I decided to explore these ideas with him, and we've been together, rebuilding our marriage, ever since. Life for us has always been hard, harder than for most, I think. But I felt then and still feel today that we owed it to each other to get beyond the pain and forgive each other for being human. We've both been so let down as parents, maybe we expected our relationship to compensate for what life didn't give us. We're finally beginning to acknowledge our bitterness at the cards we've been dealt, and learning to pull together as friends."

For you, as for Paula, few life events are more devastating than your partner's betrayal. Remember, though, that your depression is like a thick morning fog, obscuring your vision, and that having suicidal thoughts is different from acting on them. If you ever feel dangerous to yourself or others, you can walk into a hospital emergency room or call a friend and announce, "I'm depressed. Please protect me." *What you want to kill is not yourself but your pain.*

Your job right now is to do your best to tolerate your despair even if you don't yet know how to relieve it. At this moment, you may find it impossible to believe what I'm telling you, but you must have faith that you can, over time, learn to value yourself again and develop authentic connections with people who matter to you.

SEX DIFFERENCES: DO THEY INFLUENCE THE WAY YOU RESPOND TO THE AFFAIR?

Men and women tend to assign different meanings to a partner's affair, which, in turn, color their emotional responses to it. It's important not to overgeneralize—what applies to some people doesn't apply to others—but there's evidence that most people react at least partially in gender-typical ways. Awareness of these biological and cultural imperatives, no matter how fluid and inexact they are, should shed some light on your reaction to the affair, and make you feel less crazed and alone. It should also help your partner understand you better.

In general, women are more likely to try to rehabilitate the relationship and keep it alive; men are more likely to end it and find a replacement. Women tend to get depressed and strike out at themselves; men tend to get angry and strike out violently at others, if only in their fantasies. Women are more apt to attribute the affair to their general unworthiness; men, to their sexual inadequacy. Women may exaggerate the significance of the affair and take longer to heal; men may compartmentalize their pain and move on.

Difference #1: Women Try to Preserve the Relationship; Men Turn and Run

Women: "Maybe we can work it out."

Men: "Don't bother to come back."

When the hurt partner is a woman, she's more likely to work to preserve the relationship[6]—in part because her culture has taught her to please others and deny herself.[7] A man tends to cut his losses and search for a replacement—someone who will give him the love and attention he feels he deserves. Typically, women silence themselves or hide from their feelings when they've been emotionally violated. Pressured to maintain the appearance of harmony, they often muffle their authentic selves and the inner voice that cries out, "I need more than this." Our society delivers the message that it's the woman's job—and measure of her self-worth—to maintain her ties to others. One fascinating study[8] shows that when girls around the age of eight are asked how they feel about being mistreated by boys, they know their anger and speak up; but somewhere around the age of twelve, these same girls, asked the same questions, respond by saying, "I don't know." This well-documented body of research demonstrates that as women get older, many of them stop trusting their intuitions when they've been wronged. If you as a woman fail to acknowledge how your partner's infidelity is harming you, if you stop speaking directly and authoritatively about your negative feelings in order to stay together, if you're afraid to "blow the whistle,"[9] you've been well-trained.

Another reason many women seek to preserve relationships, even damaged ones, is that they believe and fear that the alternative is to live alone. The famous 1986 marriage study by Harvard and Yale researchers Bennett, Bloom, and Craig[10] sent women into a state of panic over an alleged shortage of bachelors. Although Susan Faludi pointed out back in 1991 that these statistics were grossly exaggerated,[11] they nonetheless created a state of "nuptuliatis"[12] that continues today, in which women believe that their opportunities for marriage after age forty are next to nil.[13]

Divorced women suffer economically more than divorced men, in part because they assume more responsibility for raising young children,[14] in part because their former spouses are more likely to meet car payments than child support obligations.[15] Although the earning gap between the sexes is closing, women tend to fill lower-level jobs or earn less in comparable positions—77 cents to the male dollar.[16] For these practical reasons alone, many women struggle to keep their marriages afloat.

Men—traditionally more financially secure, more confident that their partners can be replaced—are less likely to take their straying spouses back. Because they define themselves less in terms of the success of a relationship, they often feel they have less to lose when it falls apart. Woman tend to silence themselves and stay; men, to flee. They cope with their injury by erasing the source of their pain.

Difference #2: Women Get Depressed; Men Get Angry

Women: "I failed at the most significant relationship in my life."

Men: "If I run into my wife's lover, I'll kill him."

Women tend to react to an affair by beating up on themselves. Men tend to react with anger, beating up those who injure them, at least in fantasy.

Women have twice as great a chance of becoming clinically depressed as men, according to recent figures gathered by the Mayo Clinic.[17] One reason for this is their tendency to direct their criticism inward at themselves rather than outward at others. Another reason is that they're more likely to define themselves in relation to others and equate their self-worth with being loved. When a relationship falters or fails, a woman is more likely to get depressed and experience a diminution of self. It's not just that she loses her partner, she loses herself.[18]

If you're a man, in contrast, you're more likely to direct your fury at your wife or at your wife's lover than at yourself.[19] Aggressive men often have to hold themselves back from acts of violence, but even passive, introspective types find themselves daydreaming about assaulting the "enemy." In either case, your anger allows you to feel powerful and in control, warding off such unsettling feelings as shame and self-doubt. Some of you will want to view your partner as a victim, manipulated by a seductive lover. By directing your rage at him, you avoid confronting the painful possibility that your partner chose to stray because she was seriously dissatisfied with you.

Difference #3: Women Feel Inadequate as Companions; Men Feel Inadequate as Lovers

Women: "I'm not good enough. I can't satisfy my husband."

Men: "My penis isn't good enough. I can't satisfy my wife."

As a woman, you're likely to attribute your husband's betrayal to your own insufficiencies as a human being, not just to your performance in bed. You're likely to assume that your partner had an affair for love, not just sex, and that the attraction was more than physical. As a result, you may assign more significance to your partner's affair than he does. When he insists, "I never loved the other woman; I never wanted to break up our marriage; my affair meant nothing to me," you'll have an awful time understanding or trusting his words, but you may want to consider that he's being honest.

If you're a man, you tend to think your wife cheated on you for better sex, an assumption that makes you feel sexually inadequate and jealous, and may lead to violence against your wife or her lover. Men tend to overlook or minimize other, nonsexual relationship issues, such as communication and intimacy, which may matter most to their wives. If you want to salvage your marriage, you might begin by asking your partner what's missing in the relationship for her, and what exactly you can do to make her feel more loved and appreciated.

Difference #4: Women Obsess; Men Distract Themselves

Women: "I can't stop thinking about his girlfriend."

Men: "I refuse to think about her affair."

Because a woman's sense of self is so closely linked to her success in her most intimate relationships, she tends to be more obsessional about affairs than a man, more likely to dwell on the deception, to the exclusion of everything else. In the process, she becomes more embittered by her partner's lies and remains more mistrustful for a longer time.[20] Actively reliving the details of the affair, she keeps her hurt and insecurity alive.

Men, in contrast, spend less time ruminating about the betrayal and more time actively engaging in physical activities that make them feel masterful and competent.[21] They seem better able to compartmentalize their pain and move on— often to another partner.

Do these sex differences really influence how you respond to the affair? If you're a man, can you feel as depressed and self-critical as a woman? If you're a woman, can you be as preoccupied with your sexual performance as any man?

Gender-specific patterns have been identified in current research, but that doesn't mean they apply to you. At times, in fact, the opposite may be true. Betrayed women, after all, are certainly capable of demonstrating their rage. Euripides knew that over two millennia ago, when he spun his tale of Medea, an abandoned wife who slays her children and her husband's lover to avenge the infidelity. Zoom ahead 2,400 years to a daytime talk show where, as a guest expert, I watched a wife stride across the stage and, in a setting less Greek but no less tragic, slug the babysitter who had slept with her husband.

As for the response of betrayed men, it would be absurd to say they don't ever obsess about their partners' infidelity or work hard to win their partners back. No single response is the property of one sex; the gender differences discussed here are meant only to help you and your partner develop a fuller perspective on each other's behavior at this impossible time. Whether you're a man or woman, the losses you've sustained are deep and complex.

Success, Emerson once said, includes the ability to survive the betrayal of someone you love. That's fine, to a point. But now it's time for you to go beyond survival and begin to heal. To start this process, you, the hurt partner, need to accept that your initial emotional response—excessive, self-incriminating, and desperate as it may have been—was entirely normal and understandable, or at least the best response you were capable of at the time, given your resources and the magnitude of your loss. *You need to forgive yourself for having lost yourself,* and re-build yourself from within.

To reforge your relationship, you also need to come to terms with your partner's response to the affair, no matter how different it may be from your own. In this chapter, your partner was asked to see the infidelity through your eyes; in the next, you're asked to see it through your partner's. Believe it or not, the person who betrayed you may also be struggling to make sense of it all.

TWO

The Unfaithful Partner's Response: Lost in a Labyrinth of Choices

"Going back to my marriage feels like a prison
sentence. But I can't abandon my kids."

"I wasn't looking to fall in love with someone else but I did,
madly. Now I can't decide which relationship to give up."

"I know I strayed, but I didn't mean to hurt you, and
I never stopped loving you. Can't we move on?"

These are some of the conflicts you're likely to struggle with now that your affair is out in the open. Clearly, they're different from the ones your partner is facing. No matter how badly you feel, the effects of your infidelity are almost never as shattering, disorienting, or profound for you as they are for the person you deceived.

Why is this? To begin with, your sense of self has not been assaulted. It's very likely, in fact, that the opposite is true—that the experience of having a lover has validated you. You may feel desired by two persons, whereas your partner feels loved by none. The affair may also give you a new sense of control over your world, with more power, more choices than ever before. Your spouse, in contrast, probably feels diminished, and threatened by an uncertain future.

Although your partner is suffering from a very different and significantly more debilitating sense of loss than you are, I'm sure you're experiencing your own definition of hell. Unburdening yourself of your secret should take a huge weight off your mind and offer some temporary relief, but you're likely to remain as conflicted as before. While part of you may be irresistibly drawn to your lover, another part may be disgusted with yourself for cheating or making your children suffer. The bitterness you thought you felt toward your partner may soften into remorse at the pain you're inflicting. You may decide to give your relationship another chance, only to discover that your partner isn't ready to let you off so easily. As you agonize over your options and the compromises that each entails, you may find yourself trapped in a minefield of choices—paralyzed, unable to stay or leave.

As you struggle to bring order to this chaos you call your life, you need to remind yourself that your partner is in no frame of mind to appreciate your predicament. Your conflict over leaving your lover, your grief at losing a soulmate or best friend—why should your partner care? These are your issues, and you need to grapple with them alone. To expect sympathy or understanding is only to alienate your partner further.

Although your partner may insist on an unconditional commitment, you're probably not equipped to make any irreversible life decisions at this fragile time (we'll deal with those decisions in the next two chapters). Your immediate task—your partner's, too—is to identify your intense and contradictory feelings, and recognize how appropriate and normal they are at this stage of your journey. Here are the most common ones; try to identify your own:

- Relief
- Impatience
- Chronic anxiety
- Justified anger
- Absence of guilt
- Guilt over the children
- Isolation
- Hopelessness
- Paralysis
- Self-disgust

Relief: "I'm tired of lying."

It's usual, once the truth is out, to feel a surge of relief. Even if you don't know where you're headed, you're likely to feel deliciously extricated from the complications that your lies and deceits created for you. You may even feel cleansed or sanitized. Andrea, a thirty-nine-year-old housewife, described her relief when her husband, Jeff, discovered her affair: "It had become ridiculous, juggling two lives. I couldn't manage the deception, never mind the pressure. If I knew I was going to have sex with my boyfriend on Wednesday afternoon, I'd make love with Jeff on Tuesday night so he wouldn't expect it again so soon. I came to dread his advances. When he finally found out, I swore off my boyfriend, and for the first time in years my life came into focus. It felt wonderful, being one person—always in one place, always where I was supposed to be."

Marty, a married, forty-seven-year-old stockbroker, was delighted to get out of the fast lane: "I had lied so much to so many people, I didn't know anymore who I was, and what I had said to whom. I couldn't keep my lives apart, or separate truth from fiction. I was always scared to death of slipping up and getting caught. I'd spend the evening with my girlfriend and then race home, cursing every traffic light, my nerves on end, knowing once again I was late and that the minute I walked in the door I'd have to pass my wife's inquisition. I was too old for this. When she finally confronted me, I was more than ready to tell the truth—I was flooded with relief."

Confessing the secret may make you, like Marty, feel whole again, but before long your feelings are likely to become more muddled and complex.

Impatience: "I've left my lover and told you everything. What more do you want from me?"

Once the affair is disclosed, you may be eager to reach out and rebuild. It's not just that you want to reconnect, but, more selfishly, that you want to stop feeling guilty every time you confront your partner's pain. Your partner, however, operating under a different timetable, is likely to be outraged by your apparent efforts to minimize the damage and move on. As marriage and family counselor Dave Carder points out, betrayed partners "need to feel anger as intense as the infidel's infatuation, anguish as intense as the infidel's joy, retaliation as intense as the infidel's deceit."[1]

Apologetic but impatient, you now may wonder, "How long do I have to put up with my partner's incessant, guilt-inducing verbal assaults that seem to resolve nothing and only pull the two of us further apart?"

Chris, a thirty-nine-year-old car dealer, felt proud, even exonerated, for confessing his sexual transgressions to his wife. At the urging of his parents, he became a born-again Christian and came to believe that his sins were washed away with his tears. Having forgiven himself, he expected his wife to forgive him, too, but she remained unmoved. "He feels pure—good for him," she said. "Now everything's dumped on me. What am I supposed to do with his deceit—rejoice?"

Shock, bitterness, rage, despair—these are your partner's more typical responses, and you'll only add to your frustration if you expect them to go away any time soon. There are no quick fixes, no magic words. What will heal you is what Melanie Beattie calls "the passage of experiences"[2]—those small, concrete acts, those cumulative moments that convince your partner that you've faced your own duplicity, your own un-beautiful self, and are safe to trust again (I discuss these experiences in Chapter 6). This takes time. For now, you need to hang in there with as much compassion and forbearance as you can muster, bearing witness to your partner's emotional chaos and, through caring acts, making your partner feel secure, valued, and willing to risk loving you again.

Chronic Anxiety: "As long as I keep busy, I'll be okay."

One way you may manage your anxiety, now that the affair is out in the open, is to plunge into a flurry of activity, sometimes purposeful, other times meaningless; sometimes to build a new life, other times to avoid thinking about it.

The greater your confusion, the more likely you are to throw yourself into compulsive activities to distract yourself. Any diversion will do—watching TV, exercising, shopping online—as long as it draws you away from the real task of confronting yourself and your life.

"After I confessed to my wife and broke off with my girlfriend, I was frantic to have a completely new life," Dave told me. "I never gave myself a chance to think, much less feel anything. In one week I quit smoking, started working out, designed a new wing off the bedroom of our house, reorganized my office, and bought a new, expensive recreational toy—a faster, sleeker boat. Change was the operative word. It took months to realize that I hadn't even begun dealing with any of the real issues."

These escapist tactics, as Dave discovered, may for a time quell your anxiety and delude you into thinking that you're in control of your life and that everything is back on track. But compulsive busyness—as I pointed out in the last chapter—is nothing but a superficial and temporary fix, a distraction from deeper, more unsettling issues within yourself and your relationship that ultimately need to be addressed if you're going to build a new life together. It's fine to keep active, and understandable that you want to start fresh: Turning over a new leaf almost always feels great. But in time you need to sort through your feelings and deal directly with the issues that made you stray.

Absence of Guilt: "I'm doing what I want to do, and it feels right."

Even after the affair is revealed, you may feel little or no guilt over your behavior, no remorse for breaking your covenant of trust.

This apparent callousness, this seeming indifference to the pain you're causing, is likely to have an explosive effect on your partner. "It's the height of insensitivity, the final insult," a patient named Glen told me, when his unfaithful wife admitted that she wasn't sorry for having the affair. "She says she wants me back, but she doesn't have a shred of regret for cheating on me. Is she totally blind to my feelings, or is it that I matter so little to her?"

There are five common reasons that you, like Glen's wife, may feel no guilt or need to apologize:

1. You've written off the relationship and are using the affair to expedite your exit.
2. You have a characterological disorder that makes you incapable of experiencing compassion or remorse for anyone.
3. You're angry at your partner.
4. You're euphoric about your lover.
5. You hold certain assumptions about infidelity that justify your affair.

The first of these reasons needs no amplification. The second is beyond the scope of this book. Let's look at the other three.

Anger at Your Partner

There could be many reasons for your anger. You may feel undernourished, taken for granted, used. You may feel you've given up too much for too little, sacrificed important goals or dreams, delayed any real personal gratification for much too long. Years of accumulated resentment may leave little room for any other emotion.

Certainly while you're having the affair, and even after it's revealed, you may feel more anger toward your partner than guilt. That's because the two emotions are inversely related: The greater your anger, the less your guilt; the more venom you direct at your partner, the less you direct at yourself. The anger you experience may be a legitimate response to the way your partner has treated you, or a defense against the guilt you feel for what you've done ("It is human nature to hate those whom you have injured," wrote Tacitus, almost 2,000 years ago). What makes it hard to know the difference is that anger always *feels* justified—it's a basic characteristic of the emotion.

Anger often has a sanctimonious edge to it, and may make you feel entitled to go elsewhere for the love and attention you think you deserve but never got at home. That was John's case, when he exploded at his wife after twenty-five years of marriage. "I've been miserable for too long and you've been a bitch," he blurted out. "I quit. I'm out of here."

John's fury felt legitimate and liberating. It blinded him to it all—his long absences from home, his lack of involvement with the children, his failure to make his wife feel important to him—and convinced him that his affair was a just reward, a way of evening the score. If he had come out from behind his anger, he might have found that he wasn't so innocent, nor his wife so flawed.

Euphoria Over the Affair

Transported by an intense sexual or emotional connection to your lover, removed from the mundane obligations of an enduring relationship, you may not care about or even question how your affair affects others. "I feel so supremely happy, so in sync with the world, I don't want to analyze it," one patient told me. "In fact, I don't want to think about the consequences at all. I just want it to last." Since it's natural to attribute meaning to our feelings, the unadulterated joy you feel may signal to you that what you're experiencing is true love at last, and leave no room for guilt. This doesn't necessarily mean that your relationship is doomed; it may signify only that the affair has a powerful, intoxicating hold on you at this moment in time. Later on, looking back, you may realize that you were caught in a whirlwind of emotions and unable to sort through them until the dust cleared.

Core Assumptions That Justify Infidelity

A third reason you may not experience guilt is that you hold certain core assumptions that justify your adulterous behavior. Some of these assumptions are likely to predate your relationship and reflect long-held ideas about love and commitment. Others may be rationalizations, conjured up to protect your self-esteem, suppress your guilt, and grant you permission to stray. To the extent that you believe them, you're likely to feel little compunction about your behavior:

- "My affair is permissible as long as I love the other person."
- "My affair is permissible as long as I don't love the other person."
- "What my partner doesn't know won't hurt him or her."
- "A one-night stand, a fling, doesn't change our relationship."
- "I only have one life to lead and deserve to be as happy as possible. It's okay to get some of my needs met from my lover, and the rest from my spouse."
- "My affair has made me a happier person and therefore a better partner."
- "My affair lets me satisfy my needs without breaking up the family. I'm doing it for the kids."

- "People aren't meant to be monogamous."
- "I have no impulse control."
- "My biological instinct is to be adulterous."
- "All men are wolves."
- "Every couple has its secrets."
- "I'm entitled to keep a part of myself hidden and separate from my partner."
- "Since my partner probably knows about my affair but isn't confronting me, it must be okay, as long as I don't flaunt it."
- "I shouldn't have to sacrifice what I need to make my partner feel secure or happy."
- "I never promised to be perfect."
- "If I commit myself fully to any one person, I'm bound to get hurt."

I encourage you to look at these and other assumptions that lie behind your feelings, and ask yourself:

- Are these ideas true?
- Are these ideas useful? Do they still serve me today?

You may discover that some of them are undermining your ability to be intimate and faithful, and decide to revise or reject them. Keep in mind that with an attitude that supports infidelity, you're more likely to stray.

A patient named Len used to tell me that all men cheat. But when he took a closer look at his assumption, he realized that he had cultivated it as a young boy in order not to hate his unfaithful father, and had continued to act on this belief throughout his adult life, weaving his way through three marriages and a succession of one-night stands. He finally came to see that he was not his father, and that this assumption, which he had cloaked himself in for over twenty years, no longer served his purposes. Believing something, he realized, doesn't necessarily make it useful or true.

Grieving the Loss of the Lover: "I'll never get over this person who made me feel so special."

After you end the affair, you may feel guilty for abandoning your lover, and mourn this person's loss for months or even years.

Your remorse is understandable. This new companion may have seemed like a lifeline to you, drawing you into a world of sexual intimacy and excitement that you thought was out of reach. You may have felt understood and cared for in a way you no longer dreamed was possible. Or perhaps you just had more fun and felt more alive. Above all, your lover may have changed the way you experienced yourself—bolstering your self-esteem in some deeply corrective way, and making you feel more intelligent, competent, attractive, sensual, adventuresome. In short, as Ethel Spector Person puts it in *Dreams of Love and Fateful Encounters*, the experience of romantic love may have helped you "overcome the strictures of the self."[3] It's natural to feel guilty when you abandon someone who gave you such a precious gift, particularly if you lured that person with promises, spoken or implied, to stay together.

A patient named John is typical in the way he wrestled with guilt over ending his affair with his thirty-five-year-old art director. "She's given me—or rather, I've taken from her—the best years of her life," he said. "She's now five years older and her chances of meeting someone else and having a child are seriously diminished. I owe her big, and I feel like a heel for abandoning her, even if it is to go back to my family."

Guilt is one emotion you're likely to feel; grief is another—grief for the loss of someone who may have restored your youthful vision of yourself and given you a glimpse of a better life. This grief can strike at any time, even years later: Something you hear, see, or smell can suddenly release a deluge of feelings.

"I was standing in line at McDonald's more than a year after I stopped seeing Dean," Alice told me, "when I became exquisitely aware that the stranger in front of me was wearing the same aftershave lotion he used. I felt physically ill and had to rush outside for fresh air."

"I assumed life would be simpler when I told Joan I was going back to my wife," Burt said. "I told myself, 'Out of sight, out of mind.' But the more out of sight she was, the more I thought of her. I kept fighting the urge to e-mail her, to accidentally bump into her. I don't regret returning to my family, but at times I still long for Joan."

Your guilt at deserting your lover may infuriate your partner even more than the affair itself: What could be more insulting, more demeaning, than living with someone who cares more about a lover's feelings than about your own? But nothing, not even your guilt, will cut your partner deeper than the way you continue to grieve your loss, even while you say you're working to recommit. This grief may not dilute your efforts to restore trust, but they may dilute your partner's. Ask for understanding now, and you can expect contempt.

Your partner, in turn, shouldn't ask for assurances that you've emotionally detached from your lover. This is something you probably can't give, and puts you in the position of having to lie or tell the truth and make your partner squirm. Your partner needs to recognize that your love for this person may have been real, and that any effort to discredit it will only generate resentment. You, in turn, need to remember that your partner is suffering and may attempt to devalue the lover only to restore lost self-esteem and woo you back.

Both of you should consider that what you, the unfaithful partner, have come to value so deeply is not necessarily the lover, but how the lover made you feel; that what you're seeking is not a replacement for your partner but an alteration of your basic sense of self; and that what you need can perhaps be found with your partner, if you're both willing to open yourselves to change. You may both have to live with the ghost of the lover, but that doesn't mean your life together can't be rich and fulfilling.

Guilt Over the Children: "What kind of role model am I?"

As a parent, you're likely to worry about the effect your affair is having on your children, and on their feelings toward you. What could be more frightening than the prospect of losing their love and respect? In your heart, you want them to see you as a parent they can look up to, not someone who is confused or lost, not someone who has abandoned them.

When Bill imagined himself telling his sixteen-year-old son about his new friend, Heather, he was overcome with guilt. His first marriage had ended when his wife was killed in a car accident, and he had brought up John, then one year old, alone. Now, six years into his second marriage, he was faced with an impossible decision. "I'm crazy about Heather," he told me, "but I don't want John to lose another mother. How can I traumatize him again, now, in his adolescence? If I tear his home apart a second time, he'll never forgive me."

For you, as for Bill, there's no risk-proof way to tell your children about the new person in your life. They probably won't understand, much less have compassion for, the idea that you were unfulfilled at home, or swept away; all they'll hear is that you're threatening the family and the security of their lives. They may try, in their own way, to justify your behavior to themselves because they need to stay attached to you, or they may turn against you for denying them their childhood.

When Tina tried to explain why she was seeing another man, her eighteen-year-old daughter turned away in disgust. "I don't understand why you can't just talk to Daddy and make him realize how unhappy you are," she said. "You tell me you hate him for being so passive, but why can't you just go to him and say, 'Look, I need you to do more for me—pay the bills, make dinner reservations, fix the toilet, whatever. Just take some of these jobs off my back.' With everything we have as a family, is this issue really so important that you can't work it out? I hate you for breaking up the family. I hate you for thinking only of yourself."

Your guilt toward your children is likely to intensify if you were a victim of your own parent's infidelity. As you think of throwing your kids into the same brutal crossfire, you're bound to relive your own childhood traumas.

This was true for Frank. When he was thirteen, his father left home for another woman, and put Frank in the position of having to choose between the two households. "I hated my father for doing that to me," he said. Thirty years later, however, Frank found himself in his father's shoes, preparing to leave his wife for his lover, and forcing his children to choose between the two families. "Do I leave the marriage and make the kids suffer, or do I stay and deny myself?" he asked. "It's like choosing between air and water."

None of Frank's solutions came pain-free, so what he did was nothing; he left neither his wife nor his lover, but simply waited for the right time to act—which, of course, never came. First he waited until his second son became a bar-mitzvah, then he waited for his daughter to graduate from high school. And so time passed. Frank never did resolve his dilemma, and he continues to feel stuck, embittered, and only peripherally involved in each of his relationships.

For you, as for Frank, there are likely to be two voices warring within you: the child, encouraging you to listen to your passions and live for the moment; and the duty-bound parent, reminding you of your greater, long-term responsibility to your family. It's hard to know which voice to listen to. Perhaps all you can do right now is console yourself with the knowledge that nothing you do will make you totally happy or satisfy all your needs; that whatever decision you make will be tinged with regret. (I'll help you resolve these ambivalences in Chapters 3 and 4.)

To get through this time, you may find it helpful to remind yourself that your kids will grow up, that you'll probably have many opportunities to talk to them about what happened, and that their feelings toward you and your affair are likely to change over time. Your own understanding of what happened will change as well, and so will the way you explain it.

Isolation: "No one's there for me."

Once your affair is exposed, your relationship with your children is not the only one that may suffer. Your parents and many of your friends may judge you harshly and cut you off from your usual sources of emotional support.

The cruelest rejection may come from your parents. "At first my mother called me every day to tell me I was making her sick," Barry told me. "She backed off only after I stopped taking her calls. Lately she tries to be supportive by asking me how I'm doing, but I can see she's looking straight through me, wondering where she went wrong, and how I got so screwed up."

If your parents are deeply religious or hold conservative values, they may treat you as a degenerate, a pariah, a family disgrace, and pressure you to stay with your partner and end the affair. You may start to wonder, "Do they care about me and my happiness, or only about abstract principles and what their friends will say?"

Some parents will blame themselves for your behavior, and turn a deaf ear to your professions of passion or pain. Domestic tranquillity—that's what they wish for you. The last thing they care to hear about are your marital problems, or your joy in the arms of your lover.

Your closest friends may also be ill-prepared to listen to your conflicts, particularly those who know you and your partner as a couple and are anxious not to take sides. Some may have moral blinders on, or feel too threatened by the fragility of their own relationships to support your feelings or come to your defense. Others will assault you with their theories about love and commitment, when all you want is a sympathetic ear.

Tina, a fifty-four-year-old professional golfer, laughed at the idea of discussing her young lover with her family, but she thought she could share her angst with her best friend, Ginny. But Ginny was no comfort: "Get a grip on yourself!" she bellowed. "You've got four kids!"

Anxious to avoid the judgment of family and friends, you may keep them at arm's length and spend all your free time with your lover and your lover's friends. This may entangle the two of you more deeply than you want or are ready for.

It's tempting to try to break out of your isolation and surround yourself with people who flatter your thoughts and feelings. But if you really want to look honestly at yourself, you need to speak to those who have no personal stake in your decisions—those who are firmly there for you, but who will challenge you to accept your complicity in your problems at home. Don't forget, however, that no matter how helpful these individuals are, they know only a part of you—the part that you've chosen to show them or that you know yourself—and they have their own private agendas and biases. Few of them know you well enough to advise you wisely or give you the support you need.

One sensible option at this vulnerable time is to consult a therapist—someone who is likely to be neutral and therefore able to respect your feelings and help you make sense of your chaos.

Hopelessness: "There's no way this relationship will ever work."

It's common at this early stage to see your relationship as an emotional death camp, with no chance of pardon or escape. You may decide to stay for many reasons—fear of being alone, guilt, the children, financial security, a sense of moral responsibility—but you're likely to assume that love is gone forever and that your partner is incapable of meeting your needs.

You may be right, but you also may be distorting the truth in favor of your lover. That's what Jerry did. The fifty-five-year-old engineer couldn't praise his lover, Cindy, or fault his wife, Judy, often enough. "Cindy seems to know what I need and what I'm thinking even before I do," he told me. "She makes me feel appreciated. She accepts me for who I am. Judy doesn't have a clue about me, and I don't think she's capable of changing. I'm going to stick it out with her because of the kids, but I feel like I'm incarcerating myself."

Jerry's *belief* that his wife couldn't support him became a self-fulfilling prophecy. He never communicated to her in ways that let her hear what he was asking for. He never gave her a chance to change. He never tested whether she could respond to his needs.

Your situation could turn out to be less bleak—but only if you don't allow your sense of hopelessness to dictate your behavior. It would be sad if, because of the way you're feeling now, you never let your partner try to please you.

Paralysis: "I don't know which way to go."

To leave or stay, to run off with your lover or say goodbye— these critical choices are likely to leave you paralyzed with indecision, unable to move or stand still. All you know is that you can't juggle two lives anymore—it's too much to handle.

Joy, a thirty-four-year-old professional fund-raiser, was married seven years when a flirtatious scene at her Christmas office party got out of hand. "I stayed late that night, drinking much too much, trying to drown out my inhibitions. When Evan asked me to dance, I was knocked over by how great he felt. Before I knew it we were kissing. I never thought about the consequences because I never expected it to go anywhere, but two weeks later we met at his apartment and had sex, and the rest, as they say, is history. I never expected to fall in love, but I have, and now I don't know what to do. My husband's a decent person, and I'm not unhappy in our marriage, but I'm not ready to give up Evan, either. I can't just jump back into the marriage and pretend I want to be there. I'm really in over my head."

Henry, the fifty-year-old chairman of a publicly held company, went through the same emotional wringer. He had agreed to stay with his wife and focus on their problems, but he couldn't keep his hands off his lover, Edie. One day, feeling lonely and confused, he asked Edie to lunch. The experience was both titillating and anxiety-provoking. "I made a fool of myself," he admitted, "fondling her under the table, giggling like an eighteen-year-old kid. But I was so hot, I couldn't control myself. I'm a grown man, the CEO of a major company, what the hell am I doing, running around, acting like an animal in heat? On one hand, I'm telling my wife, 'Let's work things out'; on the other, I'm sneaking off with Edie. And the more time I spend with her, the more confused I get."

Part of your ambivalence, like Henry's, may come from the fact that you were swept up in an affair without really understanding the consequences, or without consciously seeking it out, and now feel gripped by emotions you can't control. You may be intoxicated with life in a way you haven't been for years, and unable to extricate yourself from the excitement.

Any resolution may seem more appealing than this impossible balancing act, but nothing is clear or obvious, and every solution seems weighted with compromise. Your relationship with your spouse may not be so terrible, nor your relationship with your lover so fantastic. "If I put as much tenderness and care into my marriage as I do into my affair, would it be as good?" you may begin to wonder.

Your affair may have you soaring now, but it could slow to a crawl if the two of you move in together and have to see each other up close, in the common light of day. If you recognize each other for what you are, not what you imagine each other to be, you could find yourself shedding one unrewarding relationship for another—encumbered, this time, with alimony and visitation rights every other Sunday. Floundering like a boat that has slipped its moorings, you may want nothing more than to escape from everyone, and would gladly trade all prospects of love for a life of peace and solitude.

Trapped in your ambivalence, you can expect to find yourself bombarded with questions for which there are no obvious answers:

- "Do I still love my partner?"
- "What is love?"
- "Am I normal?"

- "Am I justified?"
- "How do I get answers?"
- "Why is this happening?"
- "How do I get out—and from which relationship?"

Love is not pure; it's made of many complex, sometimes contradictory, feelings. While part of you says, "If only I could make a clean break from my lover and commit myself to my spouse," another part rejoins, "If only I could run off with my lover and block out the past."

Whatever you decide, your partner is likely to be ravaged by your attachment to another person, and to doubt that the two of you can ever love each other again. At this stage of your odyssey, both of you need to leave yourselves open to many warring emotions, without hastily drawing conclusions about the future. Human beings aren't constructed to feel one way about anything—least of all love.

Self-Disgust: "I have nothing to say in my defense. I feel like a sleaze."

Whatever you now feel about your love life—relieved, empowered, ambivalent, trapped—you may also feel deeply ashamed of yourself for violating religious or family values that enjoined you to honor marital vows and stay the course. Having trampled on your scruples and perhaps broken your partner's heart, you're likely to feel that you've betrayed everyone who matters to you, including yourself.

Grace, married twelve years, upbraided herself for sleeping with a tennis instructor at her health club. "I was feeling so unloved in my marriage," she told me. "My husband barely touched me. Things got to the point where if he knew I was interested in sex, he'd deliberately reject me. He always had to be in control, and I was going out of my mind with loneliness. Still, being in this illicit relationship makes me feel like a tramp. I can't believe how easily I turned my back on fidelity, commitment, honesty—all the values I thought I believed in.

I'm finally getting the love, the attention, the affirmation I so desperately need, but I've broken every rule in the book to get it, and sold my soul as well. I feel more loved today, but shitty about myself."

Sometimes there's no justification for the wretched, even diabolical way you treat your partner. "I can't believe how awful I was to my wife while I was seeing Meg," Joe, a thirty-two-year-old electrician, admitted:

"I had planned this baseball party for the guys I work with—we were going to hang around, have some beer and pizza, and watch the playoffs on TV. The 'guys' included Meg; it was no secret to them we were more than friends. I knew my wife wanted no part of any of this—she was pregnant, and she hates baseball and drinking—and I was counting on her to do what she's done in the past: get out of the house for the weekend and stay with her sister.

"All I could think of was spending the night with Meg. But right before the party, Susan began to bleed. She called the doctor, and he arranged for her to go to the hospital for a D&C the following day. She didn't want to burden anyone, so she offered to spend the night in a motel so she could get a good night's sleep and I could still have my party. I agreed. I also let her drive herself to the hospital the next day."

Joe shook his head. "I know I must look totally detestable to you. There's no excuse for the way I behaved. I abandoned my wife when she needed me most. All I can say is that I got completely swept up in the affair and acted like a selfish idiot. I don't think my behavior is a reflection of my true character. I just think I was lost."

Some of you may be disgusted with yourself for trying to bring your partner down to your own level—provoking behavior as inglorious as yours to make yourself look better in your own eyes.

Sid, a twenty-six-year-old MBA student, found himself using his wife, Ingrid, to clear a path for him: "I was deliberately cruel to her, hoping she'd be just as cruel back, and I'd have a reason to leave. I wanted to implicate her, to get her hands dirty, to make her share responsibility for the breakup, so all the guilt wouldn't fall on me. I even tried to get a friend to have an affair with her, hoping it would sully her and pull her down to my level. Then I made her see a couples therapist with me so he could do the dirty work and convince her that *she* should be moving out. The worst was when she was nice to me—I couldn't bear it. When I told her I was leaving, she helped me pack my bags. I was ripping her life apart and there she was, packing my bags. Her niceness suffocated me, and I fought her off so I could breathe again."

Sid divorced Ingrid and four years later reflected on his behavior. "I was terrible to her. She didn't deserve my meanness. But I was young and didn't know who I was or what I wanted, or how to make a marriage work. What I'll always hate myself for is how I didn't just get out when I was so unhappy, but dragged her through the mud with me."

Guilt can be a healthy reminder that you've been untrue to yourself, a message to live more closely to your convictions. But when it causes you to trash yourself, you learn nothing; when it makes you write yourself off as no good, you cheat yourself of valuable self-knowledge. I suggest, therefore, that you direct your reproach not at yourself, the person, but at those specific qualities within you that you dislike or consider maladaptive, and that may have led you to treat your partner so shoddily and deceptively while your affair was going on. Once you isolate these negative attributes, you can go to work remodeling them, and open yourself to constructive change and self-forgiveness.

Among those qualities you may fault yourself for are:

- feeling so insecure, so uncertain about yourself, that you become vulnerable to the attentions of those who build you up;
- keeping your unmet needs (companionship, affection, conversation, etc.) from your partner, then going elsewhere to have them met;

- feeling entitled to have your needs met without regard for the needs of others;
- craving excitement and novelty to the point of not being able to tolerate the ordinariness, the predictability of an enduring relationship;
- ignoring or being unaware of your own personal conflicts, and blaming your unhappiness on your partner.

While you may want to explore these and other qualities that you consider unattractive in yourself, you do yourself a disservice if you focus on them exclusively and ignore your partner's role. You have no right to blame your partner for your affair—no one *makes* you cheat—but you have every right to address how your partner contributed to your dissatisfaction.

SEX DIFFERENCES: DO THEY INFLUENCE THE WAY YOU RESPOND TO THE AFFAIR?

Gender differences play a role in your emotional response to the affair, just as they do for your partner. As I pointed out in the last chapter, these differences are far from exact, but they add another layer to your understanding of your behavior.

Current research on extramarital attitudes and behaviors shows that women are more apt to have affairs for love and companionship,[4] while men are more often content with sex alone.[5] Women are likely to believe that their infidelity is justified if it's for love; men are likely to believe their infidelity is justified if it's *not* for love.[6] Women are also more likely to anguish over the affair than men are.[7]

These findings won't excuse you in your partner's eyes—your insistence that you couldn't help yourself, that you did what any man or woman would, won't get you very far—but they may help your partner get inside your head, and spark a useful discussion about the meaning of the affair and the deficiencies in your relationship.

Difference #1: Women Seek Soulmates; Men Seek Playmates

Women: "I finally found someone I can open up to."

Men: "My lover and I share so much—sex, tennis, jazz."

In general, women have affairs to experience an emotional connection that they feel is lacking in their primary relationship. They stray in search of a soulmate, someone who pays attention to their feelings and encourages meaningful conversation. Women like to talk, and they develop an intimate bond through verbal interaction. *The New Yorker* pokes fun at this proclivity in a cartoon of a woman soliciting a male hooker. "Oh yeah, baby, I'll listen to you," he says, "I'll listen to you all night long."[8] As sex therapists like to point out, a woman's arousal usually begins outside the bedroom; her partner engages her in an emotional (not merely physical) foreplay that enhances her feelings of warmth and security, and, in turn, feeds her sexual responsiveness. Women who stray often develop a close friendship with the affair-person before they become sexually involved. Once a physical bond develops, they continue to seek a more committed intimacy.

Men, in contrast, are more likely to have affairs that lack emotional attachment. They tend to enjoy doing active things, sexual or nonsexual, with their lovers, and to feel closer to them through nonverbal play.[9] Often it's a man's physical attraction to another woman, not a need for friendship, that draws him into an affair, and it's the unencumbered sexual adventure more than understanding or closeness that keeps him there. At the time of the affair men are less apt than women to be dissatisfied at home.[10] In the gay population as well, men are "decidedly more promiscuous and more drawn to impersonal sex" than females, according to Robert Wright.[11] (His Darwinesque explanation is that men can procreate hundreds of times each year, and women only once, so men don't need to be as discriminating.) As the playwright Edward Albee generalizes in *Three Tall Women,* women stray because they're lonely, men because they're men.

Both men and women can use their knowledge of these gender differences as a form of damage control. If you're a woman, for instance, you might question how directly you've conveyed to your partner how dissatisfied you are with your relationship, and exactly what you need to restore the intimacy that's missing. After learning about the affair, hurt partners often lament that they weren't ever given a chance to address their partners' complaints.

If you're a man, you might question why you got involved with another person, and how unhappy you were in your primary relationship at that time. What began as a superficial attraction may have catapulted into sexual passion, and then evolved into a strong emotional connection. You may end up replacing your partner, when you weren't that dissatisfied to begin with, only later to discover that your new relationship is as conflict-ridden as your marriage ever was.

Difference #2: Women Believe Their Affair Is Justified When It's for Love; Men, When It's Not for Love

Women: "But I loved him."

Men: "But I didn't love her."

Women are more likely to sanction their affair when it involves love; men, ironically, when it doesn't. Women tend to attach themselves more deeply to their lovers, both emotionally and sexually, which is one reason that their affairs more often lead to divorce.[12]

In general, men believe that extramarital sex is acceptable and even condoned by society as long as it's only a fling and no one finds out. They tend to minimize the significance of a sexual tryst, seeing it as an inconsequential event, an accident, a momentary release.[13]

Difference #3: Women Anguish Over Their Affairs; Men Enjoy Them

Women: "My affair has complicated my life."

Men: "My affair has given me life."

In general, women tend to experience more conflict over their sexual transgressions than men, and are less likely to believe their affairs are justified, under any circumstances.[14] As I pointed out earlier, a woman, once involved, is more likely to get emotionally entangled with her lover and to have difficulty separating sex from love. In a recent study of unfaithful wives, Carol Botwin found that women as a rule are not as liberated by affairs as men; they anguish more, experience more guilt, become more dissatisfied with their marriages, and feel more dependent on their lovers.[15]

Women who stray also suffer more from spending time away from their children. As the primary caretakers, they are more often the ones to stash the children away with babysitters or day-care providers while they rendezvous with their lovers—a deception that can make them feel doubly illicit. Women who defy traditional feminine virtues—"self-denial, self-sacrifice, self-effacement, self-restraint"[16]—are more likely to feel guilty when they act independently and put their own needs first, for whatever reason.

Men seem to be better equipped to separate their affairs from the main currents of their lives. Because they tend to spend less time thinking about people[17] and reminiscing about important moments in their relationships,[18] their affairs are often less central to them, and preoccupy them less.[19] Their ability to enjoy the nonintimate or anonymous aspects of their sexual relationships more than women partially explains their greater infatuation with X-rated movies; just as men are more easily aroused in a vacuum—by the simple sight and novelty of visual images—so they're better able to enjoy sexual stimulation with an anonymous lover, without the emotional complications they often dread. In a recent, nationwide survey of sexual behavior,

54 percent of men reported having erotic thoughts at least once a day, as compared to only 19 percent of women.[20]

If you're a woman who is having an affair, you've probably invested a great deal of time thinking about your lover. But it may be—be prepared to hate hearing this—that this investment has led you to attribute more love and specialness to your illicit relationship than it warrants. If, like many women, you have difficulty justifying an affair that's purely sexual, your guilt may lead you to exaggerate your dissatisfaction at home and magnify your love for your lover.

If you're a man who is having an affair, you may trick yourself into believing you can keep sexual relationships simple. Unfortunately for you, your lover may react in ways typical of her sex, and come to demand more intimacy and commitment, thereby changing the rules of your game. Should this happen, say goodbye to the freedom and enhancement the affair once gave you.

A Final Note

In trying to isolate specific differences between unfaithful men and women, I run the risk of magnifying, even reifying them. As we saw in the last chapter, these gender-linked differences are often blurred, and may even be reversed. There are men, certainly, who search outside marriage for female friends, not just playmates. And if Carol Botwin is correct in *Tempted Women*[21] and Dalma Heyn in *The Erotic Silence of the American Wife*,[22] there's a new breed of woman—Botwin calls them "the groundbreakers"[23]—who aggressively seeks out lovers for sex, and embraces the experience relatively guilt-free.

What I assume most of you share (or you wouldn't be reading this book) is the very human goal of sorting through the confusion and wanting to do what's best for yourself, while being reasonably fair to others. It helps to take into account your acquired or innate reactions as men and women, but there's always much more to the picture than mere gender response.

So far, you and your partner have taken the first step of giving a name to your feelings in the wake of the affair. You're now ready for the next: making a sound, healthy, informed decision about your future together. Let's begin by looking more closely at your ideas about love, and at how they can mislead you into submitting to an unrewarding relationship or tossing out a perfectly viable one.

STAGE TWO

Reviewing Your Options:
"Should I Stay or Leave?"

THREE

Exploring Your Ideas About Love

Within a single love relationship there are many endings.
—Clarissa Pinkola Estés, Ph.D.,
Women Who Run with the Wolves

Once the affair is out in the open, you need to decide whether to work on rebuilding your relationship or end it. Whichever route you choose, I encourage you to choose it deliberately and not to act on feelings alone. Feelings, no matter how intense, are based on assumptions that are often highly subjective and may prove to be unrealistic, unuseful, or untrue. What feels right to you now you may later regret as an impulsive and un-processed response that can't be easily reversed.

Two of your options are dead-end. The first is to stay together and never address why the affair happened or work to assure that it won't happen again. This is a ticket to a life of quiet, or not-so-quiet, desperation. The second is for you to stay together, with at least one of you continuing to be unfaithful, while the other fights back depression or rage. This is no more promising.

Except in those cases in which both partners freely agree to an "open" relationship, or one partner is physically or mentally incapable of serving as an active sex partner and the other one chooses to stay to provide assistance and emotional support, I have never known an ongoing affair to benefit a couple. *In fact, I have never known a prolonged affair to do anything but undermine a couple's efforts to seriously address the intimacy deficits in their relationship.*

There are really only two viable alternatives.

One is to throw your lot in with your partner and work to improve your relationship. The danger for the hurt partner is that you may be drawn blindly to your mate and insist on keeping your relationship intact, no matter what. This is an example of *unrequited love.* "I just want my partner back," you say. But will you be happy?

The other alternative is to say goodbye and begin building separate lives. The danger for the unfaithful partner is that you may be drawn blindly to your lover and insist on being with this person no matter what. This is an example of *romantic love.* "If the love I feel is this strong, it must be true," you say. But is it?

Let's look closely at these two types of love before you make any irreversible decisions. This is not a time for quick fixes.

UNREQUITED LOVE: "IF I DIDN'T LOVE HIM SO MUCH, I COULDN'T TOLERATE THE WAY HE TREATS ME."

Unrequited love is an intense but unwarranted attachment to your partner that makes you want to stay together, no matter how dysfunctional the relationship. The blind spot behind this feeling—what you fail to see—is how unloving your partner has been toward you, how shoddily you continue to be treated, and how nothing you do will change this.

Some of you hold on to these relationships, though it's obvious to any outside observer just how depriving or abusive they are. "But I love this person," you say, blankly, as if this were enough to justify your attachment.

Doggedly, sometimes desperately, you try to get your partner to stay or come back, without looking to see whether this person is good for you. Your self-esteem is so low, your sense of entitlement so undeveloped, your concept of love so limited, that you don't even think to ask: "What are my essential needs and which of them are being met, or grossly denied, in this relationship? Can my partner change in ways that matter to me? Does my partner want to change?"

Linda's husband admitted that he was having an affair with his voice instructor, but he refused to discuss it, and continued to see his lover regularly, often coming home late for dinner or staying in the city overnight. He instructed Linda not to ask him questions or create unpleasant scenes, but also not to pretend that everything was normal and loving between them. (He hated it when she was nice to him; it made him feel manipulated.)

Linda went from therapist to therapist, searching for strategies to lure her husband back. She didn't know it, but what she was really searching for was her lost self—the self that informed her that the intense pain and emptiness she was feeling came from loving someone who was brutally selfish and treated her with contempt.

When I first met Gail, her husband, Craig, had just confessed to seventeen affairs over the course of their fourteen-year marriage, and she was in a state of shock and denial. "We have a great marriage," she swore. "Craig is perfect for me." She could have been talking about how the sun comes up each day, so complete was her faith in him. As she began to sift more consciously through the wreckage of her marriage, however, her selective amnesia lifted, and her memories became more accurate and detailed. She remembered, for example, how Craig used to come to bed sticky or sweaty, and wanting sex. She would complain lightly, and he would make light of her complaints. Aghast, she now realized that he had probably had sex earlier that day with someone else and hadn't bothered to wash. She also recalled the time that Craig drove her home from the doctor's office after a mammogram for a suspicious lump in her breast. He spent the whole time chatting on his cell phone with his stockbroker and never once asked about the results—and she never once acknowledged her disillusionment and rage.

It took Gail many sessions with me before she could peel back that layer of self-denial and face how denigrated she had felt throughout her marriage, and how completely she had failed to process her suspicions. "If I didn't love my husband so much, I wouldn't be able to tolerate the way he treats me," she said one day. Her ability to acknowledge that he was hurting her was a step in the right direction, though it didn't make her love him any less.

Gail's low expectations for herself and her marriage began to make sense to her when she looked back at her relationship with her parents. Her father was a violent and abusive womanizer who taunted his self-effacing, overaccommodating wife with accusations of infidelity. Her mother's response was to stay home, work harder, and always make herself available to him sexually. "If you want to keep your husband faithful," she told her daughter, "never say no when he wants sex."

Gail grew up believing that being loved meant being owned. In her marriage, she went to work for her husband, and developed no interests outside the home. Only when she expanded her definition of love beyond what she had experienced with her parents and Craig did she began to burn inside. "I want and deserve much more," she realized.

By Eric Kaplan, © 1993 *The New Yorker*

"I know. But I think I can change him."

Like Gail, you, too, need to ask yourself, "Have I been deceiving myself about my partner's capacity for love? Have I been excusing this person's behavior too long? Is there something in me or in my past compelling me to love and ingratiate myself with people who betray or bully me?"

It's not within the parameters of this book to convince you that you have a right to a life or that you're capable of making it on your own, but if you doubt yourself, you may want to get professional help to correct your self-image before you automatically slip back into an emotional wasteland.

Of course, it also matters how you treat your partner; your negative behavior may provoke the negative treatment you get in return. If you're cold or critical, you shouldn't be surprised if your partner is cold or critical, too. You need to take responsibility for how your behavior has contributed to the distress in your relationship, and you have a right to expect as much from your partner.

Keep in mind that some people have personality disorders that make them unable or unwilling to change, both emotionally and psychologically. Gail's husband, Craig, for example, would probably be diagnosed as narcissistic. Such individuals assume that they're entitled to love, and are virtually incapable of forming authentic bonds. Feeling empty inside, they attach to others only to aggrandize themselves. They fail to grasp the concept of reciprocity—of two people giving to each other in mutually enhancing ways. Such persons often feel no guilt or remorse because they're incapable of empathy. When you express your needs to them, they're likely to take it for criticism and feel threatened, even abandoned by you.[1]

If you're in a relationship with such a person, you'll need more than good intentions or a self-help book to make your relationship work. Couples therapy is likely to be equally ineffective. Because of their difficulty confronting inner conflicts, their mistrust of others, and their inability to negotiate interpersonal issues, narcissists often cannot tolerate the intimacy of therapy and quit, or flit from doctor to doctor. If you stay in the relationship, you'll have to provide constant adulation, and even then, your partner is likely to feel deprived and wronged, and eventually replace you.

Narcissists who are psychologically unraveled by the loss of their partners may sink into a depression so deep that they become accessible to change. But before they rebuild their relationships, they must rebuild themselves. If you want to wait out this process, it's important to be realistic about how long it will take—months, years, even a lifetime may not be enough.

The narcissist is one type of damaged personality. Another is the sociopath, or antisocial individual, who compulsively lies, is irresponsible in meeting work and family obligations, and exhibits poor impulse control, often leading to physical violence and unlawful behavior.[2] This person usually can't sustain a long-term monogamous relationship for more than a year.

Other partners suffer from what is known as a borderline personality disorder. These people are often moody, anxious, insensitive, and hostile. A relationship with this sort of person is likely to make you feel chronically angry, insecure, or exhausted—assuming you're honest about your feelings.

There are other types of individuals who resist change, and with whom it won't be easy to maintain ties: those who are addicted to alcohol or drugs, who become physically or verbally abusive, who are sexually provocative in inappropriate ways, or who just refuse to take your issues seriously and work with you to strengthen your relationship. This isn't to say that if you're dissatisfied, your partner is irredeemably bad for you and you should leave. I encourage you, however, to open your eyes to the truth of your relationship, and learn to acknowledge when you've been violated. Your feelings of love should be earned; they shouldn't spring from some overactive source within you that pumps out love irrespective of how you're treated. Be wary of spinning "enabling fictions"—false narratives that make you think everything's all right when it's not, and lull you into choosing "perpetual forgiveness over the possibility of change."[3]

To avoid jumping to false and damaging conclusions about your partner, you might want to read more about dysfunctional personalities in Beck, Freeman, and Davis's *Cognitive Therapy of Personality Disorders*.[4] In the end, you have to decide for yourself whether your partner is gripped by intractable forces that make change impossible, or simply unmotivated to give you the love you need at this tumultuous time. How much is irreversible, how much a matter of training, how much is due to a permanently damaged psyche, how much to the alterable circumstances of your relationship—these are fundamental questions that you'll be better able to answer once you've dethroned your partner and opened your eyes to the deceptions and distortions of unrequited love.

ROMANTIC LOVE: "I'M READY TO RISK EVERYTHING FOR A PERSON WHO MAKES ME FEEL SO HAPPY, SO LOVED, SO ALIVE."

Romantic love is an intense but unwarranted attachment that you, the unfaithful partner, may feel toward your lover. It's likely to make you want to leave your partner, no matter how satisfying your life together has been.

"My love for the lover must be real," you assume, "otherwise I wouldn't feel such high chemistry and be willing to sacrifice so much for this person." The blind spot behind this feeling—what you fail to see—is that your so-called grand passion may have more to do with your unmet childhood needs or present-day challenges than with who this other person really is. For the sake of an exhilarating high, which you're bound to come down from if the relationship lasts, you risk discarding a potentially salvageable, rewarding, lifelong relationship with your partner.

How do you make sense of your sweeping, intoxicating feelings for your lover, and your bitterness or disappointment with your spouse? How do you distinguish between a torrid but temporary attachment and an enduring covenant of love? Why turn away from romance when it feels so wonderful, or stay with your partner when your gut instinct is to run?

If you're emotionally entangled with your lover, you're probably not interested in asking these questions; you may just want to enjoy the ride. But I invite you to read on, and explore what romantic love is and is not, so that your decision to stay or leave, which may be irreversible, is one you won't later regret.

Let's begin by looking at the emotional, cognitive, and chemical changes that may be taking place within you at the very thought or sight of your lover.

Emotional Changes in Romantic Love

Romantic love is full of "rapture, transport, transcendence, and bliss," writes Ethel Spector Person in *Dreams of Love and Fateful Encounters: The Power of Romantic Passion*.[5] This sublime connection, often referred to as high chemistry, is effortless and fills you with a sense that you've met your perfect match. "Perhaps all romance is like that," Jeanette Winterson writes in *The Passion,* "not a contract between equal parties but an explosion of dreams and desires that can find no outlet in everyday life. Only a drama will do and while the fireworks last the sky is a different colour."[6]

In romantic love, your lover often becomes the single focus of your life, filling you, body and soul. You have a strong desire to spend every free moment together, to merge, to become one. You think about your lover constantly; you want to do things for and with this person, constantly. And because people tend to assign meaning to the way they feel and behave, you interpret your reaction as true love. What else could explain your all-embracing obsession?

The more time and emotion you invest in your lover— buying presents, text messaging—the more love you're likely to feel for that person. Similarly, the less time and emotion you invest in your partner, the less love you're likely to experience for him or her.

Cognitive Changes in Romantic Love

When you fall in love, a perceptual distortion usually takes place, and you idealize the other person, assigning to him or her more positive attributes than any one person could actually possess. The object of your affection becomes beautiful, brilliant, stimulating, sensitive, and, above all, the perfect one for you. It has been postulated that these distortions serve the evolutionary purpose of bonding partners together for the essential task of child-rearing.[7] Whatever the reason, by exaggerating and selectively focusing on the positive attributes, while screening out the more questionable ones, you attach to your lover in incontestable ways that no long-term partner can compete with.

At the same time, you're likely to paint your partner in equally distorted but negative terms, as a foil for your lover.

Boring, constricted, joyless, critical—these are words with which your vilify your partner, and justify abandoning that person and attaching yourself to someone else. "The spouse, if not loathed, comes to be seen as limited," writes Ethel Spector Person. "The marriage, if not bad, is experienced as stultifying."[8] This vision may ease your way out of the relationship, but it's a vision that's likely to be warped or full of holes.

Chemical Changes in Romantic Love

Love is "a natural high," Anthony Walsh writes in *The Science of Love: Understanding Love and Its Effects on Mind and Body.*[9] In other words, your experience of intense passion has a biological base in which your body is literally swamped with amphetamine-like chemicals such as dopamine, norepinephrine, and phenylethylamine (PEA). The smittening effect of these drugs, particularly PEA, doesn't last forever, however. The body gradually builds a tolerance to them, and requires more of them than it can produce to achieve the same euphoric state. In the next stage of love, the brain releases a new set of chemicals called endorphins—natural painkillers that soothe you and create a sense of security and calm. These chemicals help you move from a heated infatuation to a more intimate, sustaining attachment.

The limitation of this biological model is that it makes the transition from romantic to mature love seem smooth and effortless, as though your brain and body chemicals carry you automatically from one emotional stage to another. In any long-term relationship, however, you and your partner are likely to pass through a sustained period of disenchantment, followed by intervals of aridity. We don't know what happens to you chemically during these difficult times, but we do know that for your relationship to survive them, you need to be prepared for, and accept, the vicissitudes of love.

CONFRONTING YOUR UNREALISTIC EXPECTATIONS ABOUT LOVE AND MARRIAGE

If your relationship doesn't live up to your ideas about love, the problem may be not with your relationship but with your ideas. Unrealistic expectations, not your partner, may be responsible for your dissatisfaction. These expectations include:

- "My partner and I should feel a deep, unspoken bond at all times."
- "My partner should be able to anticipate my needs."
- "I shouldn't have to work for love."
- "I shouldn't have to work to be trusted."
- "I deserve to be loved."
- "The chemistry is either right or wrong."
- "My partner should love me unconditionally."
- "My partner should be emotionally available to me whenever I need him or her."
- "Love is a feeling that can't be forced or manufactured. It either exists or it doesn't."
- "A good marriage is free of conflict."
- "If I'm not happy in my relationship, it's my partner's fault."
- "We shouldn't have to work at feeling sexual desire for each other; it should come naturally or not at all."
- "When passion dies, so does the relationship."

Think through these ideas about love, by yourself and with others, and ask yourself which ones you believe in, and how realistic and useful they are for you. You may brush them off as the half-baked assumptions of people less sophisticated or perceptive than you, but don't be fooled. Some of them are likely to lie behind your discontent.

It's not easy to gauge exactly how much of your unhappiness is due to unrealistic expectations (in which case *you* need to change), and how much to your partner's inability to satisfy your basic needs (in which case your partner needs to change).

This is a complex and highly subjective call that you can make only by searching deep within yourself. But your own starry-eyed preconceptions of love may be setting you up for failure when:

- you want your partner to be your friend, companion, protector, playmate, mentor, and lover—and, of course, to assume the proper role automatically and graciously, according to your needs of the moment;
- you expect your partner to do exactly what you want to do, at the moment you want to do it, and to be happily occupied when you're busy;
- you expect your partner to enhance you in ways that take you beyond who you are—making you feel wiser, more loving, more competent, but never inferior;
- you want your partner to merge with you, *be* you, but not to suffocate you with enthusiasm or dependence and, certainly, never to bore you;
- you expect your partner to know your needs and communicate them with complete clarity, even when you're being unreasonable;
- you expect your partner to forgive your human limitations, even as you reject his or her imperfections.

If you discover that you're asking too much of love but want your love to last, you're free to modify your expectations or adopt new ones more suitable to the current stage of your relationship. More modest, workable assumptions can make you more tolerant and forgiving, and cushion you against the natural disillusionments in any mature relationship.

Here is one vision of an intimate bond taken from *Grown-ups* by Cheryl Mercer. Some of you will find it somber and simplistic; others, profound and mature:

When I think about marriage, what I long for most, strangely enough, is not an elevated spiritual union with a man; that's a fantasy not readily envisioned. What seems wondrous to me instead are the small, shared rituals that bind a man and woman in familiar intimacy, the borders inside which they make love, choose furniture, plan vacations, quarrel over closet space, share the toothpaste, celebrate Christmas the same way they did last year. I've been in love myself, so I know something of what it's like to build a life together—the private jokes, the friends you share, knowing in advance which of you makes the coffee and which goes for the paper, even the comfortable tedium of hearing his or her favorite story yet again. To promise to share forever the small—not only the grand—moments of life seems to me profoundly human, more intimate even than making love with someone for the first time.[10]

DISENCHANTMENT: MOVING FROM ROMANTIC LOVE TO MATURE LOVE

Love is not static. We grow dissatisfied and move apart; affection returns and we pull together again. Some people, ignorant of the process, pull away when the good times end and assume the bad times will last forever. These people flee, mope, or drift into affairs. Others see the ups and downs as part of a dynamic process, which, when anticipated and understood, can enrich and revitalize their relationship, even give it an added punch.

If you accept that feelings of love are neither steady nor constant, but travel in natural cycles, you'll be more prepared to bear up under the turmoil that follows periods of contentment, and see beyond it. Some researchers have documented that periods of discontent come at four-year intervals.[11] Others trace the stages of love in a more linear progression, from romance to disillusion to maturity.

As psychologists Barry Dyn and Michael Glenn put it,[12] the first stage is one of expansion and promise. The second is a time of contraction and betrayal, when both of you become less compromising, less available for change, and begin to retreat into rigid patterns and routines, many of which predate your relationship. At this point you're likely to feel immensely let down with each other and caught up in a handful of well-defined, interpersonal struggles, all variations on the same few themes that repeat themselves in different forms throughout the life of your relationship. If these domestic scenes don't tear the two of you apart, or wear you down, and if you can come to terms with each other's limitations, you're likely to enter the third stage of love—one of compromise, accommodation, integration, and resolution.

Thus, somewhere after the romantic prelude, and as a prerequisite to entering a more solid, secure, intimate relationship, what must inevitably take place is a period of *disenchantment.* The person you deified turns out to have clay feet. The fairy tale you were living is now, it seems, a true-life story with no happily-ever-after. Your criticisms are likely to escalate and become more shrill, and your level of sexual excitement to decline. If you're going to bridge these choppy waters, you'll have to come to terms with the diminution of everything that once seemed so thrilling or easy when you were courting.

As the unfaithful one, you're likely to have a liturgy of complaints about your partner. But what about your feelings toward your lover? A conversation I had with an attorney who left her husband for her summer intern is typical:

"What don't you like about your lover?"

"Absolutely nothing."

"What do the two of you fight about?"

"We don't."

"When you look into the future, what conflicts do you expect to arise between the two of you?"

"I can't think of any."

If you haven't passed beyond this glorious though specious stage of romantic love, it's doubtful you'll have much in your lover to object to. That's because, as couples therapists Stuart and Jacobson put it, "Courtship is a time of maximum human deception." [13] While your body chemicals pump you up with enchantment and idealized perceptions, you remain oblivious to your lover's faults. The days of grappling with love's inevitable disillusionment still lie ahead.

Every sustained relationship has these moments of annoyance and disappointment, its gall and wormwood, if only because two people rarely have the same needs at any given moment. Qualities that you like in your partner on one day you're likely to hate on another, not necessarily because of anything your partner says or does differently, but because of conflicts within yourself. The attention you were so grateful for last Tuesday, you may resent today as a threat to your independence. The charm and gallantry you so admired on Wednesday, you may dismiss on Thursday as an excessive need for attention. Unless you're blinded by love, there is no way to ignore, or to deny, one side without the other, no way to separate out what you love from what you hate, for they are two sides of the same person (more on this in Chapter 5).

When people get divorced and remarried, they expect to be happier, but the statistics tell a different story. According to leading marital researcher John Gottman, second marriages fail at an even higher rate than first marriages: 50 percent of first marriages and 60 percent of second marriages end in divorce.[14] Add stepchildren, and the number of second marriages that fail jumps to 70 percent. It helps to keep in mind that the happiest couples in America don't resolve some 69 percent of their problems.[15]

When you're deciding whether to leave or to stay and rebuild trust, I encourage you to look beyond the moment and try to see your partner more objectively. For those of you who are swept up by high chemistry, this means seeing past the blind spots of romantic love and opening yourself up to the possibility of a less fiery, but warmer, more lasting love with your partner.

The cooling of romantic love inevitably carries with it a sense of loss, like the first days of fall, but it also opens the door to a more mature, committed relationship in which you accept what you love and hate in each other, tolerate feelings of ambivalence within the context of a loving relationship, and stay meaningfully attached even when you're hurt or upset.

Don't give up on your partner too easily. Ask yourself: "Does the problem lie within our relationship or within me? Have I fallen out of love because my partner can never give me what I need, or because I'm suffering temporarily from the loss of the *illusion* of love: the illusion that seduced me into believing that love is constant, that I would always feel positively about my partner; that I would never have to struggle with conflicts that made me question our basic compatibility as a couple." As so eloquently expressed by Clarissa Pinkola Estés in *Women Who Run with the Wolves*:

> A part of every woman and every man resists knowing that in all love relationships Death must have her share. We pretend we can love without our illusions about love dying, pretend we can go on without our superficial expectations dying, pretend we can progress and that our favorite flushes and rushes will never die. But in love, psychically, everything becomes picked apart, everything. . . . What dies? Illusion dies, expectations die, greed for having it all, for wanting to have all be beautiful only, all this dies. Because love always causes a descent into the Death nature, we can see why it takes abundant self-power and soulfulness to make that commitment.[16]

WHERE YOUR IDEAS OF LOVE COME FROM

Love is a concept as much as a feeling. How you define it, and what you expect from it, will have a significant bearing on the partners you seek and on your level of satisfaction with them.

Since your concept of love usually mirrors the way your parents or caretakers treated you, or treated each other, it's revealing to look back on these relationships and explore how they affected you when you were growing up.

According to John Money, a former sexologist from Johns

Hopkins University, all of us carry in our minds a unique subliminal guide to our ideal partner. This "love map" is imprinted in our brain's circuitry by the time we reach adolescence. If we experience a sufficient number of matchups or similarities between our lover and our map, says Money, we'll experience love.[17] The greater the similarities, the higher your chemistry is likely to be.

If your caretakers offered you a model of mature love, the odds are increased that you'll experience mature love as well. If the model was dysfunctional and you weren't made to feel safe, secure, and special, it's likely that you'll be attracted to a partner who may seem different from your caretakers, but who ends up treating you in the same stunted but familiar way, reopening the wounds of the past.[18]

John grew up with an asthmatic mother and an alcoholic father who drifted from job to job. Required to be excessively responsible, he assumed many of the day-to-day chores of running the house—shopping, cooking, cleaning up after his parents' fights. As a college freshman, he found himself attracted to a girl named Debby who was clinically depressed. He felt very comfortable, very much himself, taking care of her, and proposed on their fifth date. His bliss lasted for about six months, at which time he found himself overfunctioning, just as he had done in his youth. His selfless dedication to Debby, which had once made him feel good—needed, important, effective—now weighed him down and made him feel imprisoned and resentful.

Another patient named Mary grew up with a father who constantly criticized and demeaned her, so she found herself drawn to Peter, who made her work hard to gain approval and then refused to grant it. You would have expected her to long for the opposite—for someone who supported and believed in her unconditionally—but only a person like Peter, who made her feel like her old, familiar self—who made her experience herself as she had grown accustomed to knowing herself as a child—could stir up feelings of love. Her attachment to Peter was dysfunctional, but on some unconscious level it made her feel at home.

Your own childhood models may help explain why you, the hurt one, continue to love an unrepentant partner, and why you, the unfaithful one, are drawn to your lover.

As the hurt partner, you might choose to stay in an unfulfilling relationship because it's all you knew as a child, it's all you know today, and it feels like love to you. Trapped in the past, you fail to distinguish what's best for you from what you learned from your parents. Since you're incapable of acknowledging the neglect or harm you're experiencing, you stay with someone who offers little or nothing in return, never questioning or evaluating your other options.

As the unfaithful partner, you might resent your partner for failing to give you what you never got as a child, and go elsewhere to get these needs met, trusting your future to a lover you hardly know. Rather than work through your disillusionment with your partner and the conflicts within yourself, you seek out, or make yourself available to, someone else, someone new.

This time it feels different, you say. And blinded by intense, transcendent feelings, you believe for a while that it is. You attribute to this marvelous passion the power of healing, and experience yourself as never before. Surely this person, who seems so totally different from those who hurt or damaged you in prior relationships, will give you the sense of self, the love you've craved all your life, but which has always eluded you. So you believe.

But what's drawing you so inexorably to your lover and creating such high chemistry between you may not be perfect love, but the unfinished business of your childhood, and the promise of being freed from the abuses and deprivations of the past. High chemistry, as I've said, may be triggered by an unhealthy model of love. Low chemistry may mean that you've chosen a partner who allows you to experience yourself in a more positive, more fulfilling way than you did as a child. You may roll your eyes at hearing this, but relationships that start off with lower chemistry may be stirring up less trouble from the past, and turn out to be more satisfying and enduring in the long run.

In the end, you may decide you're better off making a life with your lover than with your spouse. Love can be transformative, one of life's preeminent crucibles of change, allowing you to evolve, expand, become your best self. An affair can reawaken you to those positive qualities in yourself that were stamped out in a depriving or abusive relationship, and give you new confidence to leave a dead relationship and claim a more responsive mate.

But before you turn your back on your partner, I encourage you to listen carefully to your fights and disappointments; they may tell the story of where you left off in your childhood development, and what you need to accomplish in your present relationship in order to heal. Before you flee, ask yourself, "Does exiting my relationship represent a legitimate path to self-realization, or is it merely an excuse to bypass my unresolved childhood conflicts?"

Regardless of your choice of partners, you're going to experience disillusionment, and you're going to have to work hard to keep your relationship alive and well. If you think otherwise, you're still deluding yourself.

In this chapter I've encouraged the two of you, both the hurt and unfaithful partner, to evaluate your assumptions about love. You may be left, however, with many reservations about recommitting. The next chapter helps you face them, and make the pivotal choice whether to stay or leave.

FOUR

Confronting Your Doubts and Fears

In the last chapter, I encouraged you to look at different concepts of love before making any irrevocable decisions about your future. Now I encourage you to confront your doubts and fears about recommitting so that they don't overwhelm you and push you blindly in a direction you'll later regret.

It's best to wrestle with these concerns by yourself. In the presence of your partner, you're more likely to defend your position than to challenge it or own up to the errors in your thinking. It's also virtually impossible to be honest with yourself when you're censoring your thoughts or couching them in euphemistic language to protect your partner's feelings. You need to see your ambivalence for what it is, not honey-coat it, or water it down.

Let's look at ten common concerns that men and women struggle with after an affair. Some are relevant to hurt partners, some to unfaithful partners. Most of them apply to both of you.

1. "Once there's been so much damage, can we ever get back together?"
2. "Now that you've been unfaithful, how can I trust that you won't stray again?"
3. "Can both of us change in ways that matter? Are we basically incompatible?"
4. "Yes, you're making some changes to save our relationship, but are they permanent or sincere?"
5. "Do you want me, or just the package (financial security, an intact home, shared parenting)?"
6. "Are my reasons for staying good enough?"
7. "Should we stay together for the children?"
8. "Doing what you did, you couldn't possibly love me, so what's the point of going on?"
9. "Isn't it wrong for me to be too affectionate, to spend too much time with you, before I'm positive I want to recommit?"
10. "Won't I be able to make a better decision about my lover if we spend more time together?"

Taking a hard, close look at each of these concerns should help you make a more informed, considered, self-enhancing decision about separating or staying together.

Concern #1 (for couples): "Once there's been so much damage, can we ever get back together?"

In the aftermath of the affair, it's normal to assume that love, once lost, can never be recaptured; that trust, once gone, can never be regained. What I ask you to do, however, is to judge your life together not by how you feel today but by how you've felt about it in the past. Look back. Were you ever happy or intimate? Can you remember what drew you to each other when you were courting? A hopeful prognosis for the future often hinges on the strength of those early years. If you were off to a strong beginning—meaning that you both tried to manage conflict constructively; that you shared loving feelings and a common vision of the future; that you had mutually satisfying sex and enjoyed a reasonable number of fulfilling activities together—there may be more hope for your relationship than you think. If you can find little to build on, however—if the relationship rarely worked for you or was seldom good—then it may not be salvageable today.

One danger in looking back on your life together is that you'll be unfair to your memories, and see them through a veil of bitterness. Be careful not to distort the past to satisfy the present. Very often unfaithful partners selectively remember the bad times to justify their affairs, and hurt partners selectively recall the good times to redeem themselves and to prove that "I wasn't as bad a partner as you're making me out to be, and our relationship wasn't as awful as you make it sound."

Try to acknowledge what was honestly good and what was genuinely bad, and try not to look through revisionist glasses. This is the time when couples make sweeping, simplistic, self-serving statements about their relationship. Those who want to leave remember: "We got married because she was pregnant," or "I always came last, after the dog and the baby." Those who want to work it out recall: "We were so excited when the baby came," or "We had great times together." If you rewrite history to justify your feelings today, you'll get nothing from this exercise.

Prophecies can be self-fulfilling. The assumption that your relationship can't be put back together, that nothing will help, may, in itself, defeat you. If you've given up on your partner, you need to be aware of this, and question whether you're creating a sense of hopelessness that's unjustified or premature. The happiness you shared is no guarantee of future joy—those honeymoon years may not survive a world of mortgages and dirty diapers. But the forecast for your relationship is brighter if you were happy once.

Concern #2 (for hurt partners): "Now that you've been unfaithful, how can I trust that you won't stray again?"

If you've been betrayed, you're likely to worry that you can't ever trust your partner or feel secure in your relationship again. Are these worries justified? Obviously, there's no foolproof formula for evaluating your risk, but there are five indicators that offer clues.

Indicator #1: Underlying Attitudes

A professed belief in monogamy guarantees little, but if your partner can't even give you the verbal assurances you need, you have less reason for trust.

When one of my patients asked her husband why he had cheated on her, he explained, "I didn't expect you to find out about it." "According to your logic," she fumed, "if you didn't think you'd be caught, there'd be no reason not to cheat. Is your conscience ruled only by the risk of punishment?" Her husband's assumption that any behavior was permissible as long as it wasn't discovered fueled her doubts that he'd ever stay faithful to her. And she was right. Less than two weeks later she found him kissing one of his old girlfriends over Kir Royals at a local lounge.

Back in Chapter 2, we looked at a list of assumptions that justify or lie behind a partner's infidelities.

I encourage you to discuss this list as a way of learning about your partner's beliefs and making educated guesses about his or her future behavior. Among the most common ones:

- "What my partner doesn't know won't hurt."
- "I only have one life to lead, and I deserve to be as happy as possible."
- "The affair lets me satisfy my needs without breaking up the family. I'm doing it for the kids."
- "People aren't meant to be monogamous."
- "I have no impulse control."
- "I never promised to be perfect."

- "Since my partner probably knows about my affair but isn't confronting me, it must be okay as long as I don't flaunt it."

Drawing from this list, a hurt partner named Leah asked her husband, "Do you still believe men are biologically programmed to be adulterous?"

"No," he said, "but sometimes people get swept away by emotions they can't control."

"What you're saying," she shot back, "is that you're not willing to be accountable for your behavior. So how can I trust you again? What I need you to tell me is, 'I'm not sure, but I turn down temptations every day. I eat salads when I crave hot fudge sundaes, I force myself to go to the health club when I'm feeling dead tired, I discipline myself in a hundred ways to keep myself healthy, and I can do the same for us.' If you're so unsure about controlling your impulses, why should I believe you won't cheat on me again?"

Having been so deeply hurt, you're probably wary of trusting your partner again too quickly. After all, there's no way to know you're not being conned; language can be used to hide the truth as well as to convey it. I suggest, however, that instead of writing off your partner's words as lies, you store them away and test them in the coming months against his or her behavior. If you're serious about trying to get back together, why not give your partner a chance to come through?

Even if your partner's attitudes on monogamy seem substantially different from yours, don't give up hope. The problem could be not that your views are incompatible, but that your partner is temporarily on the defensive and unwilling to give up ground.

When Tom's wife called him depraved for sleeping with their eighteen-year-old babysitter, he shouted back, "There are seven billion people in this world, all trying to make sense of their lives; who are you to judge me?" He didn't really believe he was justified, but he felt his integrity was under assault and rushed to protect it. He and his wife spent days verbally clawing at each other, as you and your partner may do, but their views over time turned out to be less polarized than they seemed. Tom agreed to see a couples therapist with his wife to work out his discontentment.

Indicator #2: A History of Deception

A partner with a history of duplicity is more likely to lie and deceive again than someone who has strayed only once.

When Marilyn looked back over her twelve years with Marshall, she saw that he had been double-faced from day one. While they were engaged, she had called an unfamiliar number on his BlackBerry and found herself speaking to a woman he was still dating. Shortly after Marilyn gave birth to their first child, her husband left the hospital for four hours—to bring back pizza, he said. A week later she got a call from a nearby motel, asking if she had left a pair of earrings in their room.

Marshall's pattern of lying extended beyond his sexual behavior. He told Marilyn that he had gone to college at Amherst (it turned out to be the University of Massachusetts); that he was Spanish (he was Puerto Rican); that his father was a doctor (he was a lab technician). Lying was a way of life for him, a deeply ingrained pattern that defined how he related to others. When Marilyn finally confronted him about his latest affair, he admitted it, but promised that he was a new man and would never stray again. Marilyn looked back over their life together and told him to pack his bags.

I'm not suggesting that a single affair is more forgivable than seventeen, or that having only one means it won't happen again. However, a partner with a long record of lies and deceptions is more likely to have difficulty breaking this pattern than someone who has strayed only once.

Indicator #3: An Ability to Communicate Openly

Partners who are aware of their needs and can negotiate them in a spirit of reciprocity and compromise are more likely to stay

at home and work through their issues. Partners who are unaware of their needs but expect you to intuit them, or who keep
them bottled up inside for fear of creating conflict, are likely to
let their unhappiness fester and grow. Holding you responsible
for their own feelings of alienation, they go in search of satisfaction in another person's bed.

Some partners, of course, just lack communication skills
and have no idea how to reveal themselves, having never done
so before. Life may have taught them to cover up their feelings,
avoid intimate conversation, and keep their needs to themselves. At this point, what should matter more to you than your
partner's silences, therefore, is your partner's ability to see them
for what they are—a breeding ground for discontent—and to
work with you to become more candid and direct.

It's not your job alone to break through the silences, but you
can help by encouraging your partner to open up to you and
by creating a climate of tolerance and acceptance for what your
partner has to say. Ask your partner not to protect your feelings,
but to trust you with the truth as he or she experiences it. If you
both learn to be more honest with each other and to speak more
forthrightly about your needs, you'll develop a mechanism for
resolving your problems within the context of your relationship
and reduce the chances that one of you will stray.

A forty-four-year-old financial advisor named Sam felt seriously mistreated by his much younger wife, but rather than
admit it and risk a confrontation, he repressed his anger and
sought out the companionship of a lover. The affair acted as a
catalyst, giving him the courage to speak up. Sitting with his
wife in my office, he unleashed the rage that had been caged
within him for years. "I resent the way you're always making fun
of my paunch and my bald spot," he fumed. "I resent the way
you don't even look up from your magazines when I come home
at night. I resent the way you dictate how I should spend my
money, though I make more than enough to support us both."

Sam's wife sat there, speechless, shocked. When he finally
finished she took a deep breath and said, "Okay. It's good to

hear you complain, to know what you're thinking and feeling. I never realized how much these things troubled you. I can work on correcting them—and I will."

Indicator #4: An Ability to Hear You and Empathize with Your Pain

Partners who can't get beyond their own needs and appreciate yours are more likely to cheat again. It makes sense, therefore, to ask yourself whether your partner can:

- see you as a separate person, someone other than an extension of himself or herself;
- appreciate what you've been put through, and the emotional damage the affair has caused;
- feel compassion and remorse for your pain;
- listen to your point of view, even if it differs from his or her own.

If your answer to most of these questions is no, you need to ask yourself not *"Would* my partner stray again?" but "Why *wouldn't* my partner stray again?"

Indicator #5: A Willingness to Probe the Meaning of the Affair and Take an Appropriate Share of Responsibility for It

Unless your partner is willing to explore why the affair happened and accept a fair share of responsibility for it, your hopes for a committed relationship are likely to be built on sand.

"Kevin had an affair six years ago, but to this day he refuses to talk about it with me," a forty-seven-year-old decorator complained to me. "I know almost none of the details, but it sits between us. I feel its presence. I don't believe he's cheating on me anymore, but I have no security about tomorrow, because I have no understanding of where I went wrong, or how, or whether, he's changed. And I doubt he does, either."

When nothing is learned and nothing changes, the problem remains, and so does the temptation to stray.

This section is written for hurt partners, but there's a message for unfaithful partners as well: If you want to explore why the affair happened and what caused you to stray; if you're genuinely sorry for the harm you've caused and are serious about making amends, now is the time to come forward and say so, without acrimony or prevarication. Save your counter-accusations and self-serving rationalizations for later, when you have more perspective on them; right now, they'll only make your partner question the sincerity of your commitment to change. Only when you show the inner strength to face your imperfections and accept your complicity will your partner feel secure enough to invest in a future with you.

Concern #3 (for couples): "Can both of us change in ways that matter? Are we basically incompatible?"

Assumptions take on a reality of their own. If you believe your partner is wrong for you and can't change, you're likely to write the relationship off and start looking elsewhere. But if you treat your belief as merely that—a subjective reality that may or may not be true—you can give your partner a chance to prove you wrong.

To test the truth of your assumptions, tell your partner, face to face or in writing, exactly what changes you need to feel more loved, respected, and cared for. Try to express yourself in a noncombative, noncoercive way—no threats, no ultimatums. Try also to couch your requests in terms that are positive, not negative; concrete, not global. Saying "You never make me feel important to you" doesn't communicate what you need as clearly as "You can make me feel more important to you by coming home for dinner most nights, planning fun things for us to do on weekends, and initiating sex."

Among the requests I hear most frequently:

- "Control your temper better. Tell me what's bothering you without sarcasm."
- "Stop drinking."

- "Speak up for what you want."
- "Do things with me that I want to do, even if you don't."
- "Praise me more often. Tell me what you like and love about me."
- "Show more affection."
- "Get more involved in raising the kids (pick them up at soccer practice, read them a bedtime story)."
- "Tell me what's going on in your life."
- "Show an interest in what's going on in my life."
- "Don't take it personally when I want to spend time alone."
- "Worry less about the future and focus more on today."

To make sure you know exactly what your partner wants, I recommend a commonly used communication exercise called *mirroring* or *open heart listening*. Partner A tells Partner B what's bothering him or her and suggests changes for Partner B to make. Then Partner B paraphrases what has been said until Partner A feels sufficiently understood. The roles are then reversed.

Try to listen carefully and nondefensively to the changes your partner wants from you. To decide whether they're fair and attainable for you, ask yourself:

- "What do these requests reveal about me—about what's likable and dislikable about me?"
- "Am I capable of doing what my partner wants?"
- "Am I willing to try?"
- "Will these changes enhance me as a person or compromise my integrity; will they lead to personal growth or threaten my well-being?"
- "Have I heard these complaints from others, recently or in the past?"
- "Did my parents or other childhood models behave in ways that I'm now being asked to correct in myself? Am I replicating the very same behaviors I find reprehensible in others?"

Your first response to your partner's requests may be, "You're asking me to become someone totally different from who I am." And you may be right. Partners often say, "If only you would *just . . .*" and then ask for the one quality that's totally uncharacteristic of you. At this unmoored time, however, even the most modest request may seem unreasonable. If you're locked in a power struggle, you won't want to give up an inch of ground without a fight. It may be, though, that your partner is asking for small changes that won't compromise you, but will make a world of difference in the way you experience each other.

If you've heard your partner's complaints before—from old lovers, family, friends—you may be coming face to face with something unbeautiful about yourself that restricts your ability to relate more intimately to others and that needs to change if you're ever going to sustain a mature relationship. It just may be—and this is a bitter pill to swallow—that the changes your partner is asking of you would make you a more likable human being.

At the same time, you shouldn't automatically assume that you're the only one who needs to change. If you're depressed, or desperate to get your partner back, be on guard against the temptation to agree to the impossible, or much too much. (One woman told her husband she expected him to do 90 percent of the work in the relationship, and he was so lacking in entitlement, so self-sacrificing, so frightened of losing her, that he said, "Fine, I'll do that.")

Keep in mind that your partner may be finding fault with you as a way to make sense of, or to avoid taking responsibility for, his or her own unhappiness. This should be evident when:

- your partner asks you to change for the same reasons that originally drew the two of you together (for example, your valued spontaneity is now dismissed as irresponsibility);
- your partner blames you for qualities that he or she lacks but unconsciously envies (for example, your self-effacing partner resents your ability to do things for yourself);

- your partner attempts to degrade or subjugate you;
- your partner's requests are excessive and reflect inordinate needs. (One partner told his wife, "I'm king in this community, I'm king in my company, and I expect to be king in our home." Once, when she asked him to remove his muddy sneakers before coming into the kitchen, he bristled and said, "Never tell me what to do in my own house.")

The same caveats apply to you. When *you* are the one requesting changes, you should examine the source of your discontent and not automatically assume that your partner is the problem. Before you roll out your easy list of grievances, or walk away if your partner fails to address them, you need to turn inward and question the legitimacy of your complaints. I encourage you to ask yourself:

- "Am I demanding more than my partner, or anyone, can give?"
- "Am I blaming my partner for making me feel inadequate, unloved, or insecure, when this is the way I've always felt about myself?"
- "Does it follow that because I'm unhappy, my partner has let me down?"
- "How much of my dissatisfaction is due to *me*—my unrealistic expectations, my unresolved conflicts, my excessive needs, my distorted perception of my partner and our interactions?"

People are often experts in how their partners need to change, but have few insights into changes they themselves need to make. Jay, a forty-seven-year-old businessman, is a case in point. "I can't afford my wife [Joan]," he kvetched. "Her tastes are too rich, and she makes me feel small." Convinced that he could never satisfy her, he went off with a woman half his age who asked nothing of him. To prove his generosity, he lavished her with extravagant gifts.

While Jay was debating whether to return to his wife, he handed her a list of twenty requests that began: "Show more appreciation when I give you a present, and don't make me feel I can't take care of you."

Joan was baffled. She had always thought of her husband as a financial success, and felt fortunate to share such an indulgent lifestyle with him. "When we were in Hong Kong, you went into the most expensive store and tried on a South Sea pearl necklace that cost $100,000," Jay reminded her. "You never said anything, but I knew you expected me to buy it for you. Then when we got home I wanted you to buy an Audi, but it wasn't good enough, you had to have a Lexus. You made me feel cheap."

Joan listened in disbelief. She had tried on the necklace for a lark, she was sure. As for the cars, hadn't he liked them both and told her to buy either one?

What Jay couldn't see was that he was blaming Joan for his own feelings of inadequacy—feelings that began when his father ignored him as a child, and deepened as he trailed behind his father in the family business. While there were things Joan could say to make Jay feel more successful and secure—she could thank him more enthusiastically for his gifts, and not return them, as she sometimes did—his dissatisfaction with the marriage said as much about him as it did about her. She alone could never heal his injured sense of self.

There are no simple answers to the questions, "Should I change to satisfy my partner?" or "Should my partner change to satisfy me?" What you're asking of each other could be unreasonable and self-serving, or it could be the catalyst you both need to transcend your old selves and open the way to a more profound and lasting relationship.

You may be tempted to escape the tedium and discomfort of so much self-scrutiny by exiting your relationship and attaching to someone new. But if you don't examine the issues that led to the affair, or accept a fair share of responsibility for your dissatisfaction, you may forfeit an opportunity for growth, as a person and as a partner.

Concern #4 (for couples): "Yes, you're making some changes to save our relationship, but are they permanent or sincere?"

It often happens that your partner suddenly, and completely voluntarily, makes the changes you've been pleading or silently hoping for. An overweight partner may hire a personal trainer, say, or an absent father may make time for the kids.

These changes may seem promising at first, but you're soon likely to question how heartfelt or lasting they are. You may even feel irked. "Why," you wonder, "did it take an affair and the threat of separation to get my partner to do what I've been clamoring for all these years?"

The changes may also frighten you because they seduce you into trusting someone who may let you down again. As the hurt partner, you're likely to ask yourself, "Am I being manipulated? Once I've committed myself to you again, will you assume that all is fine and revert to your old ways?" As the unfaithful partner, you're likely to worry, "Are you changing just to lure me back and trick me into giving up my friend? Once I return, will you become complacent again and leave me wishing I had left for good?"

Should your partner refuse to change in ways that are essential to you, or fail to keep promises, it may be wise to pack up and move on. But if you see that an effort is being made, you may want to put your skepticism on hold, lower your barrier of distrust, and give your partner an honest chance to come through. Your partner can't step into your life unless you open the door.

Concern #5 (for couples): "Do you want me, or just the package?"

Your wish to be wanted for yourself is probably greater than ever now, and so is your mistrust of your partner's motives. Should your partner want to recommit, you're likely to assume that it's not because of you, but because of a set of favorable circumstances that only tangentially include you. This assumption may not be conscious or correct, but it will strongly color your decision to stay in the relationship.

"Why should I take my husband back?" a patient named Gail asked me. "He's afraid of losing the kids, the lawn, the golden retriever, the fifty-four-inch TV. Who knows? Maybe he's learned that single life isn't so hot and wants someone to pick up his shirts at the laundry. I'm not sure I'm even part of the picture."

Jeff, an unfaithful partner, also doubted his importance to his spouse. "Judy wants me back because I pay her Visa bills, and she wants kids," he complained. "But it's not me she loves. Any man would do."

It's normal to wonder what role you play in your partner's decision to recommit, and to seriously consider separating if all you seem to be appreciated for are mortgage payments or meals. But if you expect to be loved *only* for yourself, and feel cheap and compromised when you're not, you have unrealistic expectations about what holds couples together.

Even when you were courting, your partner was probably drawn not totally to you, but to an idealized portrait of you, and to your ability to enhance his or her self-image. Financial and emotional security, companionship, the comfort and familiarity of home, support in times of sickness or in old age—these are all elements of any lasting relationship. All are incentives to remain together and satisfy needs as basic and deep as love itself. If you're happy at home, you won't mind being valued for what you bring to the relationship, beyond yourself; in fact, you may even feel enhanced to know you're satisfying your partner in so many different ways. If you're not happy, however, you're likely to think your partner is loving you for the wrong reasons, and feel used and unappreciated.[1]

It may be painful to admit, but after the affair you both may prefer the package to each other. There's no way, though, to assign percentages to the factors drawing you together. Should you work to reestablish an intimate connection, you're likely to see in time that your lives are entwined in a thousand different ways and that it's neither possible nor preferable to isolate this person you call yourself from the package that comes with you.

Concern #6 (for couples): "Are my reasons for staying good enough?"

You may worry that *you* are staying for the wrong reasons, too. And you may be right.

"I'm here because I'm Catholic, period," one patient conceded. "I made a commitment that was meant to be forever. And yet I feel so miserable, I have to wonder what I'm doing."

"No one in my family's ever gotten divorced," another patient told me, "and I wouldn't have any idea where to begin. But I'm terrified of staying in a marriage as debilitating as the one my parents had."

If you're sticking around only out of guilt, fear, or a sense of duty, you may want to rethink your decision, or prepare yourself for a life of self-imposed incarceration: you the prisoner, and you the keeper of the keys.

Let's look at some of these questionable reasons for staying.

Reason #1: "I can't make it on my own."

If you're staying with your partner because you believe you can't make it on your own, financially or emotionally, stop and ask yourself, "Am I being fair to myself? Am I underestimating my capacity to function, to support myself, to create a fulfilling life for myself outside this relationship?" You may be afraid to be alone but discover, when you examine your life more objectively, that you spent time by yourself before and did just fine; or that you didn't do fine, but you were younger, less resourceful, less solvent, and more encumbered than you are now.

You may perceive yourself as financially dependent on your partner, but underestimate your qualifications or wherewithal to get a job. Have you had one before? Are you exaggerating how safe and protected, how well taken care of, you've been with your partner? One woman, who believed she was unable to survive solo, realized that her husband, the great provider, had gambled away most of their life savings, and it was she who had kept the bankers from foreclosing on their home.

It's important to ask yourself what is it about being without a partner that frightens you. Often what makes the idea scary or depressing is the meaning you give it—that you're not good enough to attract someone else, that there's something basically unlovable about you. What upsets you may be less the reality of living alone than your negative assumptions about it. If you're honest with yourself, you may realize that you've been focusing on how lonely you might be *outside* the relationship, and ignoring how lonely you are *inside* a relationship that's abusive or depriving.

Reason #2: "My religion tells me that a marriage vow is inviolate and can't be broken."
Though your marriage contract has been violated, your religion may still exhort you to regard marriage as sacred, divorce as sinful, and forgiveness as divine.

Religious doctrine can give meaning to life as a source of moral certainty, spiritual fulfillment, and consolation.[2] What current research on commitment indicates, however, is that your chances of improving the quality of your relationship are better when your religious beliefs reinforce a deeply felt desire to recommit, than when they act as constraints, imposed from above.[3] When religious dogma is your only reason for staying, you may end up satisfying your faith, but not yourself, or your partner.

Reason #3: "The very idea of dismantling the relationship seems too overwhelming."
The thought of separating may be more than you can handle. "I take the iPad, my husband takes the laptop?" one of my patients asked herself, as she imagined them dividing their possessions. "It's too much for me to deal with right now." And yet, when she pictured herself living with her well-founded suspicions, she questioned which was worse, the trauma of separating or the reality of living in a damaged relationship for the

rest of her life. "One is brief, the other lasts a lifetime," she said, shortly before contacting a lawyer.

Reason #4: "I'm responsible for taking care of my partner."
Some of you may worry that your partner will be shattered if you leave. This concern may reveal a healthy desire to rebuild your relationship, but it may also cover up your fear of separating, your qualms about being on your own, your need to be needed, your hesitancy to pursue a life that works for you.

If all you're doing is sacrificing yourself, it's likely that your spouse would prefer to be free of you and have the chance to meet someone who genuinely wants to share a life with him or her. When you're not committed in a meaningful way, you can't do much to restore or nourish your partner's sense of self, and your partner is likely to be better off finding support somewhere else.

Concern #7 (for couples): "Should we stay together for the children?"

Parents agonize about the impact that their divorce and the splintering of their family will have on their children. And so they should.

Though findings depend on a child's age, sex, and level of psychological adjustment at the time of the divorce,[4] most studies confirm that children from divorced families fare worse as a group than children from intact families, at least during the first two years after the separation, in areas of scholastic achievement, conduct, psychological adjustment, self-esteem, and social competence.[5]

It seems equally clear, however, that what most determines a child's well-being is less the presence of both parents in the same household than the level of interparental conflict to which the child is exposed—before, during, and after the divorce. It appears better for children to be in a divorced family in which there are low levels of conflict than to be in an intact family in which there are high levels of conflict.[6]

In her study of ninety-eight divorced families, sociologist Connie Ahrons found that both men and women believed that staying together for the children was a mistake, that they should have separated earlier, and that their children "were better off in an honest and well-functioning household, even if it were a household that had experienced divorce."[7] Of course, people tend to spin rationales to justify their behavior; if these couples had decided to stay together and work things out, they might have drawn different conclusions.

No one would encourage you to split up capriciously, without trying to resolve your conflicts first. However, if you're staying together only for the sake of the children—if you're simply treading water in an embittered, spiritless marriage out of guilt, fear, or obligation—then, in the long run, you may not be doing your children a favor. On the contrary, you risk providing a regrettable model of love for them, one that you wouldn't want them to replicate in their own adult lives. Moreover, if you're unfulfilled in your marriage and become excessively self-absorbed and depressed, your children are likely to suffer from your emotional withdrawal.

If you decide to separate or divorce, the physical distance between you and your children may be less damaging to them than the emotional distance between you and your children. You are family, whether you share the same household or not, and your children's psychological adjustment hinges more on your emotional availability than on your physical proximity alone. If you leave home, or see your children only part-time, you should make every effort to maintain a caring involvement with them. As Joan Kelly concludes in her review of research on post-divorce adjustment, children who "begin the divorce experience in good psychological shape, with close or loving relationships with both parents," are likely to maintain their adjustment "by continuing their relationships with both parents on a meaningful basis."[8]

Your decision to leave may be less crucial to your children's adjustment than your willingness to develop a "parenting partnership" with your ex-spouse.[9] Kelly found that children who were positively adjusted before the separation were likely to maintain a similar level of adjustment after the divorce if their parents avoided direct, aggressive expressions of their conflict in front of them. Children did not become more depressed or demonstrate more deviant behavior unless "a parent asked them to carry messages, asked intrusive questions about the other parent, or created in the child a need to hide information or feelings about the other parent."[10] In other words, children managed to survive relatively unscathed unless they felt caught in the middle of the conflict.

As you consider your options, remember that your choices are not just to be unhappily married or happily divorced, but also to keep a worthy marriage intact by working out your differences and dissatisfactions. It should come as no surprise that most children, given the choice, would want their families to stay together and get along. If in your own mind there are enough good reasons to recommit, you may not only preserve the nuclear family for your children, but you may also teach them a valuable life lesson: that people who at one time hurt and even hate each other can learn to love each other again; that people can separate and then return; that interpersonal conflicts can be successfully resolved; and that a crisis in intimacy can lead to meaningful change and a stronger connection.

Concern #8 (for hurt partners): "Doing what you did, you couldn't possibly love me, so what's the point of going on?"

Convinced that your partner could never sleep with someone else and still love you, or ever love you again, you may succumb to despair or indignation, and give up on a relationship that in your heart you'd like to save.

Some of you may turn your pain inward with thoughts such as, "I'm a loser," "I can't compete," and "I'm unlovable," and write your relationship off as a terrible joke. Others among you may turn your pain outward and strike back preemptively, abandoning the person who abandoned you. The fact that your partner seems to have more choices than you, to have less to lose if the relationship fails, may only increase your wish to get the upper hand. Your anger is likely to feel empowering, and you may be reluctant to let it go, though it may simply mask feelings of self-deprecation, neediness, jealousy, or disillusionment.

It's natural to want to turn your back on someone who hurt or replaced you, and to proclaim that you're better off on your own—who among us, after all, wouldn't want to believe that this person is disposable? I urge you, however, not to make an irreversible life decision while you're feeling so bruised. Your assumption that your partner doesn't love you, or never did, may not be true. There may be reasons the affair happened that have little or nothing to do with you or with your life together. Your partner may feel more humbled and contrite than he or she is willing to admit, and want to work with you to restore the relationship, if you can be open to that possibility.

"I was about to leave my husband for straying once too often," a patient named Betty told me. "I thought, 'What's love, if it doesn't translate into loving behavior?' But he came to see, and made me see as well, that what was drawing him to other women wasn't his unhappiness with me, or his love for them, but his fear of intimacy with anyone—his worry that if he let anyone know him, he'd be seen through as a fraud. When I understood this, I felt less personally rejected and tried to be patient while he worked through his issues with his therapist. It was a beginning."

If you're sunk in depression, try to go beyond emotional self-flagellation or obsessive focus on yourself as victim, and look outward at what the affair tells you about your partner's damaged self. If you're feeling indignant, try to risk showing the soft underbelly of your anger—the fear, the hurt, the humiliation that lie beneath it. However you feel, depressed or enraged, you need to talk out your pain in a way that allows your partner to be there for you—and allows you to find out whether this person cares enough to listen and is big enough to take responsibility for his or her own share of the problem.

Concern #9 (for couples): "Isn't it wrong for me to be too affectionate, to spend too much time with you, before I'm positive I want to recommit?"

Some of you may think you should keep your distance from your partner and not be too loving until you know for certain whether you want to get back together. The problem with this strategy is that it's virtually guaranteed to drive a deeper wedge between you. After all, how can you expect to develop more positive feelings toward someone if you refuse to relate to that person in a more positive way?

When Bob started his affair with Laura, he assumed it was wrong to continue living with his wife, Susan, so he found an apartment and moved out. Unsure of where either relationship was heading, he agreed to meet with Susan once a week to keep their connection alive and negotiate practical matters such as taking the dog to the vet, visiting sick relatives, and paying household bills.

Bob avoided his wife sexually and withheld signs of affection from her (calling her on her birthday, wishing her good luck on the first day of her new job), even when he was feeling loving. "It's the respectable thing to do," he insisted, "as long as I'm involved with someone else."

Bob wasn't mad at Susan or mad for Laura, but his life centered around Laura now, and she became his sole source of companionship, as friend and sexual partner. "I suppose that would have been it for Susan and me," Bob admitted later, "but she pleaded with me not to pull away completely, and I was happy not to. I'd go home and she'd have my favorite dinner waiting for me, and then we'd take in a movie with our best friends. Or we'd sit in the living room the way we used to, sipping hot chocolate, sprawled out on our huge couch with our books. At first it felt incredibly awkward. Even weird. But gradually I realized how much I missed her. It brought back our happy times together. It helped me make a decision to stay."

You, the hurt partner, are likely to insist on some heavy talks about the meaning of the affair, and you, the unfaithful partner, are going to need to make yourself available to them to demonstrate that you care about the agony you've caused and are willing to change. Right now, however, the two of you need more than painful confrontations to get back on track, so I encourage you to put them aside from time to time and give your relationship a chance to breathe. It helps to do things that once gave you both pleasure.

A friend told me that after a marathon couples therapy session, she and her husband went off to have Chinese food together. "We were brain dead from fighting all evening," she told me. "All we did was share egg rolls and laugh at how we must look to the therapist, but it was one of the nicest, most intimate times we'd had for months."

If there are moments when either of you feels loving and wants to show physical affection, I suggest you make yourself clear and let your spouse decide whether your advances are appreciated. Although you may not be living together, you don't have to be separated emotionally, or even sexually, as long as you're both honestly trying to work through your ambivalence, and your partner doesn't think that you're more committed than you are.

I realize how incredibly scary it must be to you, the hurt partner, to make yourself vulnerable, only to risk having your feelings trampled on again. If your partner's sexual advances seem to threaten or violate you, you need, of course, to honor these feelings and keep your distance. But you still may be able to enjoy, and even nourish, displays of physical or verbal affection, separate from sex. You'll probably be more comfortable with this if, at other times, your partner is willing to confront the more stressful issues that lie between you.

Though your interactions are likely to be exquisitely self-conscious right now, avoiding each other will only build higher walls between you. You may assume that your partner doesn't want anything to do with you until you overcome your ambivalence, but you may be wrong. The pressure you put on yourself to feel absolutely certain before you share quality time may be self-induced, not something your partner requires or even expects of you.

Concern #10 (for unfaithful partners): "Won't I be able to make a better decision about my lover if we spend more time together?"

When you insist that you're spending every free moment with your lover only to find out where the relationship is going, you may be doing nothing more than putting a respectable face on lust. But you also may be genuinely confused about the intensity of your feelings and looking for a strategy to resolve your ambivalence about recommitting.

The problem with this lopsided approach is that you're likely to get more swept up in the momentum of the affair and learn little or nothing about your feelings toward your partner. If romance is what you want, go ahead, immerse yourself in your lover, but be aware of how it will tilt the scale away from your partner. In the novel *Separation*, the hurt partner captures the difference between himself, the husband of seven years, and his wife's new boyfriend: "Discovery is gone, and only recognition remains. . . . And the violence of conquest will always carry the day against tenderness, even if only temporarily. . . . Thus do those who love lose out to those who are in love." [11]

Later, as passion fades and conflicts emerge, you may see your lover more critically, and cast your partner in a more favorable light. But by then there may be no partner left to return to.

Spending time with the affair-person won't give you the perspective to make a wise choice; it will only bring you closer to that person. If you want to test the strength of your relationship with your partner, you need to invest in your partner, even though your feelings toward the affair-person may remain strong.

DECIDING TO DECIDE

You have a critical life decision ahead of you: whether to rebuild your relationship or leave. Like most couples I see, you may assume that the best or only way to resolve this dilemma is to listen to your heart. Even experts on human relationships put feelings first. When I asked a preeminent psychiatrist why he left his wife after twenty-five years to marry one of his students, he paused and said, "My lover makes me feel alive." That was it. I had expected him to pull one of his byzantine psychological theories out of his academic bag, but his feelings seemed so strong to him, so right, that he saw no reason to examine them more closely.

I encourage you, however, to make your decision in a more deliberate and considered way, one that is *cognitive* rather than *emotional*. I'm not suggesting that you ignore your feelings but that you question the assumptions that lie behind, and help create, your feelings—assumptions about your partner, about love, and about commitment.

Most couples who successfully survive an affair begin the healing process with an overarching sense of ambivalence. You won't ever start if you expect to feel 100 percent motivated or certain. What matters most is that you make a conscious choice to begin. You, the unfaithful partner, must end your sexual or romantic relationship with your lover, or at least suspend it for whatever length of time you and your partner agree upon. You, the hurt partner, must invite your partner back into your life. And the two of you must fully commit to the process of reconnecting, as outlined in this book. This doesn't mean that you have to feel certain about your future together, only that you must *behave as if* you feel certain, while you work on changing the ways you perceive and treat each other. Put your negative feelings aside, commit to each other, demonstrate your commitment by engaging in the trust- and intimacy-building strategies, and then, and only then, see whether you feel more loving, and more loved. If you wait to feel more positive before you act more positively, your relationship won't last the course.

GETTING STARTED

Even if you've made the decision to recommit, you may feel overwhelmed by what one of my patients called "the hours of restorative surgery that lie ahead." Here are a few practical suggestions to get you started.

Time Projection

Imagine what your relationship would be like if you made some of the changes your partner is asking for, and if your partner did the same for you. Small changes, remember, can make a world of difference.

Now try to picture yourself six months, a year, five years from now, enjoying each other, knowing that your decision to stay together was right. If you can imagine yourself putting the bitterness and despair behind you, and using what you've learned from the affair to inject new life into your relationship, you're more likely to make it happen.

Making a Pledge

A pledge formalizes what you've agreed on, and gives you a clear goal to work toward and measure your progress against. One couple agreed to the following:

"I care enough about you and think well enough of you to want to work this out. I don't feel 100 percent loving or certain that this decision is right for me, but those percentages are probably unrealistic given what we've been through. I promise to explore my contribution to the problems in our relationship, and to make the changes you most need, including changes in the way we communicate and relate to each other. I want you to be happy with me, and I'll work to make that happen."

Nonreactive Listening

Don't listen too closely and literally to your partner's insults. There's so much acrimony and misunderstanding between you that you're wiser to "wear earmuffs" than to react defensively and spitefully to your partner's every indictment. Try to go beyond your partner's words and hear the hurt behind them. You're both struggling to understand what happened, restore your sense of self, and achieve some equilibrium in your shared lives. No one knows the truth at this time.

LOOKING AHEAD

Reworking a relationship after infidelity isn't easy, but neither is dissolving one. For those of you who can take an honest look inside yourselves; who have shared a strong, positive history with your partner; who have struggled to support your partner's career and life stresses—financial strains, personal insecurities, in-laws, health problems, unrealized goals, and the incredible sense of inadequacy that often comes with parenting—you have a unique, perhaps once-in-a-lifetime opportunity to clean your wounds and bind together more securely and lovingly without sacrificing the memories that are golden. I urge you not to turn away from it lightly.

The rest of this book will help you transform a damaged past into a loving and hopeful future—an experience that in itself can be profoundly healing. The next chapter begins the process by helping you unravel the meaning and history of the affair.

STAGE THREE

Recovering from the Affair:
"How Do We Rebuild
Our Life Together?"

FIVE

Learning from the Affair

How frightening is the past that awaits us.
    —Polish poet Antonin Slonimski

So often we blame our partner for what goes wrong and fail to see the link between our personal, lifelong conflicts and the conflicts in our relationship—between the damage we carry within ourselves and the damage we experience as a couple.

In attempting to assign responsibility for the infidelity, hurt partners tend to think, "You were screwing around with someone else. Don't blame me." Unfaithful partners tend to think, "You weren't there for me; you drove me away." Both of you are likely to insist on your own, perhaps self-serving, certainly contradictory, and often oversimplified versions of the same conflict. The following alternating viewpoints are typical:

She: "My husband is still flirting, even after his affair."
He: "My wife is pathologically suspicious."

He: "She's always contradicting me in public. It's embarrassing and insulting."

She: "He never lets me say a word. He always has to be the expert."

She: "He ignores me and makes me feel irrelevant."

He: "She's impossible to please. If I spend any time doing things for me, she takes it as rejection."

This chapter asks you to stop pointing fingers at each other and accept an appropriate share of responsibility for the affair. It's not that you're equally culpable; you're not, if only because no one can make another person stray. But instead of haggling over the percentages—how much was your fault, how much mine—you both need to look at how you contributed to your problems at home.

In searching for clues, it helps to explore:

- how you may have been damaged by early life experiences, and how that damage may be undermining your relationship today;
- how you may have been damaged by infidelities in your own family;
- how the qualities you dislike in your partner may be related to those you like or envy, and may be missing in yourself;
- how stressful life events at the time of the affair may have knocked you off balance and contributed to your problems at home.

Let's look at your relationship through each of these prisms, and then bring your insights together in a very concrete exercise.

FACING YOUR DISFIGURED SELF: EXPLORING HOW YOU WERE DAMAGED BY EARLY LIFE EXPERIENCES, AND HOW THAT DAMAGE MAY BE UNDERMINING YOUR RELATIONSHIP TODAY

As you interacted with your parents, siblings, and other significant persons in your childhood, and as you watched them interact with one another, you developed certain dominant ways of feeling, thinking, and behaving that coalesced into the person you have come to know as you. This sense of yourself is likely to have hardened over the years and to affect how you relate to others today, although your early caretakers may be gone. Blindly, tenaciously, you may cling to this familiar self, dysfunctional as it might be. This is the person you know best, the person you've spent a lifetime *being*, the one with whom you feel most comfortable.

Here are a few of the emotions you may have experienced as a child; try to identify the ones that apply to you, and add your own:

Positive feelings: safe, contented, trusting, attended to, praised, respected, accepted, valued, encouraged to express.

Negative feelings: frightened, inadequate, mistrustful, lonely, jealous, bored, deprived, neglected, pressured, unloved, humiliated, criticized, constrained.

These and other feelings influence and define your comfort zone as an adult. The people who let you reexperience similar emotions, positive or negative, are those you're likely to seek out and be romantically attracted to today.

Along with these feelings, you're likely to have developed certain dominant schemas—ingrained perceptions and beliefs—about who you are and what you can, or should, expect from others. If you were abandoned by a parent, for example, you may have learned to expect that people you love will leave you; if you were emotionally or physically abused, you may have learned that the world is an unsafe place and that you need to guard against getting hurt again.

You also acquired specific ways of relating to others. You learned what to say or do to get what you wanted, or how to absorb or live with the pain of being turned down. You became comfortable with a certain level of intimacy (or lack of intimacy) and learned how to act in ways that preserved it. In the end you mastered, or were victimized by, your day-to-day interactions in that small, private world known as home.

You did your best to be safe and happy, given your inherited predispositions and your limited resources as a child, but if you missed out on any of the following critical growth experiences, you may never have fully developed into a healthy, secure, competent adult:[1]

1. Being safe and secure.
2. Functioning independently in the world.
3. Having solid emotional connections with others.
4. Being valued.
5. Being free to express yourself.
6. Being free to let go and have fun.
7. Living with realistic limitations.

Deprived of any of these essential experiences, you're likely to grow up with emotional wounds that affect your choice of partners and the way you relate to them. Here's how:

You may be drawn to someone who, over time, lets you replicate your early experiences with love, unfulfilling as they may have been.

In the idealized stage of courtship, this person may seem to possess the magical power of healing you—of undoing the damage of your past and freeing you from your old, familiar self. But as time passes, you may find that you've chosen someone who evokes within you the same negative but deeply rooted emotions you experienced in your childhood.[2]

You may interpret your partner's words and actions in a way that reinforces the maladaptive experiences you had as a child.

This is a variation on the to-the-person-holding-a-hammer-everything-looks-like-a-nail phenomenon, in which you see in others whatever you know or are looking for, based on your early experiences. If you were controlled as a child, for example, you may perceive your spouse as controlling, whether it's true or not. As Anaïs Nin writes, "We don't see things as they are, we see them as we are."[3] "In that sense," writes clinical psychologist Jay S. Efran, "all our perceptions are, literally, *in*-sights, including the illusion that is hardest of all to shake—that we are able to see an independent, external reality."[4]

You may unknowingly manipulate your partner into responding to you in ways that are upsetting but familiar to you.

In other words, you unwittingly prod your partner into treating you badly so that you experience yourself, the world, and others in the same distorted ways to which you're accustomed.[5] Thus, if your parents resolved conflict by ignoring you, you provoke your partner into ignoring you.

Let's look now at the seven formative growth experiences listed earlier, and see how growing up without them is likely to damage your relationships today.

You're Unable to Feel Safe or Secure

There are two common ways in which your parents may have created an insecure home environment for you:

1. They abandoned you, either physically or emotionally, and you grew up feeling chronically anxious or needy. In your adult relationships, you perceive rejection too easily and too often. Your abandonment schema says, "People I love will leave me."

2. They abused you, physically or emotionally, and you grew up feeling suspicious, intimidated, humiliated. In your adult relationships, you perceive control and sub-

jugation too easily and too often. Your mistrust schema says, "People I love will hurt me."

Let's look at how these two damaging experiences—abandonment and abuse—may affect the way you relate to your partner.

The Unfaithful Partner

Unable "to risk all and to love full out,"[6] you seek out a lover to distance yourself from your partner or lower the emotional temperature between you. Your affair reduces your fear of being emotionally dependent on someone who, you assume, will inevitably leave or hurt you. It can also keep who you are a secret from your partner, and afford you at least a temporary sense of freedom and control.

An affair can also serve to punish your partner and even the score. Having been betrayed earlier in life, you now betray the one you love to seek reparation for past wrongs.[7] If you experienced an abuse of power as a child, you now seek power yourself to make yourself invulnerable. To share power is to put yourself at risk; to wield it is to maintain control. And so your relationship becomes a domestic battlefield in which you struggle for dominance.

When Jane was ten, her mother packed her up and resettled a continent away from her alcoholic father. She never saw him again. "Jane's a great kid," she overheard her mother telling him on the phone one day. "She's yours, too. Get to know her. She needs you." Seventeen years and dozens of unanswered letters later, Jane married what she called an "emotional iceberg" who made her feel as unimportant and unloved as her father had. Throughout the marriage, she rarely confronted him with her loneliness, but retaliated through a series of one-night stands. Their marriage took on a competitive edge, the winner being the partner who needed the other less. "He thinks he's so wise," Jane confided in me, "but he has no inkling of my private life. If he can't find time for me, I'll make my own party."

The Hurt Partner

Having been abandoned in your youth, you're unable to relate to others in an intimate or authentic way, and end up clinging to your partner or making excessive demands on your partner's time. You also assault your partner with unfounded suspicions (ones that stem from your past experiences and predate your partner's affair).

Having been exposed to an abuse of power, you become overly accommodating and passive as an adult and then feel trapped and secretly resentful of a partner who seems to micromanage your life, always insisting on getting his or her way. Alternatively, you mirror the abuse you once experienced by becoming overbearing and manipulative, constantly ignoring or dismissing your partner's needs. Either way, your behavior is likely to strain your relationship and leave you feeling as alienated as you felt in the past. You may even precipitate what you fear most—being abandoned.

Sheila's father had a history of promiscuity; she remembers hiding in her room late at night, listening to her parents fighting about his betrayals. Her father never owned up to them, and her parents never split up, but the feeling in the house was always tense and sad. After two years of community college she married Sam. Each morning when he left for his high-powered job in New York, she obsessed about his secret life. Her suspicions took on a force of their own, and she found herself accusing him of deliberately staying late at the office and sleeping with his assistant. Sam found her relentless interrogations and angry outbursts impossible to deal with. "She became inconsolable," he told me. "There was nothing I could do to reassure her of my love, short of imprisoning myself in the house. After a while, she won; she wore me down. I really did dread coming home and started going out with a woman who works on my floor. I've been seeing her ever since."

You're Unable to Function Independently

Your parents discouraged you from forming your own identity, developing an independent life, or trusting your own decisions. As a result, you grew up feeling dependent, vulnerable, incompetent. In your adult relationships, you feel controlled by the emotional needs of others, and guilty or fearful when you try to strike out on your own. Your lack-of-autonomy schema says, "I can't make it by myself."

The Unfaithful Partner

An affair for you can be an act of rebellion, a way of declaring independence from relationships that feel too intimate or engulfing. Having been reared in a home in which your boundaries were ignored and privacy didn't exist, you learned to assert your sense of self through secrecy and subterfuge. Unable to be yourself in the presence of your partner, you feel a need to step outside the relationship to breathe.

David grew up without a father. His mother, a Holocaust survivor, feared losing her only child (physically and emotionally), and refused to let him bring friends to the house. Each day she walked him home from school. He experienced his mother as suffocatingly invasive, and himself as dependent and weak. Loving, to him, meant merging with another person and losing oneself. "My relationship with my mother was like that of a moth to a flame," he told me. "It was dangerous to get too close, but I couldn't stay away."

David was attracted to Muriel because, like his mother, she was frightened and insecure, and needed him so much. In their marriage, he struggled to find a way to be connected to her, yet be separate and true to himself. He needed her love to feel whole and to quell his fear of being on his own; but when he catered to her needs, he felt cramped and resentful. "I shouldered two damaged women, my mother and my wife, and sacrificed myself to both of them," he told me. It was only with prostitutes that he believed he could negotiate his needs.

The Hurt Partner

Afraid to create a life of your own, you envy your partner's separateness and feel anxious whenever this person functions independently of you. You expect your partner to enrich your impoverished life, with no help from you. Or you swing the other way, become fiercely independent, and never permit your partner to support you.

Anna, an only child, was raised by a mother who lived to protect and provide for her. When Anna was three and playing in the backyard, her mother went into the house to fold laundry. When she returned, Anna was gone. The mother found her down the street, sitting on the curb, crying. She had been kidnapped by a man who had lifted her into his car and cajoled her into giving him a hand job.

From that day, Anna's guilt-ridden mother became even more protective, crushing her daughter's every effort to strike out on her own. She was forbidden from locking her bedroom door at home or living off campus in college. Her mother's be-careful, don't-do-that attitude made it impossible for Anna to develop a sense of effectiveness or mastery in her interactions with the world. As an adult, she became engaged to a man who overfunctioned as a partner, and continued to protect her from life. But her passivity, dependence, and lack of spontaneity gradually grated on him, and he had an affair with someone who seemed more vibrant and interactive, more "real."

You're Unable to Connect Emotionally to Others

Your parents failed to interact with you in a warm, nurturing way, and you grew up in an emotional vacuum, feeling lonely, uncared for, empty. In your adult relationships, you experience others as disinterested or cold, and react by remaining aloof, drifting from relationship to relationship, or desperately seeking attention from people who let you down. Your emotional deprivation schema says, "Nobody is there for me."

Raised without skills as a loving collaborator, you're likely to be intimate with no one, including yourself. Commitment, intimacy, sharing of responsibility—these are only abstractions to you.

The Unfaithful Partner

You sleep around with the hope of finding someone who, this time, will form a meaningful and durable bond with you. To escape your sense of inner barrenness, you become compulsively sexual and crave the excitement and novelty of short-term serial encounters. Enduring relationships seem intolerably predictable and disillusioning.

Chuck grew up in a divorced home with a narcissistic father who was too busy making deals to notice him. "I don't think we ever had a heart-to-heart talk," he told me. "The one time he bragged about me, he exaggerated the truth. I struck three batters out in one inning, and he told everyone I pitched a no-hitter. The man had no idea who I was."

When Chuck turned nineteen, he got involved with Marilyn. After six months of dating, he discovered that she was sleeping with his best friend. Chuck and Marilyn patched things up and got married, but Chuck never believed he could satisfy her. Shortly after the birth of their first child, he began using escort services. Though Marilyn remained faithful, he wrote her off as cold and distant, and continued to remind her of her past infidelity as an excuse for his. Inside, he was terrified of an intimate commitment. He was sure that even if he let her get close, she'd continue to be unloving. By keeping her at arm's length, he never tested whether she could be there for him, whether she would embrace him. Anonymous sex and self-righteous anger allowed him to remain safely detached.

The Hurt Partner

Your family never taught you how to relate in a loving way, or how to reach out when you were feeling disconnected. You compensate today by withholding love or demanding more than anyone can give, and drive your partner away.

Sara grew up without parenting. Her mother was clinically

depressed and rarely left her bedroom. Her father worked long hours as an attorney eighty miles from home, and once, when she was twelve, moved into a separate apartment for several months. Neither parent showed interest in her feelings, or explained what was going on. She grew up feeling unloved, lonely, lost—deprived of a sense of family oneness, a sense of "we." The man she chose to marry was emotionally unavailable to her, self-absorbed. "Sometimes the only way to get his attention is to scream at him," she told me. Recently, he suggested that they try a trial separation. She suspects he's involved with someone else.

You're Unable to Value Yourself

As a child, your parents frequently criticized you and made you feel you didn't measure up. In the absence of praise or encouragement, you grew up feeling defective, unlovable, unsupported, ashamed. In your adult relationships, you perceive ridicule, rejection, or blame too easily. Your self-esteem schema says, "I'm not good enough."

The Unfaithful Partner

Having personal adequacy issues, you're vulnerable to the ministrations of an adoring admirer. When your femininity or masculinity is threatened (for example, a miscarriage or bankruptcy), you seek a lover to mask your feelings of disgrace or inferiority. What draws you to your lover seems to be this person's specialness, but may be only your need to restore your injured self—to feel more sexy, wanted, winning.

John, a celebrated lawyer, doted on his sons—all but his youngest, Chris. While the others followed their father to Harvard, Chris had to settle for a state university. While the others launched successful legal careers, Chris began manufacturing women's sportswear. He laughed when the family called him the black sheep, but inside he was hurting.

Chris married Rita because she looked up to him and made him feel good about himself. But when his business took a dive, she could do nothing to undo his humiliation. When she offered advice, all he could hear was his father saying, "Typical. You can't do anything right." Chris paired up with Debbie, his sales manager, fourteen years his junior, who helped him recover his financial losses and his self-respect.

The Hurt Partner
Your personal adequacy issues make it impossible for you to relate to anyone in a full-bodied, intimate way. Your negativity denigrates both of you, and pushes your partner out the door.

When Susan's parents got divorced, she stayed with her mother. But when her mother was unable to manage both a willful daughter and a full-time job, Susan was shunted off to live with her father. His younger wife complained openly about this intrusion. Susan never felt she had a home of her own or a place where she was wanted. Eventually she married Rob, and looked to him to make her feel whole. But her neediness made her difficult to love. In the end, Rob found refuge with her best friend, which only reinforced her feelings of defectiveness.

You're Unable to Express Yourself
Your parents never let you have a voice of your own. Today you try to please others, and silence yourself to avoid conflict. You're used to feeling subjugated, misunderstood, manipulated, dismissed. In your relationships, you perceive others as being controlling and insensitive to your needs. Your subjugation schema says, "My needs don't count."

The Unfaithful Partner
You keep your needs locked up inside and then silently resent how much more you give than you get back and go elsewhere to have your needs met. You succeed in keeping the peace but end up feeling victimized, unacknowledged, lonely.

Fritz grew up in a household dominated by his successful father. His mother smiled a lot. No one ever made waves. As an adult, Fritz went to work for his father and married a strong-willed woman named Roberta, whom he lavished with attention and gifts. At first the couple seemed to fit together seamlessly, but before long Roberta was attacking him for living in his father's shadow. Fritz said nothing, but finally expressed his rage by having an affair with his young bookkeeper.

The Hurt Partner

By silencing your needs, you're able to maintain a candy-coated pleasantness in your relationship. But inside you're seething with boredom or frustration. Periodically you erupt with hostility, deepening the rift between you. Your silence doesn't cause your partner's infidelity, but it puts you in the intolerable position of tolerating it.

Mindy's mother tried to keep the house as stress-free as possible so as not to aggravate her asthmatic husband. Mindy grew up learning never to rock the boat. Eventually she married Sal, an anesthesiologist with a numbing sense of entitlement, and spent her time catering to him while he catered to himself. His neglect galled her as much as his self-adulation, but she said nothing. "I can't legislate love," she told me. "If I'm good to him, he'll want to spend time with me."

No one apparently was good enough for Sal but Sal, however, and the relationship continued to deteriorate. Mindy saw less and less of him until one day she caught him in bed with his nurse.

You're Unable to Let Go and Have Fun

Your parents never let you follow your own natural inclinations and enjoy yourself, so you grew up feeling weighed down and stressed out. In your adult relationships, you shoulder too much responsibility and then feel taken advantage of. Your perfectionist strivings lead you to overdiscipline yourself or your partner. You easily perceive others as weak or lazy and unwilling to share the load. Your unrelenting standards schema says, "Everything falls on me, and I'd better do it right."

The Unfaithful Partner

Taught to be excessively responsible, even perfect, you seek out a lover who can give you back some of the childhood you were robbed of. You attribute this reawakening to the lover, when, in fact, it's because you have finally granted yourself permission to be self-indulgent or impulsive, and have replaced rigid internalized rules with ones that gratify your momentary needs.

Keith went directly from high school into a Whirlpool training program to help support an unemployed father and a disabled brother who lived at home. He resented them both. The woman he chose to marry, Michelle, had a childlike spontaneity about her and was as joyful as he was sober, but before long he resented her ability to balance work and play—to find time to exercise at the gym, call friends, linger over meals—while he exhausted himself in the factory. "She's sloughing off," he complained. "She's taking advantage of me." When he finally managed to break free of his demanding work ethic and treat himself, it was on Skype with a go-go dancer from Romania.

The Hurt Partner

Tethered to unrelenting standards, you developed compulsive habits that today drive much of the playfulness, romance, and creativity from your life. You're running so hard and fast, you have no time to smell the roses or realize that your partner is bringing a dozen to someone else.

Dorothy's puritanical father berated her for being only human. She married Ernie, who was too preoccupied with his poetry to balance the checkbook or carpool the kids to school. The more Dorothy tried to change him, the more polarized they became. Her inflexibility made him feel that he couldn't be himself with her. Her requests, like her need for order, were reasonable but unremitting. One day she told him to take out the garbage. He took out the babysitter instead.

You're Unable to Set or Accept Realistic Limits

Your parents did too much for you, or taught you to view yourself as superior to others. As an adult, you lack self-discipline, expect special consideration, and take offense when people put restrictions on you or force you to play by the rules. You easily perceive others as violating your rights, even though you're insensitive to theirs. This entitlement schema says, "I'm above the rest; I deserve as much as I can get."

The Unfaithful Partner

Your partner may be struggling to cope with your grandiosity, but, given how unaware you are of your effect on people, you're unlikely to notice. Instead, you probably see your partner as someone who fails to satisfy your needs, and you feel wronged and deprived. Having grown up without a model of mature reciprocity—of mutual give-and-take—you can't see that your demands for love are excessive, and that you fail to nurture your partner in ways that entitle you to the treatment you think you deserve. Your dissatisfaction at home, along with your affairs, seems perfectly legitimate to you, because you expect so much from your partner and so little from yourself. Avoiding the discomfort of self-examination, you're unlikely to subject yourself to therapy, or to read this book.

Howard was raised by wealthy, power-seeking parents who emphasized the attainment of status and recognition. They rarely imposed limits on him, and more than once relied on their attorneys to cover his tracks when he was caught breaking the law. As an adult, he drifted from marriage to marriage, always madly in love until the birth of children, who made him feel peripheral.

The Hurt Partner

Unaccustomed to setting internal limits or confronting your personal failings, you, too, are unlikely to be reading this book. Your energy is probably too invested in preserving an inflated sense of self, or searching for someone who will preserve it for you. You feel entitled to be taken care of, while doing little to earn it. Your partner's affair, however, may force you to confront your imperfections and give you the perspective you need to become a more lovable partner.

Michelle's mother raised her five sisters by herself and swore she'd give Michelle a more carefree childhood. Michelle was rarely disciplined and could shirk responsibility—emptying the dishwasher, getting summer jobs—with impunity. She was never encouraged to excel. "Life's short," her mother told her. "Enjoy it."

Michelle married Keith, who soon tired of her sybaritic ways and insisted that she get a job. She resented his ultimatums—until Keith started seeing other women, and she discovered that she was replaceable.

EXERCISE

It's not possible to identify in one book all the ways in which you may have been injured as a child, or all the ways in which your injuries have affected the development of your personality, your choice of partners, or your role in the affair. The fact that your parents treated you in one particular way doesn't bind you to any one set of behaviors or beliefs. However, we do tend to bring our damaged selves into our most intimate relationships, and to reenact with our partners the struggles of our childhoods. As bitter or unnourishing as they may be, they're what we know and what we tend to feed on.

It's difficult to sort out how much of your dissatisfaction is your partner's fault (treating you in ways that make you experience yourself as you did as a child); and how much is your fault (manipulating your partner into treating you in these old, dysfunctional ways).[8] To begin to make these distinctions, you need to learn more about your vulnerabilities, more about your own unbeautiful self. As a starting point, I suggest that you try to answer the following questions:

1. Which of the seven growth experiences described in this section was I deprived of?

2. What feelings (see list on p. 118) were most dominant or familiar to me as I was growing up?

3. What was going on in my relationship with my parents, significant caretakers, or siblings, or in their relationships with one another, that made me feel this way?

4. What was missing from the way my mother treated me? What was my greatest unmet need? How did this affect who I became, and the way I feel about myself today?

5. What was missing from the way my father treated me? What was my greatest unmet need? How did this affect who I became, and the way I feel about myself today?

6. What did I like most about the way my mother treated me? How did this affect who I became, and the way I feel and think about myself today?

7. What did I like most about the way my father treated me? How did this affect who I became, and the way I feel or think about myself today?

8. What did I learn about love from the way my mother and father treated me?

9. What did I learn about love from the way my parents treated each other?

10. Who were the other significant people in my life? What did they teach me about love, and how did they affect my concept of myself?

11. How do I blame you, my partner, for making me feel the way I've always felt?

12. How do you blame me for making you feel the way you've always felt?

13. How do I hurt you in ways in which you're already vulnerable?

14. How do you hurt me in ways in which I'm already vulnerable?

15. How do I provoke you so that you react to me in ways that hurt me, as I'm used to being hurt?

16. How do you provoke me so that I react to you in ways that hurt you, as you're used to being hurt?
17. What do I give you that you value most?
18. What do you most need from me to feel safe, secure, and valued?

TRANSGENERATIONAL INJURIES: EXPLORING HOW YOU MAY HAVE BEEN DAMAGED BY INFIDELITIES IN YOUR OWN FAMILY

Your experiences with infidelity as a child are likely to shape how you experience and think about infidelity today. If one of your parents was unfaithful, you're likely to have grown up in an atmosphere clouded with secrecy and tension, your boundaries blurred, your right to a secure, stable environment denied. Perhaps the babysitter you counted on to take care of you at night suddenly began taking care of Daddy at night; perhaps your father's best friend became your mother's best friend—and your stepfather. Either parent may have replaced you with a new playmate, and there was no way for you to beat the competition. Or one parent confided in you that the other was an adulterer, and implored you never to reveal the secret. The unfaithful parent, swept up in the passion of the affair, may have had little time for you, and avoided you or turned away in shame to escape your condemning glance. The hurt parent may have been too depressed, too obsessed with the affair-person, to pay attention to your suffering. Both parents may have competed for your support or forgiveness, while overlooking or discounting your pain.

Today, long after the infidelity has been acknowledged or put to rest, you may still be scarred, may still be harboring negative feelings about yourself and carrying them with you into your most intimate relationships. Riddled with insecurity, you may have trouble perceiving yourself as a worthy, lovable, special human being. It's not easy to love, or be loved, when feelings of abandonment, invalidation, or betrayal are core to your sense of self.

Let's look now at how these early patterns of infidelity may have left their mark on you.

The Effects of Previous Infidelities on Unfaithful Partners

You're more likely to have an affair if one of your parents did.[9] This may seem strange at first. Why would you emulate those who blew your world apart? Wouldn't you want to give your life the structure, the solidity you never knew? The answer is yes, of course you would, but you don't expect it to happen, so you have an affair to create a safe distance between you and your partner and protect yourself from being violated again. You learned your lesson: To love is to open yourself to pain. Being faithful makes you feel dependent and vulnerable; being unfaithful makes you feel invincible.

Mike never forgot the day his father left home. It was on his thirteenth birthday, and he found his mother sobbing at the kitchen table. Three weeks passed before his father stopped by, unannounced, to pick up his golf clubs and his Gucci ties. His mother told him what his father refused to admit, that he had moved in with another woman. Mike had never felt that his father was proud of him; now he was sure. Looking back as an adult, he realized that on that day he made a pact with himself never to love anyone so totally again—and he kept his promise. Even after he married Barbara, he remained committed to a life of promiscuity.

An affair may lift you, like Mike, into a position of power and control—what better way to avoid feeling the way your straying parent made you feel than to become that parent yourself? By identifying with the aggressor, you toss off the role of victim. No longer are you the one who was abandoned; now *you* abandon. No longer are you the one who was emotionally deprived or abused; now *you* deprive and abuse. You're out of harm's way, and in command.

Andrea knew for years that her father was an adulterer and that her mother was chronically depressed. She couldn't wait to leave home and wrap herself in the warmth of a loving, committed relationship. But one night, feeling irrelevant to her fiancé, she screamed at him, drove to a bar, and threw herself at a married man. In one swift, nihilistic blow, she tried to rise above the anguish of her past. "I don't need John [her fiancé]; he's replaceable," she told me. "All dicks are the same in the dark."

An affair may allow you to loathe yourself instead of your straying parent—to turn on yourself the rage you feel toward the parent who tore up your family. By making yourself the object of your contempt, you never have to grieve the loss of the parent who wasn't there for you. Sometimes it's easier and less confusing to hate yourself—to see yourself as weak, morally reprehensible, selfish, impulsive, "no good"—than to face the one who let you down, particularly if your self-contempt allows you to feel as defective as your parents made you feel. By directing your scorn and shame at yourself, you manage to stay attached to a parent who detached from you, and take control of your pain.

Janet never confronted the rage she felt toward her father for sleeping around while her mother was undergoing chemotherapy. Instead, she slept with her best friend's husband, turned her fury into shame, and directed it inward at herself. "I've thrown all my values out the window," she told me. The problem with hiding from her rage was that it prevented her from having an authentic relationship with anyone—her father, her husband, or herself.

It's unlikely that your family's *attitude* toward infidelity caused you to be unfaithful, but it may have laid the groundwork.[10] If you grew up in an environment in which adultery was winked at, and heard messages such as "boys will be boys" or "what your partner doesn't know won't hurt," you may be more likely as an adult to stray. Messages travel across generations.

The Effects of Previous Infidelities on Hurt Partners

It's no coincidence that so many of my patients whose parents had affairs have partners who cheat as well. By latching on to someone who betrays you, or by provoking that person to betray you, you reexperience the same rejection you experienced as a child. It's not that you take pleasure in being replaced; you don't consciously seek out abandonment or deliberately go in search of pain. What you may do unknowingly is seek out someone who treats you in a way that replicates your earlier experience of yourself. Even if your partner is committed to you, you're still likely to read into that person's behavior what you're programmed to see, and then react in ways that reinforce your preconceptions.

Eddie's overbearing father, a remorseless philanderer, made a habit of trashing his oversensitive son at every opportunity. When the boy turned twenty, he was coerced into marriage by a promiscuous and imperious woman named Alison. His attachment to her replicated his earlier experience of love: a relationship between a bully and a victim. Two years into the marriage, after Alison's third affair, he scraped together enough self-esteem to break the mold and leave her.

When Eddie fell in love with Linda, he vowed not to repeat past patterns. But he was so accustomed to being dominated that he didn't know how to tolerate such a mutually supportive relationship. "This must be love," he told me. But then he found himself orchestrating confrontations that undermined his happiness. If Linda so much as glanced at another man, he pummeled her with questions about her faithfulness. Alone in my office, he devalued her and their relationship. "I don't really love her that much," he insisted. "She's not all that attractive or special."

At the same time, Eddie berated himself for trying to destroy the best thing that had ever happened to him. Was it to restage the abandonment he had experienced first with his father and then with his ex-wife, Alison? To diminish Linda's value and make himself feel less dependent, less assailable? To test her love? To reinforce his sense of himself as an unlovable human being?

Eddie found a certain sad truth in all these explanations and talked to himself about his behavior so that he would stop contaminating their relationship. It wasn't easy. Trusting that your partner loves you and is committed to you is hard if you've been taught the opposite all your life. Having been left before, why, you wonder, won't you be left again?

History Repeated

Sometimes there can be an uncanny resemblance between the circumstances of your betrayal as a child and the circumstances of your betrayal as an adult. I don't believe people are doomed to repeat old patterns, or deliberately re-create them, but they do happen with unsettling regularity. Here are two typical experiences my patients have shared with me.

Just before Lauri was born, her father announced that he was leaving her mother for another woman. Lauri grew up ministering to a mother who was later diagnosed as schizophrenic. Thirty-four years later, when Lauri was nine months pregnant with her third child, her husband announced that he was in love with another woman and leaving home. In the hospital, Lauri gave birth to her daughter alone and, with a macabre sense of déjà-vu, brought her home to a fatherless house.

Stephanie grew up with an alcoholic mother and an unfaithful father. As a young adult, she parented them and lectured them frequently on the importance of changing their ways. To escape them, she became engaged to Hal, only to discover that he was an alcoholic who was engaged to someone else in another city. She took to lecturing him frequently about changing his ways.

Whatever the similarities between your partner's and your parent's affairs, your injury today is likely to cut more deeply—to reopen a channel of vulnerability inside you—if you experienced a betrayal earlier in your life. It's not that your sense of violation today isn't genuine or profound, but that it's contaminated by the trauma of your early experiences. That trauma needs to be acknowledged and addressed separately. You can't restore your relationship today until you strip away the damage of the past.

EXERCISE

I strongly advise you to confide in each other about your childhood encounters with infidelity. Talk through how you felt at the time, and how your experiences may have reduced your ability to value yourself and feel safe and trusting in your relationship today. Disclosing your personal histories won't make the affair less upsetting, but it may help you understand the depth and intensity of your reactions, and make you feel closer to each other—more like allies than enemies.

I also strongly urge you to discuss the affair with your children, at whatever level of detail they can digest. Encourage them to acknowledge their feelings—their grief, their anger, their confusion—and confront you with them. If you can acknowledge their pain—listening openly, without defending or explaining—you may help them avoid similar mistakes in their own adult lives. Apologize for the hurt you've caused, for your unavailability and insensitivity. Talk about yourself, knowing your partner is doing the same. Invite your children to bring up the topic again and again, as often as they need. Don't be afraid to let them see your pain or your hope for the future of your family. Later on, you may want to share with them your understanding of how you personally contributed to your marital problems. You may also want to reveal your own experiences with infidelity while you were growing up, and how those experiences marked you.

To heal the injuries of prior infidelities and move your relationship forward, I recommend that you try to separate the past from the present, and address the grievances you still hold against the person who betrayed you in your childhood. One way to do this is to write that person a letter, revising it as many times as you need until you feel it expresses exactly what you want to say. If the person is alive, you may decide to send it. Your purpose isn't to elicit a compassionate response—if this happens, great; but be prepared for no response or a defensive and hostile one. What matters most is that you acknowledge the full range of your feelings and make peace with your past.

Here's a letter that one of my patients named Mike wrote to his unfaithful father, almost three decades after his father's affair. It was Mike's way of breaking the silent pact he had made with himself never to let anyone get close to him again.

Dear Dad,

I've waited close to thirty years to bring up the subject of your leaving Mom and me. I hope it's not too late to discuss it with you. I'm not writing to blame you or to make you feel guilty; in fact, I hope that by talking about it, we can understand each other better and maybe close some of the gaps that still sit between us.

Dad, I've always wanted to ask you why you left without talking to me, why you stayed away for so long, how you couldn't have known or cared (it seemed) how that would affect me. I felt totally unimportant to you. The truth is, I always felt I didn't achieve enough to make you proud of me. Can you help me understand why you acted the way you did? Whatever the explanation, it probably isn't as bad as what I've assumed to be true.

I don't fault you for leaving, for being unhappy in your marriage, even for not knowing how to work things out with Mom. I've been married twenty-two years now; I know how hard it is to hold a marriage together. I've failed in many ways. I've even had my infidelities.

For years I couldn't face how angry I was with you for leaving me, for rarely making me feel you loved me or were proud of me, for making me take care of Mom. But I've come to realize, at least for my own self-preservation, that what you did had nothing to do with me—that I was just a kid, that I didn't do anything wrong, that I wasn't deficient in any particular way. I've learned not to take what happened so personally anymore.

When I was thirteen and you left, I decided I'd never let anyone get close to me again, and I'd never love anyone again. I kept my promise. But recently, since [my wife] Barbara found out about my affairs, we've started to talk more honestly to each other, and I'm beginning to feel I don't have to keep her at a distance anymore, and that I don't want to live such a controlled and insulated life. I'm reaching out to her, as I'm reaching out to you today.

If you'd like to respond, I'd love to hear from you. If you can't, I just want you to know—and I just want to say it out loud for myself—that I'm not going to invest my energy in hurting anymore, in feeling unsafe anymore, in keeping the world at arm's length anymore. I forgive you for the unhappiness you must have felt to leave. I even forgive you for leaving the way you did. I wish you a better life now. I wish myself a better life now.

By the way, the kids are doing great. I welcome your involvement with them. I'm sure they'd like to know you better, too.

Love,

Mike

UNDERSTANDING THE FLIP-FLOP FACTOR: SEEING HOW THE QUALITIES YOU DISLIKE IN YOUR PARTNER MAY BE RELATED TO THOSE YOU LIKE OR ENVY, AND MAY BE MISSING IN YOURSELF

As disenchantment sets in, you're likely to screen out your partner's positive qualities and selectively focus in on the bad. You may even forget that the positive ever existed. If the two of you are going to make it, you need to learn that the qualities you like and dislike in your partner are often flip sides of the same attribute, that you can't have one without the other, and that your dissatisfaction may say as much about your own unresolved inner conflicts as it says about your partner's.

Becky was initially attracted to Steve's stability, but over time grew to hate his lack of spontaneity. What she failed to see was that both qualities sprang from the same root. The problem was not that he had changed but that she had imposed different meanings on the same behavior; one day loving the security and structure he gave her life, the next day hating how constricted he made her feel. When she looked back at the chaos of her childhood—her father was addicted to drugs, her mother had manic episodes—she realized that the qualities she criticized her husband for (his inflexibility, his joylessness) were linked to the ones she counted on him for (his predictability, his dependability) and lacked within herself.

Vicki spent her childhood trying to please her hypercritical parents. In college she was drawn to a man who, unlike herself, seemed totally self-sufficient. After they married, she catered to his needs and encouraged him to ignore hers. It wasn't long before she felt overwhelmed and unsupported, just as she had felt at home. She now viewed her partner's attributes differently. What had passed for self-sufficiency she now saw as selfishness. What had passed for independence she now saw as aloofness.

I call this phenomenon—that a certain basic personality trait triggers both what you love and hate about your partner—the Flip-Flop Factor.[11]

The qualities that you consider negative are the "flop" side of the equation. The qualities that appealed to you when you were first attracted to each other, or that still appeal to you today, are the "flip" side. Put them down next to each other and you'll discover that neither side exists in isolation; that what you consider the good inevitably keeps company with the bad; and that the attributes that repel you may also attract you, when looked at from another angle.

Here are some negative attributes that you may have experienced once as positive:

Negative Attributes ("Flop" side)	Positive Attributes ("Flip" side)
lacks spontaneity, passion, and a sense of adventure; boring	stable, reliable, even-tempered, content
constantly seeks approval; unassertive, ineffectual, weak	considerate, attentive, accommodating
spaced out, self-absorbed, irresponsible	creative, flexible, spontaneous
joyless, compulsive, materialistic, driven	disciplined, productive, effective, responsible, successful
depraved, needy, oversexed	uninhibited, sexual, passionate
uncommunicative, secretive, lifeless	calm, peaceful, mysterious
narcissistic, attention-seeking	affable, socially skilled, gregarious
depressing, burdensome	deep, thoughtful
silly, superficial	fun-loving, capricious
suffocatingly invasive, needy, controlling	attentive, generous, giving, involved
cold, removed, unloving, selfish	independent, confident, stable, strong, self-reliant
hysterical, unstable	expressive
arrogant, controlling	masterful, competent

It's important for you to see how your unresolved personal conflicts make you dwell on the flop side, and block you from ever feeling content with anyone, including yourself. Maggie Scarf refers to "the unacknowledged, repudiated, and thoroughly unintegrated aspects of one's own personality," and explains, "What was once unacceptable within the self is now what is so intolerable and unacceptable in the partner. The war within each member of the couple has been transformed into a war between them. And each believes that peace and harmony could be achieved, if only the other would change." [12] In other words, the qualities you hate in your partner may be related to those you hate in yourself. They also may be related to qualities you lack, and envy your partner for having.

The story of Keith and Michelle illustrates some of these points. Keith's father did everything he could to avoid a hard day's work, and flitted from one disastrous get-rich-quick scheme to another. Keith resented his father for not carrying his weight and identified with his mother, who held the family together with her paycheck from Stop & Shop. Love, to Keith, was another word for self-sacrifice.

As an adult, Keith was hard-driving, goal-oriented, ambitious. But though he could move swiftly and efficiently from point A to point B, he often sensed that something was missing. "I'm driven and irritable too often," he told me. "Life simply isn't much fun."

Keith was initially drawn to Michelle for her light-heartedness, her warmth, her ability to enjoy the moment and be satisfied with her lot—the qualities he most lacked in himself. Before long, however, he began to dwell on the flop side of these attributes. What had once seemed spontaneous in her now seemed irresponsible; what had once seemed fun-loving now seemed undisciplined. He resented having to support her and her photography habit. If she could play, why shouldn't he? To make his point, he rented a studio apartment for his "late nights at the office" with a neighbor's wife. There, for the first time, he escaped his overly conscientious, constricted self. He didn't want to break up his marriage, but he didn't know how to feel better in it. After Michelle found out what was going on—she saw that he was withdrawing large sums from ATMs and confronted him—Keith began looking into himself. What he discovered was that his dissatisfaction said as much about him as it did about Michelle.

"I realize she's not the source of all my unhappiness or the only one who needs to change," he acknowledged. "My father was a financial drain on us, and I don't want my wife to be one, too. But I know I'm oversensitive about this, that Michelle isn't my father, and that she's good for me—the way she makes me laugh and helps me see there's more to life than making money."

Keith refused to let what he considered Michelle's irritating attributes poison their relationship, and worked to recognize what it was about them that he found appealing.

"I'll always get annoyed at how she ducks responsibility," he told me—"how she comes home and, instead of putting the groceries away or folding the laundry, calls her friends or checks her e-mail. But I've come to accept that the good comes packaged with the bad, and though I hate how undisciplined she can be, I admire how much she enjoys life, unlike me."

To reinforce his new understanding, Keith drew up a ledger, stating on one side what bothered him, and, on the other, what he admired or envied about the same characteristics. Here's what he wrote:

Michelle's Negative Attributes	Michelle's Positive Attributes
procrastinates	lives for the moment
lacks discipline	spontaneous
uninterested in making money	relationship-oriented
slovenly	easygoing
irresponsible, spendthrift	carefree
naive	optimistic
expects to be taken care of; spoiled	improves the quality of our lives in nonfinancial ways

Now let's turn to Michelle. She hadn't been entirely happy with the marriage, either. Although it was Keith who strayed, she more than once had fantasized about sleeping with someone else herself.

Michelle's mother, burdened with responsibilities as a child, had encouraged her daughter to live for the moment. Michelle was not grateful. "My mother expected nothing from me," she complained. "It was like she thought I didn't have a creative bone in my body, like I was good for nothing but good times."

Michelle was drawn to Keith because he seemed to believe in her artistic talent. He was focused and entrepreneurial, unlike her, and helped her organize and direct her energies.

Turn the clock ahead three years, and these same qualities of his were driving her nuts. "I used to think he was so productive," she told me. "Now I think he's just a workaholic. He encouraged me to develop a career not because he loved my photos but because he didn't want to support me."

To help Michelle appreciate the flip side of Keith's attributes—the side that drew her to him in the first place—I asked her to generate a list of his negative qualities and match them up with the ones she once loved in him. Here's what she came up with:

Keith's Negative Attributes	Keith's Positive Attributes
controlling, can't share power or collaborate in decision making	resourceful, competent, achieving
compulsive, driven, no fun	organized, productive, focused
insecure about money	responsible, encourages my work
materialistic	supports a high standard of living

The exercise reminded her that what she objected to was related to what she was still drawn to, and helped her to re-attach to what she liked in him. It also taught her that what she resented him for (his materialism, his compulsive work ethic) was linked to qualities she had always lacked in herself (stick-to-it-iveness, ambition). If she was ever going to feel more satisfied with him, she would have to look more deeply into her own personal issues.

"My mother never made me work a day in my life," Michelle told me. "She taught me it was my right to be dependent. Keith wants to change the rules, and I resent him for it. But I can see that he's not mean or unreasonable to ask me to pull some of my own weight."

EXERCISE

The Flip-Flop Factor can teach you, as it taught Keith and Michelle, to think differently about your dissatisfaction. It can show you that a partner who annoys or frustrates you isn't automatically wrong, or wrong for you; that though you'll believe the two of you are a bad fit at times, the opposite may be true in the long run. You chose this person—someone who may be very unlike you—for a reason. That reason may be that you're drawn to what is unaccessed or undeveloped in yourself, what you envy, what you're incapable of expressing on your own. The very attributes that you criticize are likely to be intimately related to another set of attributes that enhance you and help you transcend your limited self.

To help you see this, I encourage you to ask yourself the following questions:

1. What attributes do I dislike in my partner?
2. What does it reveal about me that I object to, or resent, these attributes? Do they represent some disavowed aspect of myself?
3. In what way are these negative attributes related to attributes that I admire, and that first attracted me to my partner?
4. What does it reveal about me that I was attracted to these attributes in my partner? Do I lack them in myself? Do I envy them?

The Flip-Flop Factor challenges you to view your differences in a new way, one in which you reconcile, tolerate, and perhaps, at times, embrace the bright and dark sides of your partner's personality, and your own.

TRACING THE TIMELINE: SEEING HOW CRITICAL LIFE EVENTS AT THE TIME OF THE AFFAIR MAY HAVE KNOCKED YOU OFF BALANCE

Identifying the critical life events that contributed directly or indirectly to the affair may help you get a better handle on why the affair happened when it did, and give you some confidence that you can prevent it from happening again.

What I mean by critical life events are personal crises or other stressful circumstances that create an emotional disequilibrium within you and alter the nature of your relationship—

events like the birth or death of a loved one, or a change in health or financial circumstances.

What may add to the impact of these life events is their congruence with stresses to which you're particularly vulnerable. If you grew up sensitive to issues of abandonment or rejection, for example, you're more likely to feel depressed when a nurturing parent dies than when your business falters. If you grew up sensitive to issues of competency or achievement, however, you're more likely to get depressed when your business falters than when you're faced with a personal rejection.[13]

These critical life events may make you, the hurt partner, difficult to live with, and push your partner further away. They may make you, the unfaithful partner, more needy and unstable, more vulnerable to temptation. Your affair may be an attempt to recover from an external crisis that undermines your sense of self, and therefore may have more to do with what's happening inside you than with any specific problem in your relationship.

Here are some common stressors that may throw either one of you off balance and precipitate an affair.

Illness or Accident

You or someone you love has a serious illness or accident, or receives a life-threatening medical diagnosis. You feel vulnerable, mortal. You panic at the thought of how much you haven't yet accomplished or experienced. Alternatively, you panic at the thought of being abandoned.

When Barry had a heart attack at age forty-two, he put his life under review and decided that time was running out. "There's so much I want to do before I die," he thought. He closed his office for the first time in twenty years and set off on a grand tour of Europe with his young secretary.

Tracey developed ovarian cancer. Her husband, Victor, suddenly felt terrified of losing her, of feeling so dependent on her. He took control of these feelings by having an affair, abandoning his wife before she could abandon him.

Death

Someone you love (not your partner) dies. You feel profoundly the loss of support and solace this person gave you, which your partner can't replace. Alternatively, you feel liberated from this person's judgment, and free to act in new, unsanctioned ways.

"When my son took his life," Kate told me, "I found it easier to focus my bitterness on my husband than to lose myself in grief. For consolation, I turned to someone else."

"Divorce was anathema to my mother, and I couldn't deal with her disapproval," Doug explained. "Within a week of her death I had left my wife and moved in with the woman I loved."

Being Uprooted

You move to a new community and suffer the loss of familiar surroundings, family, friends. You compensate by finding a lover. Or you become so depressed and withdrawn that your partner finds one.

Mark's promotion took him from Peoria to Manhattan. His wife felt isolated and abandoned, and angrily withdrew from him. Mark, having no one to celebrate his success with, felt isolated and abandoned as well, and took up with his assistant.

A Shift in Status

You experience a change in power or resources. The partner who is used to feeling more dependent gains career recognition or becomes more financially or emotionally independent. The partner who is used to feeling dominant now feels overshadowed, fears abandonment ("You're bound to leave me, now that you're no longer dependent on me"), and has an affair to feel needed or to stay in control.

As long as Michael felt superior to his wife and could put her down, their marriage, such as it was, held together. But when she addressed his complaints—losing thirty-four pounds and returning to graduate school to complete her degree—he tuned in to his young voice instructor, who restored his threatened sense of power and importance.

Personal Failure

You experience what you perceive as personal failure—the loss of a job, infertility, bankruptcy.

A week after Ron was laid off as an investment banker, he ran into his Wall Street buddies at a local bar and wound up in a motel with a bond trader. "I was on a power trip," he admitted. "I was feeling competitive and not particularly successful."

Life Transitions

You undergo major life transitions that change the nature of your relationship, such as pregnancy, the birth of a child, or the departure of children for college (the empty-nest syndrome).

"When the baby was born," Dick recalled, "nothing else mattered to my wife. I felt totally replaced. So I went off and replaced her."

Substance Abuse

You or your partner becomes addicted to alcohol or drugs.

"I didn't know that Adam was depressed about his business and medicating himself with merlot," his wife, Holly, explained, "but I did know that he seemed totally self-absorbed and uninterested in me. I was feeling so rejected and alone that when my therapist came on to me, I took it as a compliment."

Tracing the Timeline: An Example

It's usually not one isolated event that leads to the affair, but several, happening concurrently. I encourage you and your partner to work together to identify these events and to discuss, in a nonaccusatory way, how they made room for a third person.

Dean and Mary began this discussion by drawing up a chronology of critical life events and exploring how each one helped destabilize their relationship.

Critical Life Events	Responses
July	
We moved from Chicago to New Haven. Dean started a high-pressured job with a hotel chain, working for a boss he couldn't please. Mary was without family or friends.	*Dean:* "I was afraid of being fired. I felt responsible for Mary's happiness, a burden I resented. I spent too many years holding my mother together after my father left, and I couldn't bear subjecting myself to that again."
	Mary: "I felt alone and ignored. I relied on Dean to entertain me."
August–November	
Mary wanted a baby and tried to get pregnant.	*Dean:* "I went along to make her happy, but I wasn't sure I was ready. Our sex life became obligatory, temperature-controlled."
	Mary: "This was a happy time for me. Dean never let on that he was so ambivalent."
December	
Mary got pregnant. Dean visited his best friend, whose first child had just been born.	*Dean:* "I saw how exhausted my friend was, and how constricted his life had become. I felt the door closing on me."
January	
Mary's brother had a serious car accident. Dean celebrated his thirtieth birthday.	*Dean:* "I worried about all the things I'd never see or do."
	Mary: "I spent a lot of time in the hospital visiting my brother. I really wasn't there for Dean."

February

Mary had a miscarriage.

Dean: "I felt almost relieved. I didn't think I could take care of myself, much less a family."

Mary: "I felt defective and demoralized, and withdrew from Dean."

April

Dean had an affair.

Dean: "I felt free, capable, in control—like my old shining self again."

Identifying these critical life events didn't excuse Dean's affair in Mary's eyes, but it helped her take it less personally. Knowing that she was only part of the problem lifted a weight from her shoulders and gave her the confidence to risk loving Dean again. Dean, in turn, saw that his dissatisfaction had less to do with Mary than with the pressures of his new life and with his own unresolved responsibility issues from the past.

The exercise also taught them, as it can teach you, that life itself can be the enemy—that day-to-day stresses conspire against us all, and that we need to join forces against them, not against each other.

RESPONSIBILITY SHARING: AN EXERCISE IN CHANGE [14]

This exercise is a prescription for change. It helps you pull together all the abstract concepts we've been discussing in this chapter and apply them in a very concrete and graphic way whenever you find yourselves in conflict. It shows you the specific changes you need to make to manage your differences and reduce the chances that one of you will stray again.

It's not enough to change the way you act; if you're going to overcome old patterns, you also need to change the way you think and feel. I've therefore divided this exercise into three distinct and deliberately simplified categories:

1. The behavioral component—the way you treat your partner.
2. The cognitive component—the meanings and expectations you attach to your interactions.
3. The emotional component—the way you feel toward your partner.

Step by step, you'll learn to:

- identify what you do that upsets or provokes your partner;
- identify the thoughts and perceptions that feed your behavior;
- identify the specific changes your partner wants you to make;
- develop an attitude or perspective that makes these changes acceptable to you;
- observe how your feelings change as your behaviors and attitudes change.

The exercise consists of writing out or thinking through your responses to the following questions. You can do this together or separately. To make what I'm asking clearer, I've included a case study for you to follow and adapt to your own circumstances.

The Triggering Event
What actually happened? Stick to the facts; don't interpret what they mean to you.
Case Study
By the third day of their ski vacation, Keith had not initiated sex. He insisted that they get up at seven each morning to hit the slopes the minute they opened. Michelle would have preferred to stay in bed and make love some mornings, but

she went along with his plan. She wanted to stop for a nutritious breakfast, but, knowing how disgruntled he'd be, she said nothing and grabbed some muffins at a gas station on their way to the lifts. Finally, she screamed at him, "I don't even know why you wanted me to come on this vacation. All I seem to do is inconvenience you. You just want to do exactly what you want. I feel like a stranger to you." Keith just drove on.

Pinpointing the Conflict
Your Behavior: What did you do that hurt your partner?
Case Study
Keith: I focused on getting the most out of the activity, ignoring or dismissing Michelle's needs; I never made time for intimacy.

Michelle: I ignored my own needs, went along with Keith's plan, then blew up at him.

Your Cognitions: What were you thinking or assuming that made you act the way you did?
Case Study
Keith: Those lift tickets are expensive, so we should get in as much skiing as we can. Michelle's so slow in the morning. She probably wants to stop for breakfast, but if I don't mention it, maybe she'll let it go. As for sex, later.

Michelle: Keith would rather be with Jane [his ex-lover]— he's not sexually attracted to me and doesn't love me. It doesn't matter what I want. I don't have a voice in this relationship.

Your Feelings: How did this conflict make you feel? Rate each emotion separately on a scale of 1 percent to 100 percent.
Case Study
Keith: Impatient 100%, annoyed 90%, inconvenienced 100%, anxious 80%.

Michelle: Disregarded 90%, unloved 100%, resentful 100%, controlled 90%.

Resolving the Conflict

Your Behavior: What specific behavioral changes would your partner like you to make? How would your partner like to be treated differently?

Case Study

Keith: Michelle wants me to slow down. Ask her what *she* wants to do. Shape our plans to fit both of our interests. She wants me to do things for her without resenting her or feeling that I'm sacrificing myself. She wants me to learn to enjoy feeling close to her. Make room for intimacy.

Michelle: Keith wants me to tell him what I need instead of going along with his plans, feeling disregarded and controlled, and then lashing out at him. If I decide to do what he wants, he doesn't want me to hold it against him. He also wants me to understand that his compulsiveness has nothing to do with his love for me—it's who he is.

Your Cognitions: What attitude or perspective do you need to adopt so that you can make these changes willingly?

Case Study

Keith: Stop substituting activity for intimacy, doing for relating. My parents taught me little about affection. I need to think about how I want my marriage with Michelle to be different. I know I'll be too tired after skiing to make love, so I either should do it in the morning or cut the day shorter. I cheated on her, and now she needs me to show interest in her sexually and make her feel wanted. But I'm deceiving myself to think I'm doing this just for her. When I take the time to make love, I'm usually glad I did.

I gave up my childhood to take care of my parents, so I resent doing things for anyone, including Michelle. But I'm wrong to see every accommodation as a sacrifice. This isn't just my vacation.

Michelle: I know Keith. He wants to get the most for his money. I'm hurting myself, taking his behavior personally. He loves me and enjoys sex with me. He just doesn't know how to stop or slow down. He knows he's driven and doesn't particularly like this side of himself. There are times when I admire how organized and efficient he is, and appreciate his efforts to help me get my business started.

I'm not doing Keith a favor by giving in to his agenda and ignoring my own, and then hating him for bullying me. If breakfast means that much to me, I need to tell him he'll just have to get to the slopes a half hour later.

When I feel disregarded, as I did as a child, I tend to repress it and then explode. But yelling at Keith puts him on the defensive and makes it easy for him to write me off. I need to speak calmly but firmly. Shout, and he's not going to hear.

Your Feelings: How are you feeling now?
Case Study
Keith: Impatient 60%, annoyed 30%, inconvenienced 70%, anxious 30%.

Michelle: Disregarded 40%, unloved 25%, resentful 35%, controlled 25%.

You, like Keith and Michelle, need to step back from the specific content of your altercation and see how it fits into a broader pattern of conflict. Most couples argue over only a handful of issues throughout their life together. The details change, but the conflict is almost always a variation on a few well-worn themes to which you were sensitized in your early years. Like so many of the couples I see in my practice, you're likely to be amazed at how often these themes repeat themselves—at how you continue to misperceive and interact with your partner in the same maladaptive ways and experience the same painfully familiar emotions, regardless of the argument. Keith, for example, came to recognize his tendency to emphasize productivity over intimacy, to see every accommodation as a sacrifice, and to withdraw emotionally. Michelle came to see her tendency to dislike restrictions and schedules, to feel disregarded or unvalued, and to dismiss her feelings and then flare up.

By responsibility sharing—identifying the recurrent thoughts and behaviors that upset them, working out concrete alternatives, and writing new scripts—Keith and Michelle learned to manage and, at times, rise above their conflicts. This effort required hard work, commitment, self-awareness, openness, and maturity. It didn't just happen. But as they began to make changes in service of their relationship and their more integrated selves, they elicited more positive responses from each other and bonded together more solidly.

I hope that you, too, will work to understand yourself and your partner better, to pool your accumulated wisdom, to develop compassion and forgiveness for each other's limitations and damaging early experiences, and to design a better future together, based on a deeper awareness of who you are and who you're struggling to become. In short, I hope you share responsibility for feeling more satisfied and loved at home.

Now let's turn our attention from the lessons of the past to the present, from understanding why the affair happened to learning how you can recover from it. The next chapter addresses the very concrete task of restoring trust.

SIX

Restoring Trust

Hearts are not had as a gift but hearts are earned
By those that are not entirely beautiful.
—William Butler Yeats, "A Prayer for My Daughter"

Trust is not a gift. It must be earned, and not with verbal reassurances alone, but with specific changes in behavior. You,
the unfaithful partner, need to demonstrate to your partner
through bold, concrete actions that "I'm committed to you.
You're safe with me." You, the hurt partner, need to open
yourself to the possibility of trusting again, and reinforce your
partner's efforts to win back your confidence. You can't punish
forever, you can't be cold and distant forever, or your partner
will give up trying to reconnect. You need to spell out exactly
what your partner can do for you, and give this person a road
map back into your life.

When I speak of trust, I'm referring, of course, to your belief that your partner will remain faithful to you. But there's another kind of trust that matters, too—the trust, essential to you both, that if you venture back into the relationship, your partner will address your grievances and not leave you regretting your decision to recommit.

The first part of this chapter teaches you to change your behavior in ways that rekindle both kinds of trust. The second part challenges some common assumptions that sabotage your ability to act in trust-enhancing ways. By taking both steps—changing your behavior, and overcoming your resistance to change—you greatly increase your chances of getting the affair behind you and rebuilding a loving relationship.

PART ONE: CHANGING YOUR BEHAVIOR

If you're going to change your behavior toward your partner, you may have to act at times *as if* you feel more loving, secure, or forgiving than you really do. If you wait until your affection returns, you may very well outwait the relationship. Give in to your doubts and fears, and your relationship may die. Change your behavior first—act in a more conscious and positive way—and loving feelings may follow.

In the past you may have come home at night, grunted hello, silently rifled through the mail, and dashed upstairs to wash up or return a few calls. You weren't necessarily shutting out your partner—you were perhaps only trying to depressurize after a long day's work. But now, in the wake of the affair, and in service of a more nurturing relationship, you need to do more. Like the choreographer of an intimate dance, you need to think through exactly what you'd like to see happen between the two of you, and act in ways that will make it happen. You need to reveal what's important to you and retrain yourself to treat your partner in ways that say, "I like you. You matter to me." If this sounds like a lot of work, it is; but it probably demands a lot less time and effort than you squander on fighting.

There are many things you both can do to restore trust. I find it helpful to divide them into two categories—what I call *low-cost behaviors* and *high-cost behaviors.*[1] As you might expect, the low-cost behaviors are generally easier to produce because they demand less of you emotionally. High-cost behaviors require a much greater sacrifice.

Low-Cost Behaviors

Below is a list of some low-cost, trust-building behaviors that you may want from your partner. Some of them your partner may already do, others your partner may rarely or never do. Using these behaviors as a starting point, make your own list of what you want from your partner, and write it in the center column of the Trust-Building Chart on page 163.[2]

You, the hurt partner, need to request behaviors that make you feel more cared for, appreciated, and secure ("Tell me when you run into the affair-person"; "Show me affection at times without making it sexual"). You, the unfaithful partner, need to request behaviors that reassure you that your efforts to restore trust are paying off ("Tell me when you feel more optimistic about our future together") and that your partner is trying to address your dissatisfaction at home ("Show understanding of my need to spend some time alone"; "Tell me when you like the way I interact with the kids"). Be sure to address all aspects of your relationship—communication, free time, finances, sex, the children and other family members, personal habits, and so on. Many of the behaviors you request, your partner may also ask of you.

Here's a sample list:

- "Provide me with an accurate itinerary when you travel."
- "Limit your overnight travel."
- "Tell me when you run into or hear from the affair-person."
- "Tell me how you find me attractive."

- "Show me what pleases you sexually."
- "Tell me when you feel proud of me, and why."
- "Call or text me during the day."
- "Tell me how you feel—share your intimate thoughts with me."
- "Tell me when you feel happy or more optimistic about our future together."
- "Come home from work in time to have dinner with the family."
- "Spend more time in foreplay—kissing and touching."
- "Tell me what upset you during the day."
- "Tell me what pleased you during the day."
- "Focus on what I'm saying, and don't be distracted when we talk."
- "Tell me when you feel I've let you down."
- "Work on letting your anger go and getting back on track with me."
- "Take a massage class with me."
- "Show me affection outside the bedroom."
- "Buy new furniture for the bedroom (where you brought the affair-person)."
- "Talk to me directly about your feelings. Don't clam up and withdraw or attack me. Don't use humor or sarcasm to make your point."
- "Ask me how I feel; don't interpret my behavior or assume you know how I feel."
- "Hold me and show understanding when I'm upset; don't give up on me."
- "Make some fun, new weekend plans for us."
- "When you speak to me in a demeaning or contemptuous tone, apologize as soon as possible."
- "Tell me when you feel insecure about us, rather than assume I'm deceiving you."
- "Read and discuss a self-help book with me about making our relationship better." (Among those I'd recommend are *Try to See It My Way* by B. Janet Hibbs,[3] *Feeling Good To-*

gether by David D. Burns,[4] and *Getting the Love You Want* by Harville Hendrix.[5]

In putting together your own wish lists, be sure to:

1. *Be as positive and specific as possible.* Make your list more than a litany of complaints. If you indicate only what your partner does that irritates or hurts you, you're not communicating what you want and are bound to throw your partner on the defensive. Concentrate on what you want your partner to *do*—on those specific, observable behaviors that will bring you closer together. For example, instead of requesting something general or negative ("Don't be so controlling"), tell your partner in *positive* and *specific terms* exactly what you need ("Go along with my agenda at times, even if it's not exactly what you want to do, and be gracious about it").

2. *Respect your partner's requests as being important to him or her.* Each list is extremely personal; what comforts you (for example, "Call me during the day and show interest in how I'm feeling") may only annoy your partner. The changes you're asked to make may seem frivolous or gratuitous to you, but you need to respect that they matter to your partner.

3. *Respond to different requests on different days.* Vary the requests you choose to fulfill. Don't repeat one or two and ignore the rest. Remember: The small, caring things you do for each other from day to day make a tremendous difference in the way you feel toward each other. So do their absence.

4. *Put your lists in a visible place.* Display them on the home page of your computer, inside a closet door, or in some other accessible spot so that you're constantly reminded to satisfy each other's requests.

5. *Record the date on your Trust-Building Chart each time your partner satisfies one of your requests.* It may sound compulsive, but by acknowledging your partner's conscious efforts to please you, you reinforce them and increase the likelihood that they'll continue. You also may correct a cognitive error in yourself known as *selective negative focus,* in which you dwell on

the negative and screen out whatever contradicts it. It's normal for you to recall the bad times more vividly than the good, to sum up the day more in terms of moments that disappoint you or fire up your mistrust, than in terms of those that reinforce a feeling of well-being. By recording the dates of your partner's actions, however, you remind yourself that change is possible. Should you despair of moving forward, and believe, "I'm the only one who's trying," or "Nothing I do matters anyway—I'll never be forgiven," you have only to refer back to the dates on the chart for a reality check that should make you feel more appreciative, hopeful, and patient.

6. *Do what your partner requests, whether or not you feel hopeful about the future.* There may be times when reconnecting seems impossible—when you look at your partner and wonder, "Can you really change enough for me to love you, or for me to feel loved by you, again? Do you really care about me, or are you just going through the motions?"

Try to hang on at these moments. Your doubts may be fed by your own fears and insecurities. They may also be triggered by a partner as scared and hurt as you are, who is ignoring your needs temporarily to test your resolve and gauge the depth of your commitment. If you stop trying because your partner has, you give that person a chance to blame you for the breakdown of the relationship. If you continue to fulfill your partner's requests and refuse to get derailed, your partner will be forced to confront not you, but his or her own resistance.

7. *Add new requests to your list and discuss them as you learn more about yourself and about what you need to feel secure and loved.* When Martha's husband took her to an office party, he abandoned her to the crudités and hardly spoke to her all night. The next day she added the following request to her list: "When we go out together, touch base with me frequently, put your arm around me or hold my hand if you're feeling loving toward me, and make me feel you're proud of me by introducing me to your friends."

Trust-Building Chart

(Partner A's name) Did It Today								Trust-Building Behaviors	(Partner B's name) Did It Today							

As you interact in more conscious ways, you'll recognize additional behaviors that please or upset you. Add them to your list. The more information you can give your partner about what matters to you, the more you enable your partner to make you happy.

Let's look briefly at how one cohabitating couple, Arlene and Tim, used low-cost behaviors to restore trust.

Arlene wanted to feel more loved, and Tim wanted to feel more accepted for who he was. Arlene had slept with a colleague at work—not to replace Tim, she insisted, but because she felt lonely and neglected. Her list of low-cost behaviors was relatively short, but it got to the heart of what Tim could do to make her feel more cherished:

- "Smile at me and give me your full attention when you talk to me."
- "Speak to me in a warmer, more loving tone of voice."
- "Invite me to join you in fun activities; make plans in advance so I can look forward to them."
- "Take my hand when we walk."
- "Tell me when you feel love for me."
- "Tell me why you love me."

Tim's list, also short, voiced his need to feel that he could be himself, that "there was room in our relationship for me to be me":

- "If I'm quiet, ask me what's on my mind; don't assume I'm withdrawing from you or feeling critical."
- "Show understanding of my need to work a few hours at the office on weekends."
- "Realize that I talk more slowly than you, and don't interrupt me. Paraphrase my point of view; help me to open up."
- "Show more interest in what interests me—politics, for example."

- "Do more to share the costs and the work of keeping up our condo."

Nothing that Tim and Arlene put on their lists, or that you and your partner put on yours, should be taken as a demand or a requirement—so don't be afraid to write down everything that matters to you. Talk over what you're asking for and what you expect the positive impact to be. Once you're clear about your partner's requests, try to adhere to as many of them as you can and to act in new ways that you know will be supportive. I encourage you to see yourself at a crossroads, deciding which route to take by asking, "How would I normally handle this situation? What's my usual pattern? What response does it evoke in my partner? What would happen if I behaved differently?"

When Arlene felt her old urge to pounce on Tim at a restaurant for being so silent and self-absorbed, she stopped and asked herself, "What on Tim's list can I do to make him feel more accepted? Am I taking his behavior too personally?" Instead of berating him, she took his hand and said, "You seem lost in your own thoughts. What's going on?" Appreciating her efforts to reach out to him, he was able to tell her that he had been watching the couple next to them and thinking how bad he was at making conversation. Remembering her list of requests, he revealed his true feelings—that in spite of his silence he was feeling close to her. He then took her hand and kissed it.

Low-cost behaviors can inject fresh blood into your relationship at a time when you've been hemorrhaging. This is likely to create a dramatic surge in trust, and allow you to feel more hopeful and connected. Unfortunately, the transfusion is seldom enough to revitalize a damaged relationship, and the effects often fade within weeks. While you both should continue with these low-cost behaviors—you need them to jump-start your relationship and get you to believe in each other again—you, the unfaithful partner, must be prepared for some greater sacrifices.

High-Cost Behaviors

As we saw in Chapter 1, the hurt partner shoulders a disproportionate share of the burden of recovery once the affair is revealed. While you both may struggle to make sense of what happened, it's you, the hurt partner, who almost always has a heavier emotional load to carry. It's your job to control your obsessions, calm the rage inside you that continues to scream out at the pain of rejection, restore your lost sense of self, act in ways that are attractive to your partner, risk being vulnerable and intimate again, and forgive yourself as well as your mate.

In contrast, you, the unfaithful partner, typically want to be done with it: You've confessed, you've pledged fidelity—why, you wonder, shouldn't you be trusted now? More often than not, you feel relieved, cleansed, ready to move on. You may even feel emotionally strengthened by an affair that has reaffirmed your desirability. In short, it's in your interest to trust and forgive, while it's in your partner's interest *not* to trust and forgive, at least not too quickly.

Both of you need to exchange low-cost behaviors as a way of correcting and sharing responsibility for what went wrong in your relationship. High-cost behaviors are the responsibility of you, the unfaithful partner, alone. They're the sacrificial gifts, the penances, that you must consider making to redress the injury you've caused and rebalance the scale. It's not enough for you to say, "Trust me, honey—I'm here to stay." You have to back your claim with dramatic gestures that are "expensive"— in other words, that require real sacrifice and will probably make you feel uncomfortable and vulnerable.

These high-cost behaviors shouldn't be arbitrary or punitive. They're specific actions that your partner requests of you, or that you commit to on your own, which give your partner reason to believe that you won't stray again and that investing in the relationship isn't a foolish waste of time.

Here are some examples:

- "Don't contact or associate with the affair-person's circle of friends or relatives."
- "Quit the club or association to which the affair-person belongs."
- "Transfer some of your assets into my name."
- "Put some of your money into a joint account."
- "Assign your secretary [the affair-person] to someone else, and if that's not possible, find another job."
- "Go on a romantic vacation with me."
- "Pay for me to complete my college education."
- "Show me your monthly bank statements, credit card statements, and phone bills."
- "Get into therapy and discuss starting a family with me."
- "Do whatever it takes to give up drugs or alcohol (enter an inpatient detox facility or regularly attend AA meetings)."
- "Move to another town with me."
- "Explore in therapy the effects of your father's/mother's infidelity on you."
- "Get into couples therapy with me and work to figure out exactly what the affair says about you, about me, and about us."
- "Answer all my questions about the affair-person in front of a therapist, so I'm more certain that you're telling the truth."

The difference between high- and low-cost behaviors is totally subjective, and varies from one person to the next. What one of you finds easy to comply with ("Register the car in my name"), another may find threatening and compromising. How critical a particular behavior is for you depends in part on the circumstances of the affair. If your wife financed her weekly rendezvous from a personal account, you may find it essential to have access to her bank and credit card statements. If your husband was sleeping with his secretary, you may require him to change jobs, or secretaries.

It can be particularly stressful for you, the unfaithful partner, to negotiate high-cost behaviors that threaten your sense of self, as defined by your income or career. Compromise is possible, however, as the following case illustrates.

Roy, an established attorney in a small suburban community, had a history of one-night stands, usually with women he picked up in bars. One night his wife, Barbara, came home early and found him in bed with his latest find. When she shared her humiliation with a friend, she discovered that everyone in town already knew about her husband's womanizing—neighbors, the owner of her favorite restaurant, even her son. "I was so publicly disgraced, I couldn't imagine functioning in this community anymore," she told me.

Roy seemed sincere about controlling his sexual addiction and entered individual and couples therapy to prove it. But Barbara was nervous about the future. A proud woman nearing retirement age, she felt incapable of creating enough financial security for herself to maintain a fraction of her current lifestyle. "What if Roy not only cheats on me again but leaves me?" she asked. "What if I feel I have to leave him? How would I support myself?"

Barbara considered cutting her losses, ending the thirty-six-year-old marriage, and going after the best settlement the courts would grant her. Both partners clearly wanted to stay together, however, so I encouraged Barbara to voice her anxieties directly to Roy, and to construct with him a list of high-cost behaviors that would directly address those anxieties. What she asked for was this:

- "I'd like him to continue in therapy."
- "I'd like him to transfer 75 percent of his assets to my name." (She needed this display of commitment to allay her financial concerns and convince herself that he was serious about staying faithful.)
- "I'd like him to seek a new job in another community, and resettle there with me." (She felt publicly exposed in her hometown.)

Roy was willing to stay in therapy and get help with what he, too, saw as a problem. He also felt comfortable transferring most of his assets into Barbara's name to demonstrate his commitment in a tangible way. They went to an attorney and worked out an agreement.

The third request—relocating—was the one he had serious trouble with. He found it outrageous, even manipulative. He was established professionally, and moving meant a loss of status and income. He saw, however, that he risked losing Barbara if he gave her too little too late, and that she was asking him to agree to a fresh start not to hurt him but to help her believe in him again and overcome her sense of shame.

In the end, he pursued a transfer to another town. Fortunately, by the time it was granted, Barbara felt reintegrated into the community and didn't want to leave. Roy's willingness to forfeit what mattered so much to him—to do what it took to help her trust him again—was sufficient for her. His high-cost behavior didn't by itself restore trust, but, combined with other behaviors, it served as a bridge to recovery.

Stalemate: When You Can't Agree on High-Cost Behaviors

Sometimes you won't be able to agree on high-cost behaviors because of the meanings you attach to them—meanings that have as much to do with early childhood wounds as with your current conflict. One of you, for example, may insist on being made to feel number one all the time because you were ignored in your youth, while the other may refuse to make anyone feel special because of a childhood spent catering to a parent's needs. What one of you demands, the other may categorically refuse to do.

Should you reach an impasse, you need to step back and examine how your personal issues—the ones we discussed in Chapter 5—may be getting in the way of a meaningful compromise. That's what Ed and Miriam did.

Ed's affair with his secretary lasted nearly as long as his four-year marriage. When Miriam found out, he promised to be faithful, but Miriam found it impossible to trust him as long as he and the secretary worked together.

Ed tried low-cost behaviors first. He left work by six, as his wife requested (when he was having the affair, he often stayed late); he assigned himself another secretary; he called his wife during the day to let her know where he'd be; and he frequently invited her to meet him in the office for lunch.

These behaviors didn't go far enough for Miriam, however. She needed something more persuasive. If he couldn't work in a different office from the affair-person, then, she felt, he should quit and find another job. Ed panicked. He had just been offered stock in the company and had a solid future there. Miriam was pregnant. This was not the time for reading help-wanted ads.

They were at a stalemate. Ed saw his wife as emotionally overwrought and unforgiving. Her high-cost requests were, to him, mean and senseless, meant only to control him. "Even if I meet all her demands, she'll never trust me again, so what's the point?" he told me. Both of them refused to budge.

To move them forward, I encouraged them to ferret out those personal issues that led them to hold such uncompromising positions. For Ed, this meant confronting his deep-rooted sense of inadequacy, stemming from a lifelong rivalry with his high-achieving siblings. His lack of self-confidence made him doubt his worth in the marketplace. For Miriam, it meant confronting a lifelong sense of violation. "Not only did my stepfather molest me," she told me, "but my mother knew and chose to stay with him. She chose him over me. What Ed did was bring back all the bitterness and grief. I see I'm looking to him to make sacrifices not just so I can trust him again, but so I can erase all those years of suffering."

These personal reflections helped them soften their positions. As this book went to press, Ed was looking for a new job and working to step out from under the shadow of his siblings. Miriam, appreciating the scope of his sacrifice, was becoming more patient and trusting, and learning not to hold him responsible for everything bad that had happened in her life.

As with Ed and Miriam, you need to explore why certain sacrifices seem essential, and others impossible to fulfill. You also need to appreciate what they mean to your partner, and try to work out a compromise.

PART TWO: OVERCOMING YOUR RESISTANCE TO CHANGE

As much as you may like the idea of using the trust-building exercises, I guarantee that you'll resist carrying some of them out. It's not that you're a bad person or that you don't want the relationship to improve, but that your deeply wired assumptions are likely to get in the way. Some of them may stop you from communicating your needs, others may stop you from satisfying your partner's needs. Still others may force you to discount whatever it is your partner tries to do for you. Let's look at nine common cognitive blocks:

1. "I don't have the right to ask my partner to change for me."
2. "If I say what I need, I'll just hurt or anger my partner, and create more conflict. It's better to keep my dissatisfaction to myself."
3. "My partner should intuit what I need. I shouldn't have to spell it out."
4. "I can't ask for love. If I have to, I don't want it."
5. "If my partner does what I ask, not spontaneously but only out of a conscious desire to win my trust, it doesn't count."
6. "My partner is responding to my requests only to deceive me and get me back. As soon as I start trusting again, we'll be back where we started."
7. "I shouldn't have to acknowledge my partner's trust-building behaviors."

8. "My partner hurt me/let me down and should change first."
9. "I can't and shouldn't act in trust-building ways when I'm so angry."

Cognitive Block #1: "I don't have the right to ask my partner to change for me."

This common attitude is dysfunctional because it silences you and cuts you off from your partner and yourself. It robs you of the chance to find out whether your partner is willing to respond to your grievances, and it robs your partner of the chance to make good.

Look inside yourself and ask, "Why do I find it so hard to request something from my partner, something just for me? Where did this lack of entitlement come from? Did a parent ignore or punish me when I tried to speak up? Did I grow up in a household where I learned not to burden others with my needs? Was one of my parents a model of self-effacement?"

I encourage you to act against this cognitive block and prepare a full list of changes you want your partner to make for you. You may discover that you have been trapped in your own head, have imposed an isolation on yourself that's unnecessary, and have denied a basic need to be cared for, for much too long.

Cognitive Block #2: "If I say what I need, I'll just hurt or anger my partner, and create more conflict. It's better to keep my dissatisfaction to myself."

The wish to keep peace at any cost is a common but dangerous obstacle to restoring trust and intimacy. It was Teri's attitude after her affair. She needed her alcoholic husband to know that she had strayed because he was unavailable to her, and that she'd never be satisfied at home until he addressed his addiction. But she kept silent and hoped the whole mess would go away.

Over time, Teri came to see that a request for change was not an attack on her partner's character but a gift in service of their relationship. She traced her fear of confrontation to her father, who taught her to obey his authority and punished her for speaking up. "I need to be honest with you in a way I was never allowed to be with my father," she told her spouse. "I'm afraid of alienating you, but I've pushed you even further away by cheating on you and not telling you straight out how I need you to change."

Talking so openly drained the process of its terror and taught Teri that unless a person risks conflict, there can be no closeness, no resolution.

Cognitive Block #3: "My partner should intuit what I need. I shouldn't have to spell it out."

This assumption is a recipe for misunderstanding and disappointment, as it was for a patient named Helen. When her husband, Richard, returned to her after a month-long fling, he was not wearing his wedding ring. The meaning to Helen was clear: He was still ambivalent about recommitting and wanted women to think he was still available. Her pattern, however, was to say nothing and privately burn. "He knows it's important to me," she told me. "Why should I have to bring it up?"

I encouraged Helen to add her request that he wear the ring to her list of low-cost behaviors, and to discuss it with him. What she discovered was that he had lost the ring and was afraid to let her know. Once the issue was out in the open, he bought a new one and was happy to wear it.

It's important to realize that your partner is not a mind-reader, that it's your job to articulate your needs, and that if your partner doesn't always anticipate them, it doesn't mean your partner doesn't love you.

Cognitive Block #4: "I can't ask for love. If I have to, I don't want it."

It's relatively easy to ask your partner to take out the garbage or call during the day; it's much harder to ask your partner to say, "I love you."

Most people dismiss expressions of love when they're given on demand and feel demeaned when they have to ask for them. But if it's important for you to be told you're loved, be sure to add this request to your list. Just make clear that you want to hear loving words only when they're sincere. You need to free yourself to speak up for whatever you need most.

Cognitive Block #5: "If my partner does what I ask, not spontaneously but only out of a conscious desire to win my trust, it doesn't count."

Some of you may devalue your partner's efforts to restore trust when they're not gratuitous expressions of love but deliberate gestures meant to rebuild the relationship. "I want my partner to behave naturally, and do things that spring from the heart," you say. The problem with this attitude is that, the harder your partner tries, the less sincere it will seem to you. By valuing *feelings* of love more than *actions* that convey love, you limit your partner's ability to reach out to you in the only way that may be possible at this time.

I'm reminded of an incident with my son Max when he was six. We had gone skiing in Vermont for the day. As I watched him whiz by, I overheard a group of adults marveling at his performance, and felt a surge of love for him. Turn the clock ahead eight hours, and we were pulling into the garage at home, exhausted and soggy. The thought of waking Max from a deep sleep, dragging him upstairs, and putting him to bed was almost more than I could bear, and I considered for a moment letting him spend the night in the car. Frankly, I felt more fatigue than love. But what I did was force myself to act *as if* I felt love, and patiently got one very cranky child into bed. Looking back, I realize that this self-instructed kind of love was deeper, stronger, than the spontaneous feelings that had swept over me earlier that day. Those feelings were real but cheap; they asked nothing of me.

It's when we coach ourselves to act in loving ways in service of our relationship (even if we don't happen to feel very loving at the moment) that we pass the true test of love. It requires more to act loving when we don't feel that way. It asks us to go deep inside ourselves, to tug at our resources, and to deliver what truly matters to us. Acting out of a sense of enduring attachment and commitment to another human being can be very loving indeed.

Cognitive Block #6: "My partner is responding to my requests only to deceive me and get me back. As soon as I start trusting again, we'll be back where we started."

Some of you are likely to doubt the sincerity of your partner's efforts, and dismiss them as exercises in deception. "My partner's trying to please me only to lure me back," one unfaithful partner told me. "She needs my income." "My partner's changing only so I'll take him back," a hurt partner explained. "He's afraid the divorce settlement will strip him of his assets. He'll change now, but not for long." The problem with this attitude is that it makes growth and recovery impossible. If you don't give your partner an opportunity to change, to earn back trust, how will you ever know what's possible? If you always read duplicity in your partner's high- or low-cost behaviors, how can you ever be comforted or reassured by them? The idea is not to get rid of your skepticism—that would be unrealistic—but to suspend it long enough to give the healing process a chance to take hold.

Cognitive Block #7: "I shouldn't have to acknowledge my partner's trust-building behaviors."

Some of you may resist recording your partner's behaviors on the Trust-Building Chart, on the grounds that mature adults shouldn't need to be coddled. "Why should I acknowledge it every time my wife does something nice for me?" a hurt partner named Tom asked me. "Why should I pat her on the back for trying to clean up her own mess? She's not a child. If she chooses to act in a loving way, she should do it without expecting me to tell her how great she is."

What Tom, like you, may come to accept is that everyone needs praise and recognition; everyone needs to know that labors of love are noticed and make a difference. If you refuse to acknowledge what your partner is doing in service of the relationship, you discourage the very behaviors you want to produce.

Cognitive Block #8: "My partner hurt me/let me down and should change first."

This you-change-first attitude destroys the natural flow of a mature relationship, in which one partner usually does more for the other at any given moment, without keeping score. It also reduces you to petty, vengeful, highly competitive behaviors that destroy your ability to enter into the trust and caring exercises. Refusing to take the initiative may satisfy your sense of indignation, but it will do nothing to heal your wounds. I encourage you, therefore, to develop an attitude that says, "The best way to change my partner's behavior is to change my own first." In essence, I'm advising you to create an environment in which your partner is most likely to fulfill your needs. If nothing comes of it, at least you'll know you did your part.

Cognitive Block #9: "I can't and shouldn't act in trust-building ways when I'm so angry."

There may be times when you're too committed to your anger to be constructive, and you refuse to play the game of forgiveness or reconciliation.

"I don't feel loved or loving, so how can you expect me to act as if I do?" an unfaithful partner asked me. "I can't imagine even taking my wife's hand."

"I'm too mad to even look at my husband, much less work on exercises with him," a hurt partner said.

These defiant attitudes are understandable but counterproductive. They may allow you to feel less vulnerable and exposed, more self-righteously irate, but in the end they deny you the opportunity to test what you and your partner are capable of creating together. I encourage you, therefore, to step back and ask yourself whether your refusal to do the exercises is a result of *emotional reasoning*—a cognitive error by which you assume that because you feel something strongly, it must be true; that because you're furious at your partner, you must have a right to be.

Since you'll never feel angry without feeling right—it's a basic characteristic of anger—I suggest that you don't waste time debating whether your anger is justified, but ask yourself instead, "Is it useful? How will it serve me?" This may be one of those times when it makes sense not to be true to your feelings, but to act in service of your life together, knowing that more loving feelings may follow once you act in loving ways. As the poet and author Robert Bly said, "We make the path by walking." [6]

LOOKING AHEAD

The process of restoring trust can take a lifetime, but this doesn't mean you'll have to struggle with trust issues on a daily basis. Your relationship is likely to feel fragile and tentative for several years after the affair is revealed, but during that time you can expect to experience many reassuring, joyous moments as well.

Trust is a delicate, elusive gift that can be earned only over time, through commitment and continued effort. I ask you to be courageous and make yourself available for change. You may have only one opportunity to engage your partner in the healing process, so I encourage you to seize it, and respond with your most confident self—the self that allows you to address your partner's grievances and act *as if* you believe the two of you are capable of reconnecting more solidly and lovingly than before.

As a patient of mine once said, "You can have trust without intimacy, but you can't have intimacy without trust." With trust comes the knowledge that "I can give myself to you knowing that you won't harm me—that you'll support me and what matters to me. I can open myself up to love you because I feel safe with you and valued by you." The exercises in this chapter should help you restore this basic sense of security. But you need to learn more—for example, how to communicate more constructively, how to renew sexual intimacy, how to forgive. The rest of this book takes you on this greater journey.

SEVEN

How to Talk About What Happened

Many couples make the mistake of thinking they can rebuild their relationship after an affair simply by having enjoyable, positive experiences together. Although good times are critical to healing—you need to make room for playing and relaxing—they're no substitute for talking out your pain and dissatisfaction, and being listened to and understood. Unless you open yourself to your partner's feelings and communicate your own, your positive interactions will be like frosting on a stale cake. Let's turn, then, to the subject of this chapter: how to talk and listen more intimately—how to talk in a way that lets your partner know who you are and what you need, and listen in a way that encourages your partner to be open and vulnerable with you.

Learning constructive communication techniques is the easy part (I list several of them at the end of the chapter); being *willing to use them* is the challenge. "I know exactly what I should say to my partner to turn the whole argument around," you

may say, "but I'll be damned if I'll do it." Behind your resistance are likely to be certain long-held, dysfunctional assumptions about talking and listening—assumptions such as, "If
I tell you how you've hurt me I'll push you even further away,"
or "If I listen, you'll think I agree with you." Unless you confront these assumptions, learning new techniques will be like
shuffling deck chairs on the *Titanic*.

INTIMATE TALK

It's time now for honest, personal, and deeply revealing talk
about the affair, not only if it was recently revealed, but also
if you went through the trauma long ago and never discussed
it in any depth. Unless you drag it out of the closet—out from
between the two of you—you'll never give it a proper burial.
It's also time to talk about old grievances. For some of you, this
means going beyond depression to unleash your unacknowledged fury. For others, it means going beyond fury to convey
your unacknowledged sadness, fear, or shame. All of you must
admit your share of mistakes for what went wrong.

Two Dysfunctional Ways of Talking: Silence and Storm

There are two common, dysfunctional ways of managing your
thoughts and feelings. One is to silence yourself—to keep
everything bottled up inside. The other is to storm—to emote
without restraint. Let's look at them, and at the assumptions
that feed them.

Silence

If you're having too many conversations in your own mind,
you're probably not having enough conversations with the
person you should be talking to—your partner. Silence may
insulate you from further harm or disappointment, but it may
also rob you of the chance to feel understood, have your needs
satisfied, admit your mistakes, and reconnect. Disclosing what
you feel and need is an act of love, a prelude to intimacy. Speaking your mind "by telling all one's heart" is not only an act of

ordinary courage, as Annie Rogers calls it,[1] it's basic to letting your partner back into your life.

Let's look at two common assumptions that may block your ability to speak up:

1. "If I tell you what's bothering me, it will push us further apart."
2. "If I admit how I contribute to our problems, you'll think less of me or hold it against me."

Assumption #1: "If I tell you what's bothering me, it will push us further apart."
The Hurt Partner

You may be so pleased to have your partner back that you'll do anything not to risk being abandoned again, even if it means bottling up your rage and inner chaos. But topics not aired don't evaporate; they poison the space between you.

"For me to feel close to Howard again," one hurt partner said, "our marriage has to change. I need to feel more than safe. I need to be able to be myself, and that means talking openly about my feelings. But Howard doesn't want to talk, and I'm afraid to annoy him. He tells me, 'Then was then, now is now; I just want to move on.' So I don't push it. But we don't move on, either."

"A year after Joe's affair ended, I heard that his girlfriend had a baby," another hurt partner told me. "Ever since, I've been secretly gathering information about her from my daughter, who works in the same department. Is Joe the father? I can't help wondering. Every time I look at him, I'm dying to ask, but I don't. I can't. So it sits between us—the child he wouldn't have with me, the child he may have given her."

For you to heal and forgive, you must be convinced that your partner grasps how deeply you've been violated. For that to happen, you must talk about the affair and how it has affected you on the most personal level. It may help to refer to the list of nine losses in Chapter 1 and to discuss which ones you've experienced since the affair was revealed. Don't bludgeon your partner with your anger to avenge your losses or to detract from your complicity, but let your partner see what's going on inside you as a step toward reconciliation. *When you let your partner hold your pain, you can begin to let it go.*

The Unfaithful Partner

You may silence yourself to avoid conflict, but don't confuse peace with intimacy. Keeping your discontent to yourself is not loving or protective; it only leaves you both vulnerable to another betrayal. If you're waiting for a less volatile time to speak up, forget it; time will not make your task any easier. Vent your concerns now, or the cancer will grow.

Vanessa knew she was miserable months before she took on a lover, but said nothing. Instead, she lamely invited her husband to spend time grocery shopping and running errands with her. Her husband, oblivious to the mounting crisis, politely turned her down. What Vanessa didn't tell him was, "Look, I'm lonely. I need more of you. You're totally absorbed in your job and I feel irrelevant to you. This is serious. Listen to me." If he still didn't get it, she could have told him, "I'm thinking of having an affair. I'm finding myself attracted to other men"; or "I'm thinking of leaving you. I'm telling you not to threaten you but to keep us together."

If Vanessa had revealed herself sooner and with more directness, she might not have needed to seek companionship elsewhere. But it was hard for her to speak up when she had been taught all her life to silence her discontent. "Silence is golden," "Don't rock the boat," "Fighting's not worth it," "Things will clear up on their own, over time"—these were the messages she was raised on. What no one told her was, "No conflict, no closeness; confront your grievances or you'll be left with nothing but the illusion of tranquillity."

Assumption #2: "If I admit how I contribute to our problems, you'll think less of me or hold it against me."

The Hurt Partner

You may have a hard time admitting complicity, given how betrayed and violated you probably feel, but your acceptance of an appropriate share of responsibility will release you, at least in part, from the role of victim. It can be empowering to know that, instead of waiting passively for your partner to change, you, too, can do things to make a difference.

The Unfaithful Partner

You may be equally reluctant to accept responsibility, but your partner needs to know that you understand and regret the harm you've inflicted. If you were selfish or insensitive, or if you were led on by unrealistic expectations and excessive needs that were beyond your partner's (or anyone's) responsibility or capacity to fulfill, now's the time to admit it and apologize. Remember, *the single most precious gift that you can give your partner as reassurance that you won't stray again is your willingness to delve into yourself, confront your personal issues that led to the affair, and acknowledge them openly and responsibly.*

Here's what some of my patients said to begin this process; you'll want to search for explanations of your own:

- "I fell apart when my business began to fail. I felt totally humiliated."
- "When Mom died, I didn't know how to reach out to you and tell you how miserable and alone I felt, how much I needed you."
- "I never confronted your anger, just as I never confronted my father's. I was the wimp, and I let you step on me. I hated you for that because it was easier than hating myself."
- "I never felt attractive, sexy, or smart. I relied on the flattery of other women to make me feel desirable."
- "Frankly, I don't know why I had the affair, but I'll get into therapy and find out and share what I learn with you. It's

partially your job to make me happy, but it's not your job to keep me faithful. I'll take care of that—I promise."

You both may be loath to reveal what you profoundly regret or feel ashamed of—it may seem to make you less lovable, more open to attack. But the opposite is usually true.

I remember how painful it was for me to learn this lesson, back in fifth grade, when infidelity, I thought, meant not being able to make a baby. I had just gotten my first pair of eyeglasses. As I went off to a sleepover pajama party, my parents warned me to take good care of them. I tried. But when it came time to bed down, I couldn't find a safe place to put them among the blankets on the basement floor, so I stuck them under my pillow, thinking no one would step on it. I was wrong. When I returned home the next day, I was worried that my parents would be angry at me, and apprehensive about admitting my stupidity, so I made light of my mistake. "You're never going to believe what happened," I crowed as I walked through the door. "You were right!" And I held up my smashed lenses. Well, of course, my parents were furious—not because my glasses were broken, but because I came across in such a cavalier, irresponsible, arrogant way. If I had revealed my true self, I would have said to them, "Look, I feel terrible about these glasses. I really did try to take care of them but used bad judgment. I know they're expensive, and I'm sorry for what happened." They would have forgiven me, I'm sure.

Candor and self-scrutiny can be just as disarming for you, and make you seem more likable, more human, in your partner's eyes. It can also make your partner less defensive, and, in turn, more willing to confront his or her own contribution to the affair. The more you blame your partner, the less responsibility your partner is likely to assume. Allow yourself to be vulnerable and you invite your partner to be vulnerable, too.

Storm

When you silence yourself, you muzzle your discontent; when you storm, you assault your partner with it. Behind the storm, as behind the silence, may be certain maladaptive assumptions that give you permission to vent without control, and virtually guarantee that your partner will ignore you or fight back. Let's look at a few of these assumptions:

1. "I need to get my feelings off my chest—it's unhealthy to censor them."
2. "Unless I rage, you won't hear me or understand my pain."
3. "I am who I am."
4. "I have to feel satisfied before I stop."

Assumption #1: "I need to get my feelings off my chest— it's unhealthy to censor them."

Some therapists still argue that the unrestrained expression of emotion is cathartic—a kind of verbal blood-letting that exorcises poisonous feelings trapped inside you. However, most professionals today believe that the relentless, uncontrolled outpouring of anger breeds only more anger, both in the partner who is venting and in the partner who is under attack.[2]

I'm not suggesting that you should always lower the volume or that it's always bad or wrong to storm. Your partner can't understand your experience if you wrap it in a smile. Unremitting rage is off-putting, though, and by modulating your voice and choosing your words carefully, you give your partner no excuse *not* to listen. You may need to release bitter feelings before you can cultivate more loving ones, but there are ways of doing this that don't create more bitterness. (I list some of them under Suggestions at the end of the chapter.)

Assumption #2: "Unless I rage, you won't hear me or understand my pain."

You may automatically assume that the squeaky wheel gets the oil; that to be heard you need to be dramatic and make a scene. You may be right—your partner may refuse to pay attention to you unless you rave, and then write you off as crazy or unreasonable. When this happens, you're left with no adaptive outlet and are bound to feel even more infuriated.

But you may be wrong—your raging, even if it gets attention, may shove your partner away and leave you feeling more lonely and unsupported than before. If you speak more calmly and directly, your partner may listen to you more closely and feel your pain or discontent more palpably than when you storm.

Martha could have told her unfaithful husband, "You exposed me to a life-threatening disease because you're a selfish pig. You've never cared about anyone except yourself." What she said instead was, "I don't feel safe inside my own body. Do you understand how crazy that makes me feel? You could have exposed me to AIDS. I can't imagine what could have been so important for you to have put my life at risk."

Assumption #3: "I am who I am."
You may insist that you're an "emotional person" who can only relate in the fiery way you do. Such labels, though, are only excuses to justify dysfunctional behavior and give you license to storm. If you want to get your message across, you need to stop hiding behind the false and convenient assumption that you can't change.

Assumption #4: "I have to feel satisfied before I stop."
Many of you get drawn into conflict and then can't disengage principally because you assume you must feel satisfied before you stop. This idea forces you to stay locked in battle long after the troops should have gone home. The problem with this strategy is that it's likely to leave your partner feeling battered and defensive, and unwilling to concede your argument or discuss it with you further. If you want to be heard, you need to stop once you're understood, whether you feel satisfied or not. Don't think that by slugging it out and going one more round you'll drive your point home. You're more likely to get jabbed back, or send your partner fleeing from the ring.

A word of precaution: The rage that the affair has unleashed may lead to violence against your partner or against yourself. Some of you, even those with no history of physical abuse, may find yourselves unable to control it, and act in ways that shock and endanger you.

Torben and Kathy found themselves unable to talk rationally about his affair. One night before bed she became hysterical and threatened to kill herself. Torben, overcome with guilt, held a knife up to his throat and told her, "Finish me off. I'm bad." While Kathy stalked into the bathroom for a bottle of sedatives, Torben smashed a dish on the floor. A chip flew up into his face, ripping open his lip. They both stopped and looked at each other, dumbfounded. "My God," they thought. "What are we doing? What's happening to us?"

These flare-ups, as extreme and uncharacteristic as they may seem, frequently follow in the turbulent wake of an affair. At a time when your emotions are roiled up, your sense of self traumatized, your relationship ruptured, you must learn to recognize the early signs of escalating violence, and disengage before your confrontations spin out of control. Don't drink and fight; alcohol will only intensify your hostility. Don't threaten divorce; your relationship is too fragile to tolerate this kind of intimidation. If you see that your emotions are overheating, remind yourself that you may not have the communication skills or self-control to discuss a subject as flammable as infidelity, and step back from whatever it is that's upsetting you. Call a temporary truce with words such as, "I can feel the tension mounting between us. Let's agree to stop here and get back together at five tonight to talk more. I really do want to hear what you have to say."

It's important to agree to disengage, but also to agree to re-engage at a specified time, so that the person who is venting doesn't feel shut out.

How Your Past Affects the Way You Talk Today
To understand why you silence yourself or storm, look back at how your family communicated with you and with one an-

other. From these interactions you learned ways of expressing yourself. Here are a few examples:

- Your parents were always screaming at each other, and you grew up fearing confrontation.
- You had several feisty siblings who taught you that the only way to be heard is to shout.
- You learned from a self-effacing mother to silence your needs.
- You learned from an explosive, overbearing father to rail back.
- You learned from a critical mother that the way to win approval is to say what others want to hear, and ignore your own voice.
- You learned from an absent father that to get attention you have to nag, scream, or cry.

When you communicate with your partner today, you're likely to reenact scenes from your childhood that reinforce these early lessons. If you grew up feeling misunderstood, for example, you may silence what you need and guarantee that your partner doesn't understand you. If you grew up feeling unsupported, you may yell and make sure that your partner doesn't listen.

Breaking these lifelong patterns may seem risky, like swimming in unprotected waters. But by taking the plunge, you free yourself to interact in more intimate ways and allow your partner to hear you and take your needs seriously, perhaps for the first time.

Here are two contrasting scenarios. In one of them, Curtis is stuck in silence. In the other, Sarah talks back to her silence, and works to overcome it.

Scenario #1: Curtis and Alice
Curtis and Alice both brought into their marriage a maladaptive style of communicating. It was a perfect fit, each allowing

the other to play out a well-rehearsed role, until Curtis's affair brought the curtain down.

Curtis's dominant father took care of his family and created a home environment that was ostensibly conflict-free. If Curtis ever felt resentful, he never acknowledged it to anyone, including himself. When he married Alice, he put up the same sweet, self-effacing facade that he presented to the world in his youth. He submitted to her wishes, as he had submitted to his father's, and taught her to ignore his needs. His married life seemed conflict-free.

Alice also grew up with a domineering father, but rather than shy away from him, she learned to sling back insults as fast as they were thrown. She and her father fought hard and often. In her marriage, she stepped into her father's shoes and frequently found herself storming at Curtis for being so soft and unassertive. She came to despise him for not standing up to her.

Twenty years into their marriage, when Curtis mismanaged a major business investment, Alice blasted him with contempt. Curtis said nothing, but then expressed his stored rage by leaving her and moving in with his accountant. When I saw him two months later, he was still furious at Alice for not supporting him. "After a lifetime of catering to her moods," he told me, "the *one time* I asked for something back she had nothing to give." I pointed out that in their years together he had never given her any warning, any corrective feedback, that he was unhappy, or asked her to be accountable to him. Never had he said, "Listen up. I need you now. I've been there for you, and if you can't find the compassion and humanity to be there for me, I'm leaving you." I asked him how, after so many years of teaching her *not* to be there for him, he could expect her to act differently.

Curtis could still have opened himself up to Alice—she deeply regretted the way she had treated him and wanted him back—but he silenced himself, as usual, and continued to attend to his needs alone, outside the relationship.

Scenario #2: Sarah and John

Sarah's story has a more satisfying ending. Growing up with a diabetic mother, she assumed the role of the invisible child, never imposing her needs on anyone. Her anger built up on occasion to what George Eliot called "the roar which lies on the other side of silence," but she always ended up feeling guilty and retreating into herself. In her marriage to John, she maintained this same alternating pattern of silence and storm.

Almost a year after coming clean about his affair with his secretary, John announced that he was staying late for an office Christmas party and invited Sarah to join him. She was livid. "You're obviously still seeing that girl," she raged. "If you were proud of me and wanted me to be there, you wouldn't have waited till the last minute to invite me, when you knew it was too late for me to go."

John, feeling battered, insisted that he had forgotten about the party simply because it meant nothing to him and he was swamped with work. Sarah wanted to believe his story but continued to trounce him.

That night, after John returned early from the party, Sarah wanted to make peace with him, but silence got in the way. "John's way of handling conflict was, as usual, to go to sleep instantly," she told me the next day. "I knew he'd be snoring any minute and I'd be up all night obsessing. By morning I'd feel sick and even more furious at him. We wouldn't talk all day, and by the time he got home from work I'd be a raving maniac. I really needed to feel close to him before I could go to sleep, but my old silent self just lay there, afraid to move. 'You idiot,' I told myself, 'why can't you just say you're sorry and ask him to hug you? You always have trouble asking for anything—why is it so hard? Talk to him.'

"And I did. I turned to him and said, pathetically—are you ready for this?—'I can't sleep. Do you mind if I turn the bed light on, so I can read?' 'No, that's fine,' he said, and closed his eyes.

"I lay there thinking, 'I can't believe you! The last thing you

want is to read. Get your act together. Tell him what you want.'
So I shook him awake and said, 'John, this is stupid. I feel terrible about our fight tonight—insecure about us, angry at myself for picking a fight with you. Please don't go to bed and leave me stranded. Just hold me.'

"John opened his eyes, smiled, and made a space beside him. This time I accepted his invitation.

"It's hard to believe how difficult it was, simply speaking up for myself. I had to overcome something deep inside me that sealed me off. I had lived my whole life that way, silencing myself or blowing up. When I finally found my own voice, I gave John a chance to be there for me, and I experienced myself in a new way—more connected, more supported."

Saying Goodbye to the Affair-Person

Many unfaithful partners choose to stop seeing their lovers without the formality of a goodbye. Whatever your reason—guilt, fear of temptation or confrontation—your partner is left believing that you're ambivalent about returning home and determined to keep your options open. This is not the best climate for restoring trust. Should the lover write or call, you and your partner are guaranteed a blow-up every time.

There are three good ways to communicate your recommitment to your partner. First, you must say goodbye to the affair-person in no uncertain terms. Don't try to protect this person by saying nothing or softening your words; leave no room for doubt. Make it clear that you want him or her to move on to another, more fulfilling relationship. Second, you must promise your partner that you'll never contact the affair-person again; or, if that's not possible, you must promise to keep encounters as infrequent and impersonal as you can. Third, if your partner wants to be told every time you and the affair-person cross paths, you must comply; otherwise, the truth may come out accidentally and seem like a secret you were trying to hide.

Talking About the Affair

When talking about the affair, hurt partners need to decide what they want to know, and unfaithful partners need to decide how to reveal it. These are potentially explosive issues that should be thought through before any conversation takes place.

The Hurt Partner

Knowing that the affair-person shares secrets with your partner—that the two of them know things you don't—may seem intolerable, and make you insist on being told every excruciating detail.

The problem with too vivid a picture is that it's likely to torment you and feed rather than satisfy your obsession. Your fascination is understandable, but before you begin the inquisition I advise you to write down your questions and ask yourself, "Will answers help me—will they help *us*—recover? Will they clean the slate or stir the pot? What is it that I want my questions to achieve?"

"I wasn't so bothered that Jack was collecting X-rated pictures of women," a patient named Tracey told me. "But when I found images of people having anal sex, I began to wonder if he did these things with his kinky girlfriend. I decided not to ask him because I wouldn't know what to do with the answer—there's only so much enlightenment a person can take. But I did need to find out if he could ever be satisfied making love with me, given that there are limits to what I'll do to make him happy."

Most hurt partners, unlike Tracey, have a knack of going after information that will make them suffer. "Do you still think about her?" "Did you enjoy sex with him more than with me?" "Do you ever think about her when we make love together?" "Do you have any doubts about our future together?"—these are the sorts of self-destructive questions that only drive the knife in deeper. What's the point?

When hurt partners become experts in entrapment, everyone loses. A thirty-six-year-old production editor named Jill was no exception. "Howard's affair [with his sales rep] had been over for two years," she told me, "but I still felt the need to check on him. He had promised to keep his conversations with her light. After a sales meeting, I tried to trip him up. I started off slowly, like I was smelling his tracks. I asked him, 'Have you seen Janet lately?' I knew he had, and he admitted it. And then, laying my bait: 'Is she still seeing that boy from Arizona?' If he knew the answer, I'd know their conversation had crossed the line. But Howard tried to move the subject to safer ground. 'I'm flattered that you think such a young girl could still be interested in me,' he said. I wasn't going to let him off so easily, so I shot back, 'Actually, you're the one who seems flattered that such a young thing would be interested in you.' I kept at him until he threw up his hands and walked out of the house. There was nothing he could have said to reassure me, I realized. I was going to nail him, whether he was guilty or not."

The best advice I can give you is to keep the focus on your relationship, not on the affair-person. Try to ask questions such as, "What do you need from me to feel more loved and cared for?" "What's missing in this relationship for you?" and "How do you like to be touched?"—questions that will help you get the affair, and your obsessions about the affair-person, behind you.

A patient named Ann came to this same understanding. "When I heard about Frank's fling," she told me, "I wanted to march into the slut's office and humiliate her the way she humiliated me. I wanted to scream in front of all her customers that she's a fucking whore. But I decided not to lower myself, and wrote her a letter instead. I wanted her to know I'm a real person with real feelings, and what she did was wrong. I didn't send it, though, because the truth is, she's not the problem, and she's not the solution. Whether she ever understands what she did to me, or ever even acknowledges my existence, isn't going to help me or my marriage."

The Unfaithful Partner

When it comes to answering questions about the affair-person, I believe that it's the person you betrayed, not you, who has the right to decide what you reveal. You should respond in whatever detail your partner wants. If you try to hide or soften the truth to protect your partner's feelings, you're likely to be seen as controlling, evasive, or deceptive. Go ahead and point out that the truth can hurt more than heal, but don't expect your partner to listen to your advice or trust your judgment.

Respecting your partner's wishes is not, of course, a license to be cruel. Choose your words with sensitivity, and try to give feedback that will point your relationship in a positive direction. If your wife asks, "Am I as good a lover?" it would be pointless and callous simply to say, "No." It would be entirely instructive, however, to say, "Sex was better with her and me than it's been with us for the past few years, but that's because it was forbidden and because sometimes I feel you don't want to be with me."

INTIMATE LISTENING

Intimate listening means putting your own feelings and beliefs on hold, stepping into your partner's world, and seeing yourself, and the affair, from your partner's point of view. It means asking yourself, nondefensively, noncompetitively, "What is my partner trying to convey to me? What does this person want me to understand?"

To listen meaningfully, you need to see your partner not as the enemy but as someone who also may be hurting, and whose message to you is not "You're awful," but "You matter to me. I need you to understand." You may want to remind yourself that you're not discussing the Truth, in some ultimate sense, but two different ways of looking at it. Your partner's take on things may be different from yours, but if you're ever going to get closer, you have to learn to hear it.

An unfaithful partner named Marsha found that entering into her partner's mindset did not come naturally, but she coached herself to do it. When her husband, Bob, told her, "You don't make me feel loved," her first instinct was to lunge back, "What! After all I do for you!" But instead, she tried to enter into his misery and show interest. "It upsets me to hear you say that," she said. "What do I do that makes you feel that way?" To herself she said, "Let him talk. He's revealing something important about himself—and perhaps about you. It doesn't matter whether you think he's wrong or unfair. If you want to get closer, you need to listen and try to appreciate what he's saying."

There are many ways of letting your partner know you're listening, but I recommend two in particular. They're called the Cross-Over Technique and the Disarming Technique.

The Cross-Over Technique

Couples often fight without knowing what they're fighting about, or rush in to dispute their partner's point of view before they understand it. The Cross-Over Technique is meant to help you, the listener, hear what your partner is saying, and you, the speaker, feel that you're being heard.

Here's how it works. When you're discussing a subject and one of you starts to get irritated or upset, either you or your partner calls a stop, and the two of you "cross over." This means that you both stop pressing your points—stop pushing your positions onto each other—and try to enter each other's phenomenological world. "So this is what *you* want *me* to understand," you say, in effect, as you try to paraphrase or mirror the most significant aspects of your partner's message, both in content and spirit. Your partner then rates how completely he or she feels you got the message, on a scale of one to ten. Nine is a pass. If you fail, your partner repeats the part of the message you didn't seem to hear, and you try to "capture" it, as many times as necessary, until your partner is satisfied. Don't be insulted or frustrated if you don't get high grades at first. It's often only after you mirror back the message that your partner realizes what he or she didn't say; you may not have heard it because it was never said. A distraught partner may also need you to repeat the message several times before feeling understood.

Roberta and Neil had difficulty negotiating how to spend their free time; when they tried to talk it out, they ended up not talking at all. Neil (the hurt partner) often wanted more time together; Roberta often wanted less. Neil saw her as cold and rejecting; she saw him as insecure and needy. One day, when she insisted on going off by herself to run errands, their tempers flared. Neil, applying the Cross-Over Technique, listened to her closely and then tried to mirror back what she said. "You'd like me to let you go off by yourself some of the time and not take it as personal rejection," he said. "You see my wanting to be with you as a way of checking up on you and reassuring myself that you're not cheating on me again. This doesn't feel loving to you; it feels imprisoning."

Roberta, in turn, listened to Neil and mirrored his sentiments: "You want me to understand that I create a lot of your insecurity by constantly pushing you away, and never making you feel special to me. You'd feel better about letting me go off by myself if some of the time I sought you out to do fun things with me."

Both partners had listened well, and both felt heard.

The Disarming Technique

This other listening technique[3] reduces your sense of polarization on any given issue, and helps you find some common ground to stand on. Like the Cross-Over Technique, it helps to deescalate conflict by forcing you to concentrate on what your partner is telling you rather than on what you plan to say in your defense.

In this exercise, you take turns ferreting out the truth in your partner's position—the part you genuinely agree with—and acknowledging it in a gracious and convincing way.

Ed and Miriam clashed over his working for the same company as his ex-lover, Sandy. One day, during a couples session in my office, I asked them to try the Disarming Technique. Instead of defending himself or trying to duck a confrontation, Ed acknowledged what he believed to be true in Miriam's position. "My situation at work must drive you crazy," he told her. "It's got to be even harder for you to trust me and stop obsessing about Sandy when you know I'll be running into her every day. I can understand how you'd like me to find a job somewhere else, even if I earn less."

Hearing Ed validate her point of view made it easier for Miriam to do the same for him. "I realize you're in a bind," she said, "that you want to please me but worry about finding a good job somewhere else. I know I say the money doesn't matter to me, but then I spend plenty. It's got to be hard to leave a good, secure job. It takes more energy and confidence than you feel you've got right now."

It was a turning point for both of them. Neither had ever acknowledged what was reasonable in the other's position. This admission made them feel vulnerable, but it helped deescalate their conflict and turn them into collaborators, working on a common problem.

What you, too, need to see, is that, whatever you're arguing about, there's often some truth in what your partner is saying. It's your job to find it, and affirm it. Your affirmation is likely to pull the two of you back from extreme, self-righteous postures, and bring you closer together.

Ultimately, you both must learn to be good listeners and receive your partner's grievances as gifts in service of the relationship. To renew ties, you have to know each other better, and this means accepting as valid what your partner feels and seriously considering what your partner wants from you. If the two of you can talk openly, without always pouncing on each other or going on the defensive, you'll develop a mechanism for managing conflict that will make you feel more cared for and understood throughout the life of your relationship.

Why You May Not Want to Listen

Let's look at three common assumptions that may reduce your ability to listen to your partner's complaints. (By listening, I mean *intimate* listening, which is not just a willingness to hear your partner's words but a willingness to appreciate your partner's perspective.)

1. "Listening to your complaints is the same as saying, 'You're right.' "
2. "Listening to your complaints is giving you a license to rage."
3. "Listening to your complaints is the same as saying, 'I forgive you.' "

Assumption #1: "Listening to your complaints is the same as saying, 'You're right.' "

Listening doesn't mean you agree; it just means you care enough to try to understand what your partner is saying. If you confuse listening to your partner's message with validating it, you won't listen, and you won't know what you're disputing. Unless you hear your partner's complaints, you can't begin to understand or respond to them.

Assumption #2: "Listening to your complaints is giving you a license to rage."

Some of you may worry that listening will make your partner more combative; if you're the type who feels threatened by conflict, you're not going to want to fan the flames. But listening can be disarming. Empathy—another name for intimate listening—does not intensify conflict, it softens it. Your partner, feeling acknowledged and understood, is likely to relax, trust you more, and respond to you in a more loving way. Try it. You may discover that listening is one of the most powerful resources you have.

Assumption #3: "Listening to your complaints is the same as saying, 'I forgive you.' "

Some of you may have trouble listening because you equate it with forgiving. But don't confuse the two. Listening, as I've said, means only that you're willing to open yourself to your partner's version of the truth, not that you accept it, or that you pardon or exonerate your partner's behavior. Listening can clear a path to forgiveness, but it's only a beginning.

How the Past Affects the Way You Listen Today

As you grew up, you became accustomed to hearing certain messages, implicit or explicit, in the way your family talked to you, or to one another. Some were personally enhancing ("I respect your opinion," "You make sense to me," "We don't have to agree"). Others, like the following, were debilitating:

- "You'd better watch out."
- "Now you've made me good and mad."
- "You're an idiot."
- "You can't make good decisions."
- "I've had it with you."
- "You're unlovable."
- "You don't know what you're talking about."
- "You should be ashamed of yourself."
- "It's your fault."
- "What's wrong with you?"

When your partner speaks to you today, you're prone—programmed, in a sense—to interpret what you hear in these familiar, sometimes dysfunctional ways, thereby distorting your partner's message and losing your ability to respond in an objective and constructive way.

Josh, a fifty-eight-year-old attorney, is a case in point. His father was a bully who micromanaged his every move. Today, when his wife, Amy, speaks to him, he often hears "interference," "control," and "subjugation." Amy insists that she's only speaking up for herself and trying to be helpful. Though the incidents vary—she might suggest that he forego onions on his sandwich a half hour before a cocktail party or ask him to lower the volume on the hotel TV—the personal meaning that Josh attaches to her words is always the same. He can't talk out his reaction, because he's not aware of how he's contributing to it; all he knows is that Amy makes him feel as manipulated and infantilized as his father did, and that he needs to get away from her to restore his emotional equilibrium. Of course, this solution will not heal them as the couple, or him as an individual.

It's important for you, as it is for Josh, to be aware of your hot buttons, filters, wounds—whatever you call them—because they may lead you to misconstrue what your partner is saying. You need to keep in mind that the message you think you hear may be quite different from the message your partner is trying to send. If you misread your partner (you hear, for example, "I don't like you and I'm leaving you" when your partner is angry or upset), you're likely to react inappropriately (you threaten divorce, for example) and incite your partner to react in ways that confirm your original assumption (that your partner doesn't like you and is leaving).

Knowing that you're vulnerable to interpreting your partner's words according to your own personal themes, you need to step back and ask yourself, "Is there another way of understanding what my partner is telling me; is there another way of processing it? Am I provoking my partner to communicate with me in the way that my parents did, so that I reinforce my early experiences?"

You can check out whether you're interpreting a message accurately by telling your partner, "What you've said makes me feel X (unsupported, belittled, controlled), but I know I tend to feel that way too easily. Am I hearing you correctly?" This gives your partner another chance to explain, and it gives you another chance to listen with an open mind.

Sex Differences in Expressing and Listening to Conflict

Men and women tend to express and listen to conflict in different ways. Although gender differences don't apply to everyone, understanding them may help you communicate more constructively and tolerate responses that might otherwise annoy or upset you.[4] Here are a few common examples:

1. Men often give advice when women want emotional support. Men view their intervention as loving or helpful. Women usually experience it as condescending or unsympathetic.

2. When men empathize, they often feel foolish or fake. They have difficulty believing that anyone would appreciate or derive any benefit from having them just listen to or validate feelings. Women empathize more naturally, and understand its value.

3. Men tend to get physiologically overwhelmed during emotional confrontations, and withdraw. When tensions rise, so do their pulse rate and blood pressure (a physiologically aversive condition), and they experience a biological need to escape. Women, in contrast, feel closer when they share their complaints, and experience a highly unpleasant arousal of their autonomic nervous system when their male partner withdraws.[5] A woman whose male partner flees from her whenever she tries to express her anger or pain is forced to make a grim choice: either to speak up and alienate her partner, or to remain silent and feel alienated from herself. "When . . . a woman is furious with her partner for his affairs, his emotional unresponsiveness, or his threats to leave, she may be afraid that if she makes her feelings known he will retaliate with even greater anger or by acting on his threats to leave."[6] A woman's silence, all too often, leads to depression and a loss of self.

These gender differences in communication are often exacerbated when the hurt partner is a woman and the unfaithful partner is a man. A woman is more likely to want to talk out her pain and, as the hurt partner, to have more pain to talk out. A man is more likely to want to avoid conflict and, as the unfaithful partner, to want to move on. Each partner relates in a way that frustrates and alienates the other.

For men and women to get around these differences, they have to cut a deal: Men can't avoid conflict; women can't flood their partners with it.

As the man, you must step into the fray and try to empathize with your partner's feelings. You must prove to her that if she speaks to you in a calmer voice for shorter periods of time, you'll work hard to stay engaged and understand her point of view.

As the woman, you must reinforce your partner's efforts by allowing his empathy to reach you and calm you down—and by cutting the discussion short. You should also consider seeing his advice-giving not as an attempt to demean or control you, but as an attempt to be helpful and loving.

"Every time things start to go well between me and Janet," Bill, an unfaithful partner, complained in a couples session, "she brings up my affair and stamps out all the good. I try to listen, but it doesn't seem to help. The hurt never goes away. Should we just keep doing this?"

"You're anxious to move on," I told him, "but when you express optimism, Janet gets scared. She's afraid of being hurt again. She's afraid that you're just trying to sweep what happened under the rug and haven't learned anything from it. She sees your optimism as self-serving and manipulative—a cheap, painless way to be forgiven. Here's what I recommend. You, Bill, must listen to Janet every time she needs to talk about her pain—if that means 5,000 times, then you need to listen 5,000 times. Your willingness to listen may lessen her pain and her need to talk about it. You, Janet, must share not just your grief, but your positive feelings—any warm, loving, hopeful feelings you experience—so that Bill feels encouraged and knows that his efforts to be there for you make a difference. If you, Bill, open yourself to Janet's hurt and anger, and you, Janet, allow yourself to heal, the two of you have a better chance of carving out a future together."

Suggestions

Here's some general advice to keep in mind as you communicate:

- Don't assume that what you're hearing is what your partner is trying to say. You may be hearing only what you know, or expect to hear.
- Learn to be an effective choreographer. Think about where you'd like your relationship to go before you begin talking, and ask yourself, "What do I need to say to get there?" Try to act against old, familiar patterns of communication that no longer serve your interest. For example, instead of turning your partner off with sarcasm ("I guess you wouldn't be interested in what I have to say"), coach yourself to be disarmingly direct ("I'd like to tell you how I feel about this; it's really important to me that you listen closely").
- What you discuss is often less important than how you discuss it. As you speak to each other, don't forget to convey, "I like you, believe in you, am proud of you, care about you. I'm interested in what you have to say and in how you feel."
- Don't jump at your partner's every word; make room for imperfect responses. Be patient and attentive when you know your partner is trying to get through to you. Go beyond the words and try to hear the message behind them.

Numerous communication techniques can help you talk and listen to each other more constructively. Many of them are spelled out in *Marriage Rules*[7] and *10 Lessons to Transform Your Marriage.*[8] Here are a few:

- Listen to what your partner has to say without *defending yourself* ("Yes, but . . ."), *minimizing* ("You're really making too much of this"), or *stonewalling* ("I refuse to talk about it").

- Don't overwhelm your partner with diatribes; take turns talking and listening.
- Let your partner finish what he or she is saying; don't interrupt.
- After you've made your point and your partner has paraphrased it, drop the argument, at least for a while.
- Stick to one subject at a time.
- Be specific. Don't say, "You always do this," or "You never do that."
- Criticize what your partner thinks or does; don't attack your partner's character (say, "I can't trust you when you lie to me about running into your old girlfriend," instead of "You're a pathological liar").
- Don't attribute motives to your partner's behavior. (It's better to say, "I believe that . . ." or "My idea is that . . . ," instead of "I'm sure that the reason you did X is . . .") Acknowledge that your assumptions are personal and may not be true. This gives your partner a chance to confirm or correct them.
- If your partner's tone is pushing you away, say so, and ask to be spoken to in a calmer or more respectful voice. Don't just walk away or escalate the conflict.
- Look your partner in the eye when you're being talked to; give your partner your full attention.
- If you can't give your partner your undivided attention—you're too busy, tired, upset—say so, and set another time to get together. Then follow through.

It's important to let your partner know what you want to hear. Here are some common requests my patients have made; feel free to add your own:

- "Tell me when you need reassurance. Don't threaten divorce as a way of getting my attention."
- "Tell me when you feel close to me or hopeful about us as a couple."

- "Tell me when you're upset; don't silence your pain."
- "Instead of getting mad, tell me calmly and directly what's bothering you or what you want."
- "Tell me what you're angry or upset about in a respectful way; don't demean me." (It's better to say, "By distorting the truth about me to your parents, you're made it incredibly difficult for me to have a relationship with them," instead of "You're a baby who needs your mommy and daddy.")
- "Talk to me about yourself, and us; don't drag in the affair-person."
- "Be honest when I ask you about the affair-person; don't try to protect my feelings."
- "Tell me how your family talked to you, and how this may affect the way you talk to me today."
- "Tell me what part of my message you agree with."
- "Don't assume I want you to solve my problems unless I ask for help."
- "Apologize openly for how you've hurt me or let me down."
- "Bring up the affair so I don't feel so alone with it."
- "Admit your contribution to our problems."
- "Tell me who knows what about the affair, and work out a plan with me for containing and managing the spread of the news."
- "Don't be afraid to let me see you cry. Don't be afraid to let me know the meaning of your tears."

Communicating openly and authentically is necessary to restore intimacy; so is being physically close to each other. The next chapter helps you to become sexually intimate again in ways that go beyond genital sex. I appreciate how scary the prospect may be of touching again—of letting your partner know you and please you, and of doing the same for your partner. But with your communication skills to help you express your wishes and fears, and your cognitive skills to keep you accurately processing what's happening between the two of you, you're well equipped to enter the bedroom.

EIGHT

Sex Again

Freud once said that when two people make love, there are six people in bed—the couple and their parents. After an affair, add a seventh: the ghost of the lover. This chapter helps you to pull your parents and the lover out from under the covers, warm up the space between you, and get sexually intimate again. By sexual intimacy I mean that in the presence of your partner you can:

- feel emotionally safe and protected, though physically naked;
- be yourself yet feel connected;
- value passion and playfulness in bed, but trust that closeness matters more to both of you than performance;
- acknowledge your own sexual fears and frustrations, and still feel accepted and respected;
- ask openly for what pleases you sexually yet set limits on what feels uncomfortable;

- have compassion for each other, knowing that what makes you frail and imperfect also makes you human.

Right now, such closeness may seem light-years away.

You, the hurt partner, are likely to hunger for the reassurance of physical closeness, while pushing your partner away to protect your vulnerable self. Nowhere are you going to feel more insecure, more undesirable, than in the bedroom, where you compare yourself to your partner's lover, magnifying this person's physical appeal and minimizing your own.

You, the unfaithful partner, are likely to miss the illicitness, the drama, the newness of the affair. After so much high chemistry, you may have trouble getting sexually aroused with a partner who seems tentative, self-conscious, or rejecting. You may be put off by the pressure that your partner puts on you, or that you put on yourself, to prove your love in bed.

As you both struggle to reestablish intimate ties, two cognitive errors may block your way. One is your tendency to attribute meaning to your partner's sexual behavior without examining the evidence (for example, a wife assumes that if her husband can't get an erection, he must be cheating on her). The other is your tendency to set such rigid or unrealistically high sexual standards for yourself and your partner that your physical relationship seems inadequate (for example, a husband assumes that his wife should always know what pleases him).

Hurt partners typically assume:

1. "If you're not interested in making love, or can't stay aroused, it's because you don't find me sexy or desirable."
2. "If you're not interested in making love, or can't stay aroused, it's because you're still cheating on me."
3. "I'll never be able to satisfy you the way your lover did. I can't compete."

Unfaithful partners typically assume:

1. "If I don't satisfy you in bed, you'll think I've lost interest in you or am still cheating on you."
2. "I had great sex with my lover. Since my sex life with you can't compare, you must be the problem."

Both of you are likely to assume:

1. "Sex should come naturally and easily. We shouldn't touch or be physical until we feel more comfortable together."
2. "If I let you touch me, you'll want to go further."
3. "If you masturbate, it means you don't love me and our relationship's in trouble."
4. "Sex should always be passionate."
5. "You should always know what pleases me sexually."
6. "If I ask for changes in the way we make love, I'll hurt your feelings. If I do what you ask, I'll violate mine. Change isn't worth it."
7. "We should reach orgasm simultaneously."
8. "We should have multiple orgasms."
9. "We should reach orgasm through intercourse."
10. "We should reach orgasm every time we make love."
11. "We should want sex with the same frequency, and at the same time."
12. "If our relationship were strong enough, and we were normal people, we wouldn't have to use fantasy or sex tools."
13. "The subject of getting tested for AIDS, or other sexually transmitted diseases, is too inflammatory to bring up."
14. "I'll never overcome the shame I feel about my body and my lovemaking."

Let's look at each of these questionable assumptions, and go through some exercises to help you think and act in more intimate ways.

HURT PARTNER'S ASSUMPTIONS
Assumption #1: "If you're not interested in making love, or can't stay aroused, it's because you don't find me sexy or desirable."

If your partner seems less than excited by you sexually, you're likely to assume that you're the cause and ignore your partner's contribution to the problem. Traumatized by the affair, you may see your partner's slightest hesitation as proof of your own sexual inadequacy.

After Mark's affair, his wife, Wendy, blamed herself for their problems in bed. Her response is typical.

"I question myself all the time," she told me. "Maybe I'm no good for Mark. I take too long to come. I don't lubricate as well as before. I'm too afraid to let go. I never believed I was sexy or attractive enough for him, and now I resent him for making me feel I was right."

Buried in self-doubt, Wendy never entertained the idea that Mark might have his own sexual anxieties, which were as central to their problems as anything inherently deficient in her. Some of these anxieties, in fact, predated their relationship. It was only when Wendy took herself out of the picture and looked outward that she realized:

- Mark had worried that his penis was shamefully small years before she met him. He had long seen himself as a sexually ineffectual, unattractive man who came too fast and couldn't please her.
- The affair put Mark under enormous pressure to perform to prove his love to her—he knew how damaged and undesirable his infidelity made her feel—and the tension may have killed his desire.
- Mark probably expected her to reject him after what he had done, and, conflict avoider that he was, he may not have wanted to initiate sex and risk being turned down.

You, like Wendy, need to be aware of misinterpreting your partner's sexual response. The problem could be not that your partner is having negative thoughts about you but that you *think* your partner is. What your partner may want most is a compassionate response to embarrassing problems, and help in overcoming them.

If you're sleeping on opposite sides of the bed, don't automatically assume your partner doesn't love you or want to be with you. Sex is only one way to relate, and right now it may be one of the most stressful. Wendy realized that though her husband was dodging her sexually, he was making an effort to come home early from work on a regular basis and planning fun things to do on weekends. You, too, should take notice when your partner wants to spend time with you and seems to enjoy your company in nonsexual ways. What's important is that you nourish and notice positive interactions. Not all of them have to be sexual.

Suggestions

1. Try to generate a list of explanations for your partner's desire and arousal problems that don't implicate you. Wendy named three:
- deep-seated feelings of sexual inadequacy;
- pressure to perform;
- fear of rejection or confrontation.

Other explanations might include:
- need to regain power or reassert control;
- wish to hurt or punish you;
- menstruation;
- medical disorders;
- fatigue or other forms of stress;
- effects of medication, alcohol, or drugs;
- compulsion to get things done before allowing time for relaxation or intimacy;
- fear of opening up and feeling vulnerable or ridiculed;
- fear of pregnancy;
- self-consciousness caused by lack of privacy (children or live-in relatives);

- puritanical attitudes toward sex (feeling whorish, dirty, or sinful);
- homosexual proclivities;
- sexual trauma from the past.

2.   Let your partner know that you're struggling to take his or her disinterest in sex less personally. In a gentle, nonjudgmental way, ask for help in finding alternative explanations that are equally plausible.

3.   It's your job as the hurt partner to reassure your mate that you're not looking for fantastic sex but for the beginning of a reconnection. Find your own way of asking, "What can I do to convince you that I just want us to move closer together?" Let your partner know that performance is unimportant, that erections or orgasms are unimportant, that what matters is that the two of you create a climate of acceptance, openness, and warmth.

4.   Try to value time spent together that is intimate but not necessarily sexual—sharing the Sunday paper, cooking a favorite meal, going for a bike ride or a walk.

Assumption #2: "If you're not interested in making love, or can't stay aroused, it's because you're still cheating on me."
Virtually all of you are likely to jump to this conclusion, though you may have no proof, only vague suspicions and a heightened sense of vulnerability and distrust. No matter how much evidence you amass to the contrary, these unsubstantiated fears will probably gnaw at you for months or even years, and make it all but impossible for you to risk intimacy.

A forty-six-year-old accountant named Jackie found herself picking apart her husband's every move, searching for confirmation of her fear that he was still straying. Her accusations increased the pressure he felt to prove his love in bed. This, of course, destroyed his desire and, in turn, reinforced her suspicions that he was sleeping with someone else. Here's how you might diagram their interaction:

You shouldn't automatically assume, as Jackie did, that because you're suspicious, there are grounds for it. If you're wrong, you're likely to poison your relationship as much as if your partner were still cheating on you.

Jackie's Assumption
"Jim is avoiding me sexually because
he's still sleeping with that girl."

*Jim's Emotional and
Behavioral Reaction*
He feels pressured to
perform and can't. He feels
frustrated and resentful.

*Jackie's Emotional and
Behavioral Reaction*
She feels angry, threatened,
and betrayed, and acts cold
and distant. She assaults Jim
with her suspicions.

Jim's Assumption
"If I don't get an erection right away, she's going to
think I'm cheating again, and I'll have hell to pay."

Suggestions

1. Try to distinguish fact from fear. Ask yourself, "How much do I know, as opposed to how much do I suspect for no reason except that I've been betrayed before?" If you have solid proof that your partner is unfaithful, it's time for some serious thinking about whether it's in your best interest to stick around. If all you have are lingering suspicions, however, counter them with evidence that your partner is reaching out and trying to reconnect—initiating conversations that matter to you, inviting you on business trips, perhaps just calling during the day to see how you're feeling. These gestures won't by themselves improve your sex life or make you feel more sexually desired, but they should help you talk back to your doubts and obsessions, and begin to trust your partner's professions of fidelity.

There could be many reasons for your partner's desire or arousal problems that have nothing to do with cheating. Some are listed on pages 210–211. It may help to review these alternative explanations and balance them against your unconfirmed fears.

2. You may not be able to erase your suspicions, but you can try to stop them from dominating or poisoning your life. Two techniques may help.

One simple but effective ploy is called *thought stopping*. As soon as you begin to think of your partner with someone else, try to break your concentration by saying, out loud or to yourself (the exact words are up to you), "Stop. Here I go again, dragging myself down. Let it go." Then, focusing your attention outward, notice or describe something upbeat or intriguing around you or recall the last time you had a warm or funny interaction with someone you care about. You can also turn inward and, breathing deeply, send messages to your muscles to loosen and relax. You may not be able to force your mind to stop thinking particular thoughts, but you can gently distract it.

The other technique—call it *challenging your assumptions*—involves the use of a Dysfunctional Thought Form. What you do is record the event as objectively as possible, as well as your immediate feelings and thoughts. You then systematically challenge, or talk back to, your thoughts, looking for cognitive errors.

Here's an example of how one wife talked herself through her suspicions and avoided an ugly scene with her husband, Jim, that would have left them further apart than before. The husband had admitted to several one-night stands on previous trips, but had been working to prove his fidelity ever since.

Objective event: When Jim got home from Zurich, he went right to sleep. He had zero interest in sex.

Emotional reaction: Scared, rejected, suspicious.

Automatic thoughts: "I bet he slept with someone while he was away. We haven't had sex for over a week—he never goes that long. He's been extra nice to me since he left—added proof that he feels guilty."

Rational response: "You're taking his behavior personally and jumping to conclusions. Maybe there are other reasons that he doesn't want you tonight. Like what? Like he's tired— he just got off an eight-hour flight. Like he has a big work day tomorrow and it's late. Like he's afraid he won't perform well and you'll get upset.

"Stick to the facts. He invited you to join him, and when you couldn't, he shared a room with one of his male associates. He called every day. He seemed really happy to see you when you picked him up at the airport, and he brought you your favorite perfume. Sure, it may not all be heartfelt—part of him may just be trying to reassure you. But what's wrong with that? Restoring trust takes time. He clearly cares about you and wants to make everything okay again. Just because you're suspicious doesn't mean he's done something wrong. Let it go. The truth is, you're tired tonight, too. If you weren't feeling so insecure, you wouldn't be that interested in sex, either."

Assumption #3: "I'll never be able to satisfy you the way your lover did. I can't compete."

It's common to compare yourself to the affair-person in the most unflattering and self-deprecating ways. Whatever you hate about your body or your performance in bed, you're likely to admire in that person, especially if you've never met. You think your breasts are too small? The lover must have huge ones. Your penis seems too soft? The lover's must be made of steel. Your lovemaking seems ordinary? Your partner and the lover must have enjoyed the wildest, darkest, most uninhibited sex, and together reached a thousand multiple orgasms.

Fantasies like these are likely to make you feel so undesirable and inferior, so convinced that you lack the goods, that you can no longer function as an active sex partner. If your sex life is ever going to get back on track, you need to see these fantasies for what they probably are: expressions of your sexual insecurities after the trauma of the affair.

The reality is that men frequently have affairs even when they're sexually satisfied at home, and women often stray not for better sex but to feel more loved, appreciated, and respected.[1] In my own clinical practice, unfaithful partners, both men and women, report that sex with the affair-person is often both awkward and infrequent, and that they only wished it measured up to their partner's wild imaginings. In an authoritative national study of sex habits in America, "the people who reported being the most physically pleased and emotionally satisfied were the married couples. . . . The lowest rates of satisfaction were among men and women who were neither married nor living with someone—the very group thought to be having the hottest sex."[2]

This isn't to say that sex with the affair-person wasn't at times more torrid than it is with you; torridness is hard to come by when you have one eye on the clock and the other on the kids. Laced with a spirit of defiance and secrecy, illicit sex is bound to seem more transcendent. But try not to be demoralized. Romantic love is a distorting and transient experience, and the heat your partner may have generated with another person would have cooled in time, as it has perhaps with you. Passion often loses its edge when it's no longer new or forbidden.

Keep in mind that if your partner has decided to recommit to you, it's likely to be because you offer something deeper, more enduring, than romantic love. You need to believe in and reclaim those aspects of yourself that your partner values in you and that you value in yourself. You need to trust that you're worth loving, and work to regain that sense of self that informs you that you're a wonderful person who has made your partner happy, and can continue to do so in countless ways.

Don't let your obsession with the affair-person distract you from what should be the real issue right now: restoring intimacy with your partner, in and out of bed. Instead of making useless comparisons, try to find new ways of injecting creativity, energy, and romance back into your *own* lovemaking; instead of competing with the affair-person, step out of the ring, bring the focus back on your relationship, and address the issues that let the affair-person get between you.

When I speak of *you*, I mean both of you; it's not your job alone to satisfy your partner or create a fulfilling sex life. Developing sexual intimacy is a two-person project.

Suggestions

1. If you consider yourself sexually inept or just uninformed, why not educate yourself? Self-help guides such as *Getting the Sex You Want*[3] or *For Each Other*[4] can teach you about your body and your sexual responses, and make you feel more competent in bed. You can watch X-rated videos (some are instructive; others exploit women as sex objects), or consult a friend or sex therapist. You can also learn from each other what gives you pleasure (see the exercise on pages 233–235).

2. Sometimes, when you're feeling insecure, it helps to work things out inside your own head. But at other times you need to share your vulnerabilities and ask your partner for help and reassurance. Try to keep the focus on yourself—on your insecurities, fears, obsessions—not on the affair-person or on the details of the affair. Instead of asking, "Did you see that woman again?" you might say, "I keep thinking about you and that woman. I'm feeling terribly threatened today and I don't think it's because of anything you've done, but you seem to be lost in your own thoughts. Can you reassure me?"

It's fair to expect your partner to reach out and try to comfort you. If your partner can't, you may want to question whether this is the person you want to spend your life with.

UNFAITHFUL PARTNER'S ASSUMPTIONS
Assumption #1: "If I don't satisfy you in bed, you'll think I've lost interest in you or am still cheating on you."

You may be right: Your partner may believe that if your response falls short, you must want to be somewhere else. But the pressure to be interested and aroused may also come from you—from your guilt, your qualms about reconnecting, your inflated ideas about what your partner expects from you. What may matter most to your partner is not your performance but your commitment.

Whatever you're feeling, try to talk it out—it may reduce the pressure you feel to perform, as well as the likelihood that your partner will misread your response.

One unfaithful partner, a thirty-nine-year-old oral surgeon named Phil, told his wife, "I feel I have to be some incredible stud to prove I want to be here, and the pressure's killing me. I wish we could just get into bed and hold each other, and then whatever happens, happens."

It may help you, as it did Phil, to explain that you're having sexual problems not because you find your partner unattractive or are preoccupied with someone else, but because you're worrying about letting your partner down. Don't be surprised or put off, though, if you continue to be accused of cheating or rejecting your partner. From the time the affair is revealed and you completely disconnect from the affair-person, it often takes at least eighteen months to restore the trust you violated.

Suggestions

Only you can provide the reassurances your partner needs to move the healing process forward. Among the things you can do:

1.   Let your partner know when you're feeling loving and glad to be together. Speak up when you feel more hopeful or positive about the two of you; don't assume your partner knows when you're happy. "I was thinking at work today how beautiful you looked last night"; "I really felt close to you when we stayed in bed talking this morning"—the exact words don't matter; the reassurances do.

2.   Describe what you like about your partner's body and lovemaking. Most people like to be complimented on their looks and to know what their partners find attractive about them. Whatever you choose to comment on—"I love how that

dress looks on you," "Your face makes me smile," "The way you're touching me feels great"—don't lie, don't fabricate, but don't hold back positive feedback, either. Be generous.

3. Reveal any sex problems you had with the affair-person. It may help your partner dispel the notion that everything was so terrific for you and that person if you reveal whatever sexual difficulties you may have had. The affair-person never reached orgasm, you had sex only twice in a nine-month affair, the explosiveness you experienced in bed was overshadowed by the explosiveness of the relationship—these sorts of corrective realities bring the affair down to earth and make it easier for your partner to stop obsessing and move on.

4. Reveal any sex problems you have that predate, or are unrelated to, your relationship with your partner. If your partner wrongly assumes responsibility for any of your sexual difficulties, it's important to set the record straight. Freed from blame, your partner is apt to reduce the pressure on you to perform, and even become your ally in overcoming whatever it is that sexually disables or inhibits you.

A fifty-two-year-old attorney named Arnold had problems getting an erection ever since he started taking medication to control his high blood pressure. After his affair, he avoided his wife, and she assumed he no longer found her attractive. "I've had this problem on and off ever since I started taking diuretics," he reminded her. "The problem's not my attraction to you; it's medical. And the pressure I put on myself, wanting to please you, just makes it worse."

5. Coach yourself to stay sexually involved and not get discouraged. When you're having arousal or desire problems, you're likely to want to avoid all physical contact, and may need to coach yourself to stay involved. Filling out a Dysfunctional Thought Form may help you monitor your resistance, confront your avoidance tactics, and keep yourself sexually connected.

Here's one that Arnold filled out to overcome his pattern of anxiety, shame, and withdrawal.

Objective event: It's Saturday morning. I'm lying in bed with June [my wife], thinking about initiating sex.

Emotional reaction: Anxious, angry, paralyzed, discouraged.

Automatic thoughts: "It's ridiculous, being afraid to approach June after fifteen years of marriage. But she's so sensitive and takes everything so personally that I'm scared I won't get hard, and then she'll assume I'm getting sex elsewhere or that I've lost interest in her. She even keeps a record of when we last had sex. Celibacy would be easier."

Rational response: "Of course you're feeling uncomfortable. This is going to take time. The problem, which you caused, won't go away overnight. She needs to know you're committed. If you avoid her, she'll feel more rejected, more unloved, and you'll just poison the relationship more. You may not get hard, but so what? Your erections mean too much to you—maybe to her, too. Let her know you want to be more loving and connected, but she's got to stop rating your performance (this goes for you, too). Can she accept this? Go ahead, take the first step. Reach out to her."

If you're avoiding sex, as Arnold did, you too may want to use a Dysfunctional Thought Form to help you overcome your fears and frustrations. Above all, however, you need to be patient, persist, and convey again and again the message that you're committed and want to work out your sexual issues together.

Assumption #2: "I had great sex with my lover. Since my sex life with you can't compare, you must be the problem."
When sex seems less satisfying with your partner than with your lover, it's common to assume your partner is to blame. You may be right; your partner may be too inhibited or reject-

ing to give you what you need. But the problem may reside within you.

There are a number of ways in which you may be undermining your love life at home. Let's look at four of them.

1. *You continue to make unfair and unproductive comparisons between your partner and your lover.* This is a contest you need to stop. As long as you expect prescribed sex with your partner to compete with proscribed sex with your lover, you're going to be disappointed and excuse yourself from the real task at hand: revitalizing your love life at home. Yes, sex is usually hotter and spicier in an unfamiliar bed, but so what? Passion cools, disenchantment follows; if you had stayed with the affair-person, you probably would have run up against many of the same intimacy problems you're having now with your partner. Familiarity can breed boredom, even contempt. This is a reality you need to confront, whoever your partner is.

2. *You fail to nourish intimacy outside the bedroom.* If you don't make your partner feel valued and loved outside the bedroom, how can you expect your partner to warm up to you inside the bedroom? Before you complain about your sex life, you should show your partner at least as much tenderness and regard as you lavished on the affair-person.

No one could accuse Chuck of such sensitivity. When he got home from work, he typically left his wife to bathe the two kids, read to them, and tuck them into bed, while he chortled on the phone with his business manager. When his wife finally crawled under the covers, he was waiting for her, bathed and ready for sex. "By that time, I was so furious at him," she told me, "the last thing I wanted was for him to touch me. He accused me of being frigid—and I was—but he never understood how cold his self-centeredness made me feel."

3. *You don't know how to arouse your partner.* As great a lover as you may fancy yourself, you may have no clue how your partner needs to be stimulated to become aroused. Though you assail your mate for being unresponsive, the problem may be that you're pushing the wrong buttons, and your partner,

knowing how sensitive you are to criticism, is afraid to give you corrective feedback. If you want to be a better lover and improve your sex life, you need to consult the real expert—your partner—and ask for a lesson.

4. *You blame your partner for your own sexual or intimacy problems, which predate your relationship.* It's so much easier to point a finger at your partner than to look in the mirror and ask yourself how you've contributed to your sexual dissatisfaction. It's unfair, though, to fault your partner alone for making you feel unesteemed, unsexy, or inadequate, when you've felt this way for as long as you remember.

Suggestions

1. If you're plagued with thoughts about the affair-person, try the thought-stopping technique I recommended earlier. As soon as you find yourself obsessing, break your concentration by calling out "Stop," or some similar expression, and diverting your attention to another subject.

2. Instead of focusing on the affair-person, explore what it was about your experience with that person that affected you in such a powerful way. Did you feel young, potent, wanted, alive? These may be clues into vulnerabilities and yearnings you need to address if you're going to be satisfied in any relationship.

3. Use the Dysfunctional Thought Form in this chapter to challenge your unrealistic ideas about love and romance.

4. Learn to broaden your concept of intimacy beyond the thrill of sex.

COUPLE'S ASSUMPTIONS

Assumption #1: "Sex should come naturally and easily. We shouldn't touch or be physical until we feel more comfortable together."

These "should" statements are so unrealistic and self-defeating that they're bound to put your sex life on ice; by the time it thaws, one of you is likely to be gone. If you expect to feel relaxed in bed now, you're dreaming. What's more likely is that you're feeling nakedly self-conscious—stripped of your defenses and embarrassed in each other's presence.

"So what do I do?" you ask. "Submit to something I feel unready for, that may give me more discomfort than pleasure?"

Yes, exactly. Intimacy building is an active process. It requires a conscious attitude, a deliberate choice, a cognitive decision to get more closely connected. The process begins when you decide to begin, not necessarily when you feel motivated, confident, or certain. You can't just wait around, asking yourself, "How can I open myself up to someone I have such conflicting feelings toward? How can I be intimate with someone who has caused me so much harm?" You need to go beyond these feelings, take chances, and engage each other physically. Becoming more intimate outside the bedroom may help restore trust, but it doesn't automatically translate into greater sexual intimacy. You need to take your partner's hand, caress, kiss, and allow feelings of intimacy to flow between you. *You need to begin acting not according to the way you feel but according to the way you would like to feel.*

Reaching out to each other may leave you feeling vulnerable; sealing yourself off may make you feel safe. I urge you, however, not to wait until you're more comfortable before you begin to touch again; comfort comes with an accumulation of healing experiences, not with time. Getting physical is likely to feel awkward at first, but awkward is exactly what you should be feeling as you demonstrate your willingness to stretch emotionally and take risks. Reenacting old, familiar patterns—avoiding intimacy, maintaining a barrier of distrust—may feel comfortable, but is often highly dysfunctional.

Suggestions

1.   I can't stress this point strongly enough: To get closer, you have to begin touching again. You might begin by telling each other, face to face or on paper, exactly how you would like to be touched. Your requests are likely to be very idiosyncratic, so don't expect what pleases you to necessarily please your

partner. Try to satisfy at least one of your partner's requests every day.

Common examples include:

- "When you come into the house, kiss me on the mouth."
- "Take my hand when we walk."
- "Rub my feet with oil."
- "Give me a massage."
- "Hug me for a few moments."
- "Sleep or lie near me with one arm around me."
- "Run your fingertips gently over my eyelids and eyebrows in bed."
- "Brush my hair."
- "Stay in bed with me for a few minutes after the alarm goes off; lie in my arms with your face close to mine."
- "Touch my shoulder or waist when you walk with me."

2.   Sex therapist Warwick Williams suggests that couples work out a "physical trust position" in bed. You begin by agreeing on one or two positions that both of you find safe, and then experiment. The idea is to combine physical closeness and trust. Among the positions Williams recommends are:

- One of you curls up on your side while your partner holds you from behind (the "spoons" position).
- You both lie on your sides, facing each other, holding hands (you may want to hug or close your eyes).
- One of you sits up, comfortably supported, cradling your partner's head in your lap, and stroking your partner's hair.[5]

You can talk or not, wear clothes or not, have sex or not. The idea at this point is to reestablish physical contact and engender trust. Remember: You can only get so close to someone you don't touch.

Assumption #2: "If I let you touch me, you'll want to go further."

You may worry that once you begin to touch, your partner will ignore the limits you set, turn up the heat, and try to force a simmer into a boil. Not wanting to go further than feels comfortable to you, you put up barriers, and forfeit an opportunity for closeness.

"After I found out about Jeff's affair, he kept wanting to make love, but I wouldn't let him near me," Leah told me. "I even made him sleep in the guest bedroom. The truth is, I wanted to feel him next to me, to fall asleep with his arms around me, but I didn't trust that he'd stop there, and I wasn't ready for anything more. To make love meant, 'I've forgiven you. Everything's fine now between us.' And it wasn't. I suppose I was testing him. If I refused to have sex with him and he went elsewhere, I'd know he wasn't truly repentant and didn't really love me for myself. After what he did, I earned the right to make him prove himself."

Jeff saw Leah's behavior in a different light. To him, she was being manipulative—pushing him away to control and punish him despite his genuine efforts to convince her of his commitment. His frustration turned to anger. To protect his self-esteem, he stopped initiating sex. Both partners felt alone and trapped. (In the next section, we'll see how they resolved this dilemma.)

While you, like Leah, may not feel ready for intercourse, you need to decide what you *are* ready for. Sex and celibacy are not the only choices. Remember, to rebuild intimacy you have to get physically connected again. Withholding sex may help you regain the power or equity that you lost because of the affair, but power and equity make poor bedfellows. A scale tipped in your favor is still off balance.

While you, like Jeff, may love to make love, you may need to agree to your partner's timetable while the two of you rebuild trust and intimacy in other ways.

Suggestions

1.　You need to tell each other what feels comfortable sexually, and then prove to each other that you respect each other's limits. Find some concrete way of signaling when you only want to touch or when you want more. One couple came up with their own playful solution: The aroused partner took a ceramic frog they had bought on their honeymoon and placed it on the other's night table; the "invited" spouse was free to take the leap or not. Another couple decided that since it was the hurt partner who felt more ambivalent and vulnerable, that person, for now, would always be the one to initiate genital sex.

2.　A popular exercise called "sensate focus"[6] may help you to begin touching again and to learn how you like to be touched, while eliminating the pressure to feel aroused, perform any specific sexual acts, have intercourse, or reach climax, until you're both ready. Set aside an agreed-upon amount of time—I suggest fifteen to twenty minutes, no longer—during which one of you massages or touches the other in nongenital areas. Both of you should be fully clothed. The next time, reverse roles, one person always giving pleasure, the other always receiving it. The person receiving pleasure need not say or do anything except to signal occasionally in some way—lifting a finger, saying "mmm"—when the touching feels good.

When you're comfortable with this exercise, you can try it with your clothes off, but again without genital touching. That comes next, with the understanding that before you agree to intercourse, both of you have to give the green light—the frog—first.

Assumption #3: "If you masturbate, it means you don't love me and our relationship's in trouble."

Now is a good time to discuss your attitudes about masturbation. No topic comes packaged with more myths, ranging from the idea that touching yourself causes pimples to the notion that it permanently alters the size, shape, and color of your genitals and saps your ability to have good sex. Though masturbation is still condemned by various religious and cultural groups, most people do it at some time in their lives, though they tend to conceal it. In a study of twenty-four couples reported in *The Kinsey Institute New Report on Sex*, 92 percent of the husbands and 8 percent of the wives believed their spouses never touched themselves, when in fact all of them did.[7] Among the thousands of people interviewed by Kinsey in the 1940s and 1950s, some 94 percent of males and 40 percent of females admitted having masturbated to orgasm. More recent studies have corroborated these figures for men, but found that the percentage of females who masturbate has increased to around 84 percent.[8] Most couples reported that masturbation did not make them feel less loving toward their partner, or detract from the quality of their lovemaking, but served as a supplemental component of a sexually active lifestyle.[9] Another recent study of sexual habits in America reported that, of men and women between the ages of twenty-four and forty-nine, 85 percent of the men and 45 percent of the women who were living with a partner said they had masturbated during the past year.[10] Of those people who had regular partners for sexual intercourse, one man in four and one woman in ten said they masturbated at least once a week.[11] The same study reported that married people were more likely to masturbate than people who were living alone.[12]

Let's return to our couple, Leah and Jeff, who were struggling to set boundaries for touching in the previous section. One night Leah walked in on Jeff and found him masturbating. She became terribly upset and accused him of behaving like an animal. Jeff didn't know whether he was more embarrassed or annoyed. "It's better than sleeping around," he told her. "Sleeping with you doesn't seem to be an option."

Leah thought about Jeff's response, and later, in a couples session, told him that she resented the pressure he put on her to make love whenever they touched.

"Fine," he said, "but you've got to give me some other outlet."

"Your masturbating scares me," she explained. "It's another

secret, another way you have of keeping yourself from me and showing that you don't need me."

"That's not what it means to me," Jeff said. "I see it as a healthy alternative to forcing myself on you or getting satisfied elsewhere. What else do you suggest?"

The solution they came up with was that they would sleep in the same bed, but Jeff would respect Leah's need to postpone intercourse. Leah, in turn, agreed to hold Jeff and kiss him as he touched himself. The compromise seemed to work. At the next session Leah told me, "Being there together takes the threat away, and I'm glad to have him back in bed with me. It's not ideal but it's better than where we were."

Suggestion

As a couple, it's important that you find mutually agreeable sexual options. Don't set traps for each other or issue ultimatums; set alternatives. Try to keep an open mind about what should happen sexually between you, and be creative about satisfying each other's needs for closeness and sexual release. What matters most is not that you engage in any particular sexual act, but that you problem-solve as friends and build a sense of partnership.

Assumption #4: "Sex should always be passionate."
This idea reflects an idealized, romantic standard that's impossible to meet on a consistent basis. Imposing it on an already fragile relationship is bound to leave you feeling disappointed, insecure, and critical of yourself and your partner. The reality is that sex after an affair will probably not be passionate, but graceless and trying. Hurt partners are unlikely to act with abandon when they fear *being* abandoned. Unfaithful partners, as we've seen, are likely to be inhibited by the pressure to perform, and distracted by memories of the affair-person.

What you should both keep in mind is that, given what you've been through, any kind of touching, with or without genital sex, can be incredibly intimate and courageous. Don't heap so much onto a fire that's just trying to catch hold. The emphasis now should be less on producing a high flame than on allowing yourself to rekindle tender feelings.

After her husband admitted sleeping with his friend's wife, Carol wanted their lovemaking to be white-hot. When it fell short of her expectations, she felt frightened and let down. "Nothing is clicking," she told me. "We're just going through the motions. Something's very wrong."

What was wrong was not the sex, but Carol's extravagant notion that she and her husband must feel some intensely erotic connection at all times. This unreasonable expectation made it impossible for her to enjoy or even find comfort in the pleasure he gave her.

Carol's experience was further contaminated by the personal meaning she attached to passionate love: that it proved her attractiveness and desirability in the eyes of her husband. Passion assumed an overcharged importance because she looked to it for reassurance of her specialness to her spouse. Lovemaking, to her, was not a way to reconnect but a chore, a performance, a test. How could it not disappoint her?

If you, like Carol, need to have a "ten" experience in bed, you're likely to have nothing more than a "three." Sex in movies and magazines is often portrayed as a fiery furnace when in real life it's more like central heating with an irregular thermostat.[13] To make your sexual relationship warm and loving you need to take off more than your clothes, you need to shed your exacting expectations.

Suggestions

1. Ask yourself, "Why is passion so important to me? What meaning do I assign to it that it seems so weighted with importance? Does it signify that my partner is genuinely happy to be with me? Finds me attractive? Is less likely to stray? Has forgiven me?"

It may take the pressure off you to realize that these and other meanings are subjective—that a passive partner may be happy, faithful, and forgiving, and that a sexually aggressive partner may be miserable, unfaithful, and condemning. By reframing the meaning of passion, you may be able to accept and enjoy lovemaking that's less intense than you dreamed it might be, but just as loving.

2.   Work on developing an expanded, more useful, and realistic definition of intimacy that goes beyond high chemistry and includes feeling of tenderness, caring, understanding, and respect.

3.   One of the greatest sexual turn-ons is a turned-on partner. Conversely, one of the biggest turn-offs is a partner who is sexually dead. It follows that if you want more passion from your partner, you need to be more passionate yourself.

Assumption #5: "You should always know what pleases me sexually."

This idea is convenient because it lets you dump the burden of responsibility for your sexual satisfaction in your partner's lap and then blame your partner when your needs aren't met. Nothing could be more dysfunctional, since those needs will remain unknown until you speak up.

My prescription, then, is this: If you want to be more satisfied in bed, you need to take a more active role in making it happen—it's not a job for your partner alone.

I invite you to:

• become an expert in what your body likes;
• convey this information with sensitivity and candor;
• respond to your partner's efforts to please you, however fumbling, in a complimentary and encouraging way.

Phil, a forty-three-year-old antiques dealer, had mastered the maladaptive pattern of holding his wife responsible for intuiting his needs, then holding her in silent contempt when they weren't met. "Last night Susan held my face tightly in her hands, and I realized just how much I hate it when she does that," he told me. "It reminds me of my mother. She must know it drives me crazy, but she's been doing it since the day we met."

Phil confronted his response on a Dysfunctional Thought Form. "Why must she know?" he wrote. "You've never told her. You never told anyone. You keep everything to yourself and then complain that no one understands you. You've done this your whole life, first with your mother and now with Susan. Let her know what you like. Give her a chance to please you. In your heart you know she wants to."

Many of you, like Phil, have trouble telling your partner what you want physically—you think you're not worth it, you're worried about getting rejected or reproached, you're afraid to hurt your partner's feelings, you're stuck in the belief that "if I have to ask, it's no good." It would be wonderful, of course, if your partner could always intuit what you want and give it to you freely. The problem is that no one can read your mind. At times like this, when you're feeling so estranged, you need to learn to be direct and assertive, more there for yourself.

Suggestions

1.   Sometimes it's best to communicate your needs by example rather than words—to *show* your partner exactly what feels good to you. Men can demonstrate how they like oral sex, for instance, by sucking their partner's finger, and women, by kissing their partner's mouth. The idea is to go beyond language, to touch your partner in erotic or playful ways, and give this person a chance to feel what you would like to feel.

2.   Name two irksome things your partner does in bed that you've complained about in the past. One of my patients told her husband, "You squeeze my nipples even though I've told you this hurts me, and you bury your chin bone in my neck when you're on top of me." Her husband explained that when they made love, he got absorbed in the moment and didn't realize he was hurting her. He seemed more than willing to change.

3.   Take notice of those times when you want to ask your partner to please you, but don't. Write down whether you be-

lieve your silence is worthwhile, how it makes you feel, what it accomplishes. Do the same when you speak up. Try to make your partner aware of your struggle, and ask for encouragement in communicating what matters to you.

Assumption #6: "If I ask for changes in the way we make love, I'll hurt your feelings. If I do what you ask, I'll violate mine. Change isn't worth it."

What could be more delicate than asking for, or agreeing to, new sexual behaviors—a different way of touching, say, or a new position or technique? Those of you who want changes may say nothing for fear of upsetting your partner and causing a further rupture in your relationship. Those of you who are asked to change may refuse, feeling insulted or manipulated into doing something that violates you. Is it any wonder that you both stay stuck in the past, dancing the old unbeautiful dance?

Asking Your Partner for Sexual Changes

"I want Tim to know that I've never been able to climax through intercourse, that I much prefer oral sex," Carol told me, "but if I tell him, I'm afraid he'll think he's a lousy lover and try to prove himself again with someone else. I'm willing to fake orgasms to keep him around."

Tim had his own secret. "Lisa [the affair-person] did something incredible that I wish Carol would do," he told me. "She moved her pelvis up into mine while we were making love, as though she were meeting me halfway. It made me feel wanted. Carol just lies there, like she's sacrificing herself. Whether she's angry at me, embarrassed to be physically aggressive, or just bored, I have no idea. I'd love to tell her what I want, but she'd know I learned it from Lisa. It doesn't seem worth it, making her feel more insecure than she already does."

You, like Tim and Carol, may decide to keep your sexual wishes to yourself and not risk provoking an ugly confrontation. But your silence is likely to increase the emotional distance between you, even more than your lackluster sex life.

A peaceful facade is no substitute for intimacy. Hiding what you want may protect your partner's feelings, but if your goal is getting closer, not just getting by, you have to voice what matters to you, even if the truth stings. In the end you may discover that your partner wishes you had spoken up sooner, and welcomes the chance to satisfy you.

Considering Your Partner's Requests for Sexual Changes

Asking for sexual changes won't bring you closer unless you're also willing to entertain them. I don't mean necessarily agreeing to the changes your partner wants, but being willing to consider them with an open mind.

That's what a patient named Marilyn refused to do. When her unfaithful husband asked her to douche so he could enjoy cunnilingus with her, she flashed back, "My vagina is a self-cleaning oven. If you don't like the way it smells, get your nose out of there."

Your resistance to change, like Marilyn's, may be understandable, but it may deprive you of an experience that could bring you both pleasure, and move you closer together. If your partner is making genuine efforts to become more sexually intimate, and backing them with loving gestures outside the bedroom, I suggest that you view requests for change not as criticism, a put-down, or an unflattering comparison with the affair-person, but as a *gift* in service of your relationship.

At the same time, you shouldn't agree too quickly to changes that seem repugnant or premature, or that otherwise seem to compromise your integrity or well-being. "The idea of oral sex has always made me gag," one straying partner told me. "But I feel I've got to do it to convince my husband I'm back for good." "My husband wanted sexual surprises," a hurt partner explained, "so I met him at the airport wearing nothing but a raincoat. He got an enormous kick out of it, but I never felt so cheap in my life. I had gone too far."

It's not reconstructive for you, the unfaithful one, to satisfy your partner only from a sense of guilt, or for you, the hurt one, to satisfy your partner only from feelings of insecurity and a desperate wish to please. Neither of you should feel you have to respond sexually just to prove your love or commitment. Both of you need to respect each other's right to say no.

Suggestion
To help you communicate your sexual preferences, I encourage you to share your responses to the following list of behaviors, which many partners consider pleasing. Rate each behavior on a scale of one to three: one = not pleasing; two = somewhat pleasing; three = very pleasing. Be sure to add your own requests to the list, in language that is positive and specific, not negative and global. Saying, "I hate how fast you move into intercourse," is less helpful than, "I'd like you to kiss and stroke me for at least ten minutes before we go further." Remember, communicating what pleases you only informs and directs your partner, it doesn't require your partner to do it.

I would like you to:

Partner A	Partner B	
_____	_____	come to bed bathed and smelling clean.
_____	_____	take a shower with me before we get into bed.
_____	_____	brush your teeth before coming to bed.
_____	_____	stop smoking cigarettes a few hours before we get into bed, and use mouthwash.
_____	_____	wrap your legs around me when I enter you.
_____	_____	lick my ear, finger, nipple . . . in this way (explain).

		ask me to show you how I want to be touched.
		kiss me on the mouth for a while before touching my genitals.
		run your fingertips lightly over my body.
		reassure me that I'm not taking too long to reach orgasm.
		be patient with me and make me feel you want me to come, even after you've come.
		gently stroke my testicles.
		use lubrication on my clitoris.
		suggest we make love in a new place.
		put on romantic, relaxing music.
		dance with me slowly before we get into bed.
		whisper in my ear how much you love me.
		talk dirty to me.
		come to bed naked.
		come to bed wearing something sexy.
		come on to me when you feel aroused (don't just ask me if I'm interested).

_____	_____	ask how I feel before you come on to me.
_____	_____	make love to me in front of the fireplace.
_____	_____	snuggle with me in bed for at least ten minutes after we make love.
_____	_____	stimulate me orally while I do the same to you.
_____	_____	show me how I can please you orally in ways that are acceptable to me.

Assumptions #7–10: "We should reach orgasm simultaneously." "We should have multiple orgasms." "We should reach orgasm through intercourse." "We should reach orgasm every time we make love."

When I ask my patients, "Do you believe any of these 'should' statements?" many say, "Don't be ridiculous." Yet when these expectations aren't fulfilled, these same people are often disappointed. When I ask why, they respond, "Well, I don't believe these ideas intellectually, but I believe them emotionally," or "I don't believe them for others, but I do for myself."

The fact is, many of you hold yourselves to relentlessly high sexual standards. It's no wonder that lack of sexual desire is the common cold of sexual disorders: Who has the energy to start when the finish line is beyond reach?

One of the most common misconceptions is that women who are uninhibited or sufficiently aroused not only should be able to reach vaginal orgasm, but prefer it to manual or oral stimulation.[14] In reality, most women, anatomically, don't get the clitoral stimulation they need through intercourse alone, and therefore cannot reach orgasm this way—ever.

Men, too, often find that they need or prefer other kinds of stimulation than what they get through intercourse, but they're ashamed to admit it. This overemphasis on orgasm through intercourse puts pressure on them to make it happen. When it doesn't, they're often left worrying that they'll never get their needs met with their partner, or that there's something deficient about themselves or their bodies.

Jerry blamed himself for never being able to bring his wife to orgasm. "For years I believed Ann couldn't come because of me," he told me. "I wasn't big enough, I came too soon, the chemistry wasn't right. My own negative feelings about my performance—about myself—were one reason I had an affair with Sally. She came to climax so quickly through intercourse—it made me feel virile, and vindicated. But as we spent time together, she let me know she needed other kinds of stimulation and taught me things about a woman's anatomy I was totally ignorant about. I couldn't believe how little my wife and I knew about our bodies—about how to give and receive pleasure. I realized I had run away from our sexual difficulties; I might not have, if I had seen them as problems to be solved."

Another unrealistic idea is that you should reach orgasm every time you make love. According to one of the most recent national sex surveys, most Americans fantasize about the incredible sex in other people's lives, and have an exaggerated sense of what is normal. The study found: "Despite the fascination with orgasms, despite the popular notion that frequent orgasms are essential to a happy sex life, there was not a strong relationship between having orgasms and having a satisfying sexual life." Some 75 percent of men said they always reached orgasm during sex with their partners, while only 29 percent of women said they always did. Yet the percentage of men and women who reported being extremely satisfied both physically and emotionally was equal—40 percent. As the researchers point out, orgasm could not be the only key to sexual fulfillment, or men and women would have reported different levels of satisfaction.[15]

What often matters as much as orgasm are your *ideas* about

orgasm. Rigid, unrealistic expectations are likely to leave you feeling frustrated, dissatisfied, and defective. You're more apt to have a loving, intimate experience when you emphasize the process rather than the results. As British writer Leonard Woolf pointed out, it's the journey, not the arrival, that matters.

Suggestion
Let your partner know how you'd like to reach orgasm, and give up the notion that there's one superior way—through the magnificent penis.

If you, as a woman, want to climax through intercourse but have been unable to, try stimulating your clitoris while your partner enters you either from above (holding himself slightly over you) or from the side (lying behind you). It may help to use lubrication, saliva, or gel; the notion that there's something shameful about needing lubrication is another popular misconception.

If, as a man, you have difficulty reaching orgasm through intercourse, try lying on your back and having your partner stimulate you orally, manually, or with a vibrator. You can also touch yourself while your partner strokes your testicles or kisses your nipples. What may be causing your problem is your attitude that real men come only through intercourse.

Both of you, men and women, need to figure out what makes sex pleasurable for you—what works, what doesn't—and adopt a nonevaluative attitude that says, "Any way we reach orgasm is fine and perfectly normal as long as we both feel comfortable with it. There's no one right or better way."

Listen to your bodies. They'll tell you what they like.

Assumption #11: "We should want sex with the same frequency, and at the same time."

After an affair, prepare yourselves for sudden and seemingly inexplicable shifts in levels of sexual desire. Unfaithful partners may completely lose interest in sex while hurt partners may experience a magnified need for it to overcome their doubts about themselves as lovers. The opposite is also true: Unfaithful partners may be hungry to resume sexual relations, while hurt partners may feel afraid to risk such intensity of feeling.

One hurt partner, Barbara, found that after her husband's affair she had an insatiable need to make love. "I want to wear him out so he won't have the energy for anyone else," she told me. "I want to prove to him that I can make him happy, that I can be as hot as his lover."

Her husband didn't know how to react. "I'm trying to strike a balance," he told me, "sometimes giving in to her, even when I have no desire, just to make her feel secure; sometimes telling her I'm not up for sex but reassuring her of my commitment and love. But when she senses I'm not totally interested, she starts wondering why. We always enjoyed each other in bed, but this neediness of hers is putting me off."

One unfaithful partner, Bob, went into a protective shell after revealing his affair and lost all sexual desire, not just for his wife but for anyone. He stopped masturbating as well. "I've just shut down sexually," he told me. "Maybe this is my way of punishing myself for what I've done, of controlling my urges so they don't get out of hand again."

At first, his wife worried that he had lost interest in her. Then she worried that when his interest returned, he would leave again.

As with these two couples—Barbara and her husband, Bob and his wife—your satisfaction with your partner may have less to do with different levels of desire than with your assumptions about them. If you believe that two sexually compatible people should want to make love with the same frequency 100 percent of the time, you're likely to be alarmed by your differences and go in search of satisfaction elsewhere. If you believe that two people rarely have the same physical needs at any given moment, you're likely to be more tolerant of your differences and negotiate them within the confines of your relationship.

The pressure to match your partner's needs is compounded

when you're both a woman and the hurt partner. Pop culture tells you it's your job to satisfy the man or he'll replace you. "Thus it falls to the wife to match his [her husband's] 'drive,' pretend to match it, or suffer a penalty," writes Dr. Thelma Jean Goodrich. "Even in therapy, the wife's deviation from the husband's 'drive' is typically seen as the problem to solve." When your husband invites you to make love, therefore, you may want to check in with yourself and ask, "Am I answering with a good wife voice, a scared voice, or my own voice?" Your partner, in turn, should question, "Is my wife having sex as a kindness to me, out of fear of losing me, or out of her own desire?"[16]

There is nothing maladaptive about accommodating to your partner's sexual timetable as long as it doesn't make you feel compromised, coerced, or resentful, and you're not alone in working to rebuild the partnership. I see nothing dysfunctional in you, the betrayed wife, having sex at times to please your husband, even out of fear of losing him, as long as he's trying to make you feel more secure and loved. What is unacceptable is when one of you always ignores the other's rights and privileges, or accedes to the other's needs. Relationships seldom thrive without a spirit of equity and reciprocity.

Keep in mind that your level of sexual desire will vacillate throughout your life, regardless of your gender or your role in the affair. As we age, we experience normal fluctuations in desire caused by hormonal changes. Men typically reach their peak frequency of sexual expression between mid-adolescence and their mid-twenties, at which point it gradually declines. Women reach their sexual peak later—typically between ages thirty and forty, usually followed by a gradual decline that continues until old age, with perhaps an increase in desire for at least a few years after menopause.[17]

Transitional life events also influence your levels of sexual desire. "I felt like a sexual nonentity after my child was born," a patient named Betty told me. "I became the milkman, nursing day and night, totally bent on giving my baby a healthy start.

Sex was the last thing on my mind. Eric [my husband] infuriated me, constantly pressuring me to come to bed with him—he seemed to need me more than the baby did—and I hated it when he fondled my breasts. Now, eighteen years later, the baby's in college and the tables are turned. Eric's working overtime to make ends meet, and I'm more hot to trot than he is."

Nothing may feel more alienating than your partner's lack of desire, but your tendency to read the worst into it will only push you further apart. I encourage you to look beyond your partner's apparent disinterest, beyond your own immediate needs, and work out a way of sustaining intimacy despite your periodic disappointment or frustration. Part of becoming intimate is learning to remain attached to your partner in caring ways, even when your partner can't or won't satisfy your every desire.

Suggestion

Distressed partners often develop polarized perceptions of each other's sexual responsiveness; one person is seen as a stone, never wanting sex; the other is seen as a rabbit, constantly wanting it. This exercise—I call it "the Rabbit and the Stone"—will help you develop a more realistic sense of each other's sexual desires, and reach a compromise that satisfies both of you.

First, I'd like each of you to write down how often you *ideally* would like to have sex (meaning if you weren't influenced by how often you believe your partner wants it), and how often you believe your partner *ideally* would like it. Then, write down the frequency level you would be willing to *settle for* (meaning how often you would be willing to have sex to accommodate your partner). Next, write down the frequency level you believe your partner would settle for. What the two of you are likely to discover from this exercise is that your range of responses is narrower than you expected, and that a solution agreeable to both of you requires less compromise than you feared.

Here's what one couple, Valerie and Todd, found:

1. How often does Valerie want sex?

   Valerie's response: once a week.
   Todd's response: once a month.

2. How often would Valerie settle for?

   Valerie's response: once or twice a week.
   Todd's response: twice a month.

3. How often does Todd want sex?

   Valerie's response: every day.
   Todd's response: two or three times a week.

4. How often would Todd settle for?

   Valerie's response: three times a week.
   Todd's response: once a week.

The couple found themselves laughing at their mistaken notions about each other, and arrived at the following compromise: They would have sex at least once every five days to satisfy Todd's level of interest, but not more than that, in deference to Valerie's (unless she wanted to). Each partner was responsible for initiating sex every other time. When it was Todd's turn, he usually approached Valerie that same evening; she often waited the full five days. It was agreed that if either of them refused to do as promised, that person would think through his or her objections on a Dysfunctional Thought Form, discuss them with the other partner, and set another date.

Once, when Valerie wanted an extension, she wrote down the following negative thoughts: "I'm angry. When his mother came to visit, he dumped her in my lap even though I had a report that was overdue. He doesn't value my time and expects everyone to bow down to his schedule."

She then talked back to herself: "You've been nursing your resentment all week—why are you withholding sex now? You need to confront Todd as soon as you get angry with him and give him a chance to address what's bothering you. Don't fall into the trap of turning Todd into your father, who always put himself first, and becoming your mother, who stayed with Dad only for your sake and cloaked her rage in coldness. Tell him what's upsetting you, as you do in therapy, and ask him to mirror your feelings. Then do the same for him. Don't use sex as a weapon. If you're direct, he's more likely to support you."

Instead of pushing Todd away, Valerie listened to her more resourceful self and explained her anger and acknowledged her own dysfunctional behavior patterns. On the fifth day she initiated lovemaking, as she had agreed.

Assumption #12: "If our relationship were strong enough, and we were normal people, we wouldn't have to use fantasy or sex tools."

Many of you are likely to believe that the only proper way to have sex is with both of you focused on, and being stimulated by, each other. Normal people, you assume, should not need or want sexual gadgets or mental machinations to get aroused.

Conversely, you're apt to believe that if you like or need sexual enhancers—vibrators, X-rated videos, and so on—your relationship is in trouble or you're perverted, cheap, disloyal, strange, or sick.

The fact is that there are as many different ways to arouse your body as there are to cook a chicken—probably more. The problem with rigid proscriptions for sexual behavior is that they're likely to close you off from some of the most playful and sensuous aspects of lovemaking. And at a time when your relationship is so strained, playfulness and sensuality should not be dismissed lightly.

It's been said that the most important sex organ is the brain, because what goes on in your head significantly affects your body's sexual responses. If, while making love, you fill your mind with thoughts that are spicy, even forbidden, you're more likely to get aroused than if you're thinking, "My partner never puts his dishes in the dishwasher." That's unlikely to work up much of a lather.

Sexual fantasy is a natural activity that can distract you from your anger, your feelings of inadequacy, your thoughts about the affair-person—whatever it is that interferes with your arousal at this complicated time. It can also enhance your sexual responsiveness by sending messages to those organs that activate penile erection or vaginal lubrication.

"But shouldn't my partner be enough for me?" you ask. "Isn't it obscene to be thinking of someone else while I'm making love with my partner?" No, I would say, there's a difference between thinking about sex with others and having sex with them. As well-known sex therapists Heiman, LoPiccolo, and LoPiccolo point out, "Fantasizing about something does not mean that you will actually do it. In fact, the beauty of fantasy is that it allows you the freedom to experiment with sexual variety beyond the limits of reality."[18] The idea that if you loved someone you would never be attracted to, or think of making love with, anyone else goes against human nature. It's normal to have sexual thoughts about other people. What's important is that you and your partner look forward to lovemaking, that you make your time in bed together rewarding, enjoyable, intimate, fun; and if that includes fantasy—fine.

I would just not advise either one of you to fantasize about the affair-person, though it's unrealistic to think this won't happen. You, the unfaithful partner, have acted on these fantasies before, so it's best not to nourish them. You, the hurt partner, may actually be aroused by images of your partner in passionate embrace with another person, but these mind videos are also likely to ignite your insecurity, even if at times you find them highly erotic. When you tune in to the affair-person, it's time to change channels.

One way to do this is to train yourself to conjure up other, less threatening images. *Men in Love*[19] and *My Secret Garden*,[20] both by Nancy Friday, are filled with explicit and provocative sexual fantasies, the first by men, the second by women. Some of them may turn you on.

Another way to heighten arousal is to incorporate sexual

devices in your lovemaking. Some of you are bound to recoil at this suggestion because of the meaning you ascribe to it. If you're ever to enjoy these enhancers, you need to see them in a new light, as John, one of my patients, did.

As he and his wife, Judy, were recovering from the damage of his infidelity, she revealed that during their months of separation she had begun using a vibrator and now wanted to continue using it to intensify her orgasms during intercourse. John took her request as a slap in the face. "She's trying to get back at me for my affair," he told me. "It's like she's saying, 'I can replace you just as easily as you replaced me.'"

Judy explained that she loved making love with him but couldn't reach orgasm through vaginal stimulation alone and wanted him to touch her and stay close to her while she used the vibrator. John resisted at first, but over time, after talking it over and reshaping its meaning in his own mind, he came to accept it. At times he even got aroused watching her pleasure herself.

A hurt partner named Marge came to a similar accommodation with her spouse. Since she could see that he was working to revitalize their marriage, she struggled not to feel demeaned by his wish for visual stimulation. When he asked her to slip into the black lace teddy he had bought her and watch an X-rated movie with him, she agreed. But the next day she felt cheap. "He needs these toys to keep him aroused," she told me. "They have nothing to do with me. If he loved me and enjoyed my body, I'd be enough for him."

With help, Marge recognized the subjectivity of her assumptions, and talked back to them. "He bought me this silly, pretty thing before he had his affair," she told herself. "He's always liked to see me in sexy clothes. And he's always liked porn. That doesn't make him bad, and it doesn't make me less attractive or less loved by him. Why read something into it that isn't there?"

Ultimately, what created the most intimacy for Marge and her husband was not their use of any particular sexual enhancer, but their willingness to consider each other's idiosyncratic sexual preferences without passing judgment on them.

Suggestions

1.   Take time to develop one or two provocative fantasies that you feel comfortable summoning up while you're having sex. You can begin by using them while you masturbate or as you touch your body in the shower.

When you incorporate a fantasy into your lovemaking, try to move back and forth in your mind between the fantasy and the sensations you're experiencing with your partner. Don't get totally lost in your dream world, but don't hesitate to drift into it when you're having disruptive thoughts about your partner or the affair-person.

Have fun with this and try to let your mind go, dreaming up scenes that excite you. What makes fantasy exciting is its forbiddenness or novelty; what may work best for you are scenes that you would find frightening or morally repugnant in real life. Remember, your partner never needs to know you use fantasy or what your fantasy is. An extramarital fantasy is not an extramarital affair. I talk more about this in chapter 10 on affairs in cyberspace.

2.   Invite your partner to visit a sex shop with you on- or offline. Some of the items may disgust you, others may make you laugh. Talk about the ones you would like to try. Share your feelings about them.

Assumption #13: "The subject of getting tested for AIDS, or other sexually transmitted diseases, is too inflammatory to bring up."

In renewing your physical relationship, you're both bound to confront one of the most anxiety-riddled, post-infidelity sex issues—concern over sexually transmitted diseases such as AIDS.

Though you, the unfaithful partner, may insist that you had safe sex with the affair-person, your partner is likely to need more proof than your word and refuse to have genital sex with you until you both pass medical tests. If you resist this injunction, you're dead wrong and need to ask yourself why you're feeling so defensive. The meaning you attach to your partner's demand may agitate you, particularly if you see it as an attempt to control or punish you, but no matter how offensive your partner's intentions may seem, you have no moral right to expose another person to a disabling or fatal disease. I offer the following mindset to help you follow through: "AIDS [or any other sexually transmitted disease] is real, prevalent, and life-threatening. It's indefensible to put someone else's life at risk. Getting tested is a way of demonstrating my respect for my partner's feelings and my commitment to our relationship. I can choose to see my partner's demand as coercion, or I can choose to see how pathetically selfless and dependent my partner would have to be to agree to sex *without* knowing my health status. Besides, why should my partner trust my word that I've had safe sex when I've lied [so many times] before?"

You, the hurt partner, certainly have the right to ask your partner to be tested; in fact, it's the only responsible thing to do. But try not to use your request as a vehicle for avoiding intimate contact or of conveying your rage or anguish. If you're worried about your health, speak up. Give your partner a chance to allay your anxieties and earn back your trust.

Suggestion
Get tested—both of you. Tell your partner when you have made an appointment, and then share the results. Don't put your partner in the position of having to nag you.

Assumption #14: "I'll never overcome the shame I feel about my body and my lovemaking."

Shame often stands in the way of greater intimacy—shame about the way your body looks and shame about the way it performs. When you lock these feelings up inside you, they inhibit you from going with your natural inclinations and openly enjoying and expressing yourself in bed. To draw closer together, you need to identify what you feel ashamed about, and then risk talking about it. Revealing your deepest, darkest, most shame-laden ideas about your sexual self is bound to make you feel vulnerable, but it will give your partner a chance to contradict your assumptions and accept you for the way you are. Shame needs to be aired to be exorcised.

Suggestion
Here's a list of ideas or facts that many partners admit to feeling ashamed or embarrassed about. I encourage you to discuss them and add your own:

- "My body is ugly."
- "My breasts are too small/big."
- "My penis is too small/big."
- "I don't get hard enough."
- "My penis has a weird shape."
- "My nipples are inverted."
- "I can't reach orgasm through intercourse."
- "I'm more klutzy than sensuous in bed."
- "My needs are too kinky."
- "I make too much noise."
- "I'm too quiet when we make love. I have trouble expressing myself."
- "My pubic hair is ugly."
- "I'm too fat/thin."
- "My tush is too flat/soft/fat."
- "I come too fast."
- "I take forever to come."
- "I can't get you to climax."
- "My vagina is too stretched out/too small."
- "I've never had an orgasm."
- "I don't lubricate enough/I lubricate too much."
- "I worry my vagina tastes bad."
- "I don't know how to please you."
- "I can't tell you how to please me in bed."
- "I feel awkward showing passion."
- "I'm afraid of letting go/losing control."

- "I feel cheap when I give oral sex."
- "I'm afraid I'll choke on your penis if I put it in my mouth."
- "I'm afraid you'll come in my mouth."
- "I think about making love with someone of my own sex."
- "When I initiate sex I feel too forward."
- "I like watching porn."
- "I'd like us to use a vibrator at times."
- "I masturbate when you're not around."

As you listen to your partner's admissions, it's important to realize that you're being entrusted with deeply personal information. Treat it with the utmost sensitivity. If what your partner believes seems untrue to you, now is the time to say so. When one of my patients named Vera told her husband how much she hated the black hairs around her nipples—they made her feel unfeminine, she said—he joked, "The only hair I've ever worried about is the forest that's growing out of my nose and ears. I won't make fun of your imperfections if you don't make fun of mine."

When you confess your shame and your partner helps you reduce its sting or overcome it, you remove a major barrier to intimacy.

CONCLUSION
Fear of Intimacy, Fear of Change

After you've revised your assumptions about sexual desire, arousal, and orgasms; ousted the affair-person from your bedroom; set realistic expectations about passion and the use of fantasy; and acknowledged your own personal intimacy issues, *you still may be afraid to heal and love your partner again.*

Fear of reinvesting in a damaged relationship, fear of opening yourself up and letting your partner love you again, fear of hope itself—these are common among partners who are struggling to reestablish intimate ties after an affair.

Equally daunting is the fear of change. When you realize how old and deep your dysfunctional patterns are, how integral to your sense of self, you may say, "I am who I am. It's too late to become someone else."

"You step off the curb and begin to walk across the street, not knowing what it's going to be like when you get to the other side," one hurt partner told me. "If I become more loving, more sexual, more direct about what I need, I'll experience my husband differently, and myself, too. I'll be a different person. I've always felt ignored, disappointed, deprived. If I give that up, who will I be?"

It's natural to repeat what's familiar and well-rehearsed, no matter how maladaptive. But you may be more capable of intimacy than you believe.

If you want to move closer, you can begin by identifying and taking responsibility for how you've kept your partner at a distance, how you've sabotaged your partner's efforts to know you. You can go back before the affair, before the two of you met, and look for maladaptive patterns in the way you've related to significant others since childhood. And you can consciously coach yourself to experiment with new, more loving ways of interacting.

Try talking back to your fears. You have a small window of opportunity in which to remake yourself and your relationship. Don't squander it, blindly adhering to arrested patterns of intimacy learned in childhood. Don't waste your energy keeping your relationship cold. Ask yourself, "What am I waiting for? When will I feel more ready to love again? How many more chances will we have to rebuild our life together?" It's going to take many corrective experiences to feel emotionally safe, to restore a level of trust where you can "put your deepest feelings and fears into the palm of your partner's hand, knowing they will be handled with care." [21] But I encourage you to break the seal that keeps you apart, and begin the process.

Reconnecting More Intimately
Developing realistic expectations about your physical relationship will go a long way toward strengthening your emotional

and spiritual attachment to each other. As Mary Borden wrote so eloquently more than a half century ago: "Not all of us are born lovers, or great lovers—congenital, chronic lovers. We are normal people, feeble, fumbling, well-meaning, bewildered and lonely in the crowd of the world. What we really want is a friend or two, and a companion who will be glad when we are glad, sorry when we are sorry, stick to us in adversity and last the course."[22]

The feeling of a tender, secure attachment to your partner lies at the heart of most enduring, committed relationships, surpassing in joy and fulfillment the momentary sparks and marvels of romantic love. Thom Gunn captures love's sweet contentment in his poem "The Hug."[23]

> It was your birthday, we had drunk and dined
> Half of the night with our old friend
> Who'd show us in the end
> To a bed I reached in one drunk stride.
> Already I lay snug,
> And drowsy with the wine dozed on one side.
> I dozed, I slept. My sleep broke on a hug.
> Suddenly, from behind,
> In which the full lengths of our bodies pressed:
> Your instep to my heel,
> My shoulder-blades against your chest.
> It was not sex, but I could feel
> The whole strength of your body set,
> Or braced, to mine,
> And locking me to you
> As if we were still twenty-two
> When our grand passion had not yet
> Become familial.
> My quick sleep had deleted all
> Of intervening time and place.
> I only knew
> The stay of your secure firm dry embrace.

Sexual intimacy is inseparable from emotional intimacy, each embracing, each illuminating the other. Both ask you to be generous with acts of kindness, and to be available to each other in essential ways. Both give you the strength and vision to stay connected—to last the course—even at those times when you don't feel particularly loved or loving.

NINE

Learning to Forgive

Forgiveness, like love, is a concept as much as a feeling. If your assumptions about it are extreme or unrealistic, you may never forgive, or you may forgive too quickly. In this chapter we'll look at some of the most common of these assumptions so you can make a more considered, self-interested decision about whether you can, or want to, forgive. Keep in mind that I'm speaking not only about the infidelity, but also about the many less obvious ways in which your partner has failed you, and you've failed yourself, over the course of your relationship.

ASSUMPTIONS THAT MAY STOP YOU FROM FORGIVING

Among the most inflated ideas you may have about forgiveness are:

1. "Forgiveness happens completely, and all at once."
2. "When you forgive, your negative feelings toward your partner are replaced by positive feelings."

3. "When you forgive, you admit that your negative feelings toward your partner were wrong or unjustified."
4. "When you forgive, you ask for nothing in return."
5. "When you forgive, you forget the injury."

Dictionaries reinforce these idealized notions. *The Random House Dictionary of the English Language*[1] is typical. To forgive, it says, is "1. to grant pardon for or remission of (an offense, debt, etc.); absolve. 2. to give up all claim on account of; remit (a debt, obligation, etc.). 3. to grant pardon to (a person). 4. to cease to feel resentment against; *to forgive one's enemies.* 5. to cancel an indebtedness or liability of...." Many religious authorities and theologians would add, "to give up one's right to hurt back."[2]

These definitions, while useful as abstract prescriptions, are likely to make forgiveness seem out of reach, and leave you thinking, "If this is what forgiveness means, forget it. Only a saint could act in such an unconditional, all-or-nothing, self-sacrificial way."

As I say in *How Can I Forgive You?*,[3] forgiveness is not a pure, selfless act, a pardon granted unilaterally by the hurt party. It's a joint venture that begins when you share your pain after the affair is revealed, and evolves as you and your partner forge corrective experiences that rebuild trust and intimacy. Forgiveness is a voluntary offering that must be *earned* day after day after day.

Assumption #1: "Forgiveness happens completely, and all at once."

I'm reminded of the time when my son Aaron started nursery school. After wandering around, poking at the puzzles, he turned to me and announced, "I can't go. It's too hard." Well, of course it was—if he had to master everything that day.

When it comes to forgiving your partner, you, too, may feel stretched beyond your limits. "It would take me a lifetime," you insist. "Maybe longer." And I say, "Right. Exactly. The process of forgiving unfolds ever so slowly and continues throughout your relationship. There's no end point, no time when you can take the scaffold off your lives and say, "We can stop remembering and say our work is done." To paraphrase Kafka, the decisive moment in human development is continuous.

Maybe right now you can forgive 10 percent of what your partner did, and maybe as the two of your rebuild your relationship you can forgive another 70 percent, but never more. That's fine. "Resolution of the trauma is never final; recovery is never complete," counsels Judith Lewis Herman, associate professor of clinical psychiatry at the Harvard Medical School, in her study of psychological injury.[4] You're not necessarily a good person if you forgive totally; you're not necessarily bad if you can't. You can only give what you're capable of giving, and what your partner earns.

Assumption #2: "When you forgive, your negative feelings toward your partner are replaced by positive feelings."

Some of you may resist forgiving because you see it as "the cessation of animosity"[5]—a state in which bitterness vanishes and love and compassion take its place.

This is a romantic notion, in my view, since in all my years of practice I've never known a person who was capable of achieving such an emotional turnabout. In life, psychological injuries don't ever completely heal or disappear, nor do more positive ones magically replace them. Whether you're the hurt or unfaithful partner, the memory of how your partner failed you is likely to make you wince, even years from now. To expect to start from scratch, as if nothing had happened, is to set yourself up for disillusionment.

As the hurt partner, you're unlikely ever to feel much compassion for your partner's conflicts over the affair. You may never understand, or care to understand, your partner's grief on giving up the affair-person. This is normal. When you forgive, you don't have warm, fluffy feelings whenever you think about your partner's deception, but you're likely to be less emotionally sensitive to it, and less consumed by bitterness and anger. Your animosity becomes less central to your relationship and shares a place with other, more positive feelings. You cast the affair into the broader context of your life together, and see it for what it is—a part of who you both are but not all of who you both are. And you see that your partner is more than a betrayer, and that you're more than a victim.[6]

As the unfaithful partner, you may never completely forgive your partner for falling short of your expectations, and that's normal, too. Forgiveness, like mature love, allows for the simultaneous consideration of conflicting feelings, the integration of hate and love. When you forgive, positive feelings don't replace negative feelings; they coexist with them. Your resentment remains, but balanced against the realization that your spouse wasn't so imperfect, and the affair-person wasn't so perfect—nor were you so innocent.

Assumption #3: "When you forgive, you admit that your negative feelings toward your partner were wrong or unjustified."

Another reason you may resist forgiving is that it seems to condone, excuse, or minimize your partner's behavior. It seems to deny that an injustice has occurred, that you've been wronged, that you deserve to feel angry or hurt. It seems to say, "What my partner did to me wasn't so bad or important."

Forgiving, however, doesn't mean that you deny your partner's culpability; only that you free your partner from retribution. As Reverend Marjorie J. Thompson explains:

> To forgive is to make a conscious choice to release the person who has wounded us from the sentence of our judgment, however justified that judgment may be. It represents a choice to leave behind our resentment and desire for retribution, however fair such punishment might seem . . . ; not that the actual wound is ever completely forgotten, but that its power to hold us trapped in continual replay of the event, with all the resentment each

remembrance makes fresh, is broken. Moreover, without in any way mitigating the seriousness of the offense, forgiveness involves excusing persons from the punitive consequences they deserve to suffer for their behavior. The behavior remains condemned, but the offender is released from its effects as far as the forgiver is concerned.[7]

You can forgive and also stand by your recognition that your partner went too far. In fact, unless you acknowledge to yourself that you've been wronged, there's nothing for you to forgive. "Blaming is part of getting on with life," writes Beverly Flanigan in *Forgiving the Unforgivable*.[8] "Someone can be held accountable for an injury. Someone is wrong. Someone should be identified. Then someone can be forgiven."[9]

Assumption #4: "When you forgive, you ask for nothing in return."

Some of you may refuse to forgive because you see it as a form of absolution or pardon, which is granted with no expectation of repayment. "Why should I free my partner from any obligation to repair the harm?" you ask yourself. "Why should I wipe the slate clean?"

If you define forgiveness in this self-denying or self-compromising way, you're likely to associate it with the loss of power and passive submission to abuse, and share Nietzsche's conviction that forgiveness is for weaklings—for those who are incapable of asserting their right to a just solution.[10]

Forgiveness doesn't have to make you weak, however, nor does it have to make your partner unaccountable. *If your goal is reconciliation, forgiveness requires restitution.* Should your partner be deceased or physically unavailable, you may choose to "release" this person unilaterally in order to take control of your pain and recovery. If you're trying to rebuild a relationship, however, you need to build it together. Forgiving is a two-person process; you can't forgive those who refuse to acknowledge and redress the harm they've caused you—you certainly can't have a vital, intimate relationship with them. As Judith Lewis Herman points out, "True forgiveness cannot be granted until the perpetrator has sought and earned it through confession, repentance, and restitution."[11]

A partner who wants to be physically and psychologically connected to you must work to win forgiveness through specific concrete behaviors. Unearned forgiveness, like unrequited love, reinforces the assumption that it's your job alone to stay attached, that your partner doesn't need to share the burden of recovery. If you have even a shred of self-esteem, you're likely to find this to be a dysfunctional notion.

"While reconciliation may be a desirable outcome, psychologically, forgiveness has to be earned," writes clinical psychologist Robert Lovinger in *Religion and Counseling.* "To forgive people who do not acknowledge the injury, or even worse, rationalize their injurious behavior as having been deserved, is to sustain the injury all over again."[12]

Assumption #5: "When you forgive, you forget the injury."
You may refuse to forgive your partner because you're afraid to bury the memory of what went wrong. Remembering, you think, keeps what happened from happening again. It also lets your partner know that your pain can't be dismissed too lightly.

The truth is, however, that you, the hurt partner, won't ever forget how you've been deceived, whether you forgive or not. Years later, you'll still be able to recall the exact moment of the revelation, and all the gory details of the affair. You, the unfaithful one, are likely to want your partner to forgive and forget so that you can move on to a peaceful reconciliation, but you can't rush the process. *If you don't attend to the damage you've caused, your partner probably will.*

When you forgive, you don't forget how you've been wronged, but you do allow yourself to stop dwelling on it. Your hurtful memories are likely to stay alive, but relegated to a corner of your mind. You continue to see the damage, but only as part of a picture that includes the loving times as well—the ones that remind you why you've chosen to stay together. The past may continue to sting, but it's also likely to teach some important lessons, and inspire you to do better.

Forgiving, in short, entails *conscious forgetting,* which Jungian analyst Clarissa Pinkola Estés describes as "refusing to summon up the fiery material . . . willfully dropping the practice of obsessing . . . , thereby living in a new landscape, creating new life and new experiences to think about instead of the old ones."[13]

ASSUMPTIONS THAT MAKE YOU FORGIVE TOO EASILY

Unearned forgiveness is cheap forgiveness. It's something you grant, not because your partner deserves it, but because you feel pressured to, either by others or by romantic or moralistic assumptions about what forgiveness means. Given rashly or prematurely, it buries the pain alive, and robs you and your partner of the chance to confront the lessons of the affair and properly redress each other's wounds.

Here are three common assumptions about forgiveness that may cause you to forgive too quickly or too easily, before the wrong has been acknowledged and addressed:

1. "Forgiveness is always good for you."
2. "Forgiveness shows that you're a good person."
3. "Forgiveness eliminates conflict and moves the relationship forward."

Assumption #1: "Forgiveness is always good for you."

It's commonly assumed that forgiveness is not just a gift to your partner, but a gift to yourself, in service of your best self, and that it imbues you, the forgiver, with a sense of well-being, of psychological and physical health. By forgiving, "you set a prisoner free, but you discover that the real prisoner was yourself,"[14] wrote Lewis Smedes, former professor of theology and ethics at the Fuller Theological Seminary in California.

If your partner has hurt you or let you down, you may look to forgiveness as a way of healing yourself and moving on. You may try to release your partner from the grip of your bitterness or disillusionment, and reclaim the energy that you've invested in these corrosive emotions. Forgiving, you hope, will free you from the role of victim and let you get on with your life.

This idea that forgiveness is categorically good for you is popular both with the general public and with professionals, but it hasn't held up under study. In fact, it has been shown in some cases to be anti-therapeutic, spawning feelings of low self-worth in the person who forgives.[15]

"A too ready tendency to forgive may be a sign that one lacks *self-respect*, and conveys—emotionally—either that we do not think we have rights or that we do not take our rights very seriously," writes Jeffrie Murphy in "Forgiveness and Resentment."[16] Murphy goes on to point out that a willingness to be a doormat for others reveals not love or friendship, but what psychiatrist Karen Horney calls "morbid dependency."[17] My own clinical experience confirms that unearned forgiveness is no cure for intimate wounds; that it merely hides them under a shroud of smiles and pleasantries, and allows them to fester.

Assumption #2: "Forgiveness shows that you're a good person."

You may have been taught by family or religious leaders that forgiveness is a redemptive act—a form of self-sacrifice that good people make to their enemies. By forgiving, you demonstrate your compassion and innocence, and preserve, or create, an image of yourself as martyr or saint.

Forgiveness by itself, however, is not admirable—unless, of course, you believe that silencing yourself and denying yourself a just solution is admirable. What you consider magnanimity may in fact be nothing but a way of asserting your moral superiority over your partner and freeing yourself from facing your own contribution to the affair. What you see as self-sacrifice may serve the larger purpose of putting your partner in your control, under a debt of gratitude that can never be fully repaid.

Assumption #3: "Forgiveness eliminates conflict and moves the relationship forward."

Some of you may be so anxious to reconcile that you'll do anything, even forgive. If you're a dependent personality, or if you've been raised by alcoholic or abusive parents, you've probably been trained to smooth over conflict, often by denying or dismissing your own hurt or resentment. You've learned to stay attached by burying your grievances. You forgive easily because you can't acknowledge or express your anger, and you're afraid of triggering explosive scenes, alienating your partner, and living alone.

The problem with *expedient forgiveness*—forgiveness granted without any attitudinal or emotional change toward the offender[18]—is that it's likely over time to exacerbate feelings of depression and grief, and feed an underlying aggression toward your partner. Those who forgive too quickly tend to interact with a false or patronizing sweetness, punctuated by sarcasm or overt hostility. The result is a relationship ruled by resentment, petty squabbles, numbness, surface calm, and self-denial—a relationship lacking in both vitality and authenticity.

A patient named Pat modeled expedient forgiveness when she put her husband's affair behind her long before the two of them had examined its meaning and put it to rest. "I know Henry never stopped loving me," she told me. "I don't need him to beg for my pardon." Eight years later, however, though Henry never strayed again, they were still stumbling over trust and intimacy issues.

As I've said, "making nice" settles nothing. If you want to pave the way for genuine forgiveness, you can't sweep what happened under the table. You need your partner to understand your pain, feel remorse, apologize, and demonstrate a commitment to rebuilding the relationship. *To heal, you need to forgive, but your partner must apply the salve to your wounds, first.*

SELF-FORGIVENESS

In addition to forgiving your partner for wronging you, you should consider forgiving yourself for the wrongs you've inflicted on your partner, your family, and yourself.

For you, the hurt partner, these wrongs might include:

- being overly naive, trusting too blindly, ignoring your suspicions about your partner's infidelity;
- blaming yourself too harshly for your partner's betrayal;
- tolerating or making excuses for your partner's unacceptable behavior to preserve your relationship;
- having such poorly developed concepts of self and love that you felt unentitled to more;
- hurting and degrading yourself by making unfair comparisons between yourself and the affair-person;
- feeling so desperate to win your partner back that you acted in ways that humiliated you—in front of the affair-person, your family, your friends;
- losing your sense of self; losing sight of what you value in yourself;
- putting your kids in the middle by needing them to support you, love you, and take your side against the other parent;
- being so upset by the affair that you weren't there for your children;
- isolating yourself unnecessarily; trying so hard to protect the feelings of your children and parents that you cut yourself off from their support;
- contributing to your partner's dissatisfaction at home (for example, by failing to take your partner's grievances seriously; getting buried in your career or in the needs of your children; being too critical, unavailable, or needy).

You, the unfaithful partner, should consider forgiving yourself for:

- feeling so needy, so entitled to get your needs met, that you violated your partner;

- exposing your partner—the person you love, the parent of your children—to a life-threatening disease;
- blaming your partner for your dissatisfaction, without realizing how your own misperceptions, misbehavior, and unrealistic expectations compromised your relationship;
- developing attitudes that justified your deception and minimized the significance of your actions;
- failing to confront your partner with your essential needs; acting in ways that blocked your partner from satisfying them;
- having unrealistic ideas about mature love that rendered you incapable of tolerating disenchantment in your relationship;
- having such poorly developed concepts of self and love that you didn't know how to create and sustain intimacy, or feel satisfied in a committed relationship;
- inflicting chaos on your children, family, friends.

No matter how your partner may have contributed to your unhappiness at home, you, the unfaithful partner, are solely responsible for your deception, and need to forgive yourself for the harm you've caused by violating your covenant of trust. You may also want to forgive yourself for the hurt you've caused your children. This may be an easier task if you can teach them through your own example that two people who love each other can make mistakes, take responsibility for them, and work to renew their lives together.

It may help you and your partner to forgive yourselves if you learn to accept yourselves as fallible, erring human beings— conditioned, confused, struggling to make the most of a life you neither fully understand nor control. Self-forgiveness doesn't relieve you of responsibility for your words or actions, but it may release you from self-contempt and from a "crippling sense of badness" [19] that makes you believe, "I can't do better." With self-forgiveness, you bring a gentle compassion to your understanding of who you are and why you acted the way you did, and reclaim what you most value in yourself.

A COVENANT OF PROMISES
Promises mean little by themselves, but when they're coupled with specific, relevant behaviors, they can reassure your partner of your continuing commitment to change. They can also help to keep you honest and focused. I therefore encourage you to complete the following covenant, or to incorporate it into one of your own:

> _____ [your partner's name],
> We have survived a shattering crisis that destroyed
> the integrity of our relationship. I appreciate the chance
> to work with you to rebuild something new, something
> stronger, based on a more conscious understanding
> of who we are and what we need from each other.
> I understand that fidelity alone doesn't create a
> successful relationship.
>
> I now realize how I often blamed you for my
> dissatisfaction. I didn't know how to look inside
> myself and uncover my own contribution to my
> unhappiness. I expected you to fill me, delight me,
> heal me. I didn't understand how my personal issues
> made me misperceive and mistreat you, how I made
> it impossible for you to know me or to give me what
> I needed. I alienated you at the very time that I wanted
> to love you, and that I wanted you to love me.
>
> [Add for the unfaithful partner:]
>
> I now realize how my ideas about fidelity and
> love made me think I was entitled to be unfaithful.
> I've looked back into my past and understand where
> these ideas came from, and how they served me. I no
> longer expect you to meet my idealized fantasies of

romantic love. I now understand why I strayed, and
that understanding protects me from straying again.
I commit myself to you fully, and through my behavior,
not through words alone, I'll continue to demonstrate
my commitment to you.

There always will be temptations, but I promise:

- to be the gatekeeper of my life, and take full responsibility for remaining faithful to you;
- to keep my word that I have said goodbye to the affair-person; to prove to you with words and actions that this person is not a threat to us;
- to work out my problems in the context of our lives together;
- to never cheat on you again; to make it unnecessary for you to play the role of detective any longer; to prove to you that you don't have to be afraid to trust me again.

[Add for the hurt partner:]

- I appreciate your efforts to rebuild trust and intimacy, and I promise to encourage you by opening myself up to you, by forgiving you as you earn forgiveness, and by working with you to revitalize our life together.
- I'll work on empowering myself not through anger or the withholding of affection, but through direct communication with you.
- I'll continue to ferret out and take responsibility for my contribution to the affair, and to the problems in our relationship that predated it. I realize I'm not merely an innocent victim.

[Both:]

I thought I understood that a good, loving
relationship involves genuine costs and sacrifices, that
at times I would feel deprived and frustrated, but I now

realize that I didn't really understand what loving someone meant or required.

- My commitment to you today is not based on momentary feelings, but on a full consideration of all that you bring to this relationship, and all that I need.
- Although there may be times when we hurt, or even hate, each other, I won't evaluate our relationship on a day-by-day basis. I'm with you for the long haul.
- I'll work to keep my occasional disillusionment or dissatisfaction in perspective, and to accept what I consider your imperfections. You are enough for me.[20]
- I'll try to be patient. I don't expect our recovery process to be spontaneous or easy.
- I join hands with you in working to create a shared sense of our future together, one kept alive with optimism and joy.
- I am so sorry for hurting you.
- I love you and welcome you back into my life.

_____ [your name]

WHAT LIES AHEAD: HOPE AND RENEWAL

Sometimes you need to take something apart to rebuild it in a stronger, more lasting way. Lobsters have to shed their shells to develop. Forests have to burn to stimulate new growth. And you may have needed the transformative disruption and trauma of infidelity to break out of a stale, unrewarding relationship and begin again.

A crisis, says Erik Erikson, can be a turning point; by making you vulnerable, it can heighten your potential for positive change.[21] Sometimes it takes the threat of losing something to make you realize its value. Sometimes you need to walk to the edge to realize that you don't want to jump. Until you feel compelled to leave, you may not realize you're happy where you are, and want to stay.

You probably wouldn't wish the experience of infidelity on your worst enemy, but if it helps you to uncover defects in your relationship, and grow as an individual and a partner, it may, in retrospect, seem worth it. As Jung wrote, "Seldom or never does a marriage develop into an individual relationship smoothly and without crisis. There is no birth of consciousness without pain."[22]

Last summer I bought a fancy Belgian waffle maker from a mail-order catalog. Flipping through its byzantine instructions, I flippantly concluded, "Piece of cake. I can do this." Sure enough, the first waffle came out perfect. But the second, third, even the tenth, were utter failures—one side overcooked, the other raw, the center sticking to the Teflon maze. After much trial and error, I managed to figure out—but still not master—the waffle maker. In the process I learned a valuable life lesson: Sometimes it takes screwing up to figure out how to do something right. My first waffle, though perfect, taught me nothing; it was only as I struggled to understand what went wrong that I realized how delicate, conscious, and complex a process this was.

And so it is with intimate relationships. We enter them blindly, often effortlessly, swept up with passion and an idealized perception of the partner, often cocky about our ability to keep things hot. Most of us are totally unprepared for what lies ahead, and ignorant of what's required of us to last the course. We may think we know what it takes, but, oh, how naive we are. The affair shocks us into reality. Fortunately, it also invites us to try again.

There's nothing glamorous about returning to an old, battered relationship and working to repair the damage. But after sharing so much history—after struggling to come to terms with everything that's unbeautiful about the two of you—you may now feel more connected, and more accepted and accepting, than ever before, with a wiser, more clear-sighted vision of what you want your relationship to become. Your commitment to your partner today is likely to rest on a more solid foundation than it did when you first vowed to love and cherish each other. Many people in fact would envy the consciousness and openness with which you may now actively protect and promote your intimate bond.

This is a time to rebuild, to commit yourself to a lifetime of renewal, to allow yourself to feel hopeful about your future together. This is a time to channel your energy into creating something new, something better than what you had before. Don't be afraid to nourish memories of healthy and happy times together, and to dream up new ones that will sustain you. If not now, when?

TEN

Sex, Secrets, and Affairs in Cyberspace: Living with the "New" Infidelity

When *After the Affair* was published in 1996, there was no Skype, Facebook, YouTube, Match.com, YouPorn.com, Myspace, LinkedIn, AshleyMadison.com, webcams, virtual communities, chat rooms, BlackBerries, or iPhones. There was hardly an Internet. But there was infidelity—not that everyone agreed on what that meant. As we all remember, President Clinton denied having an affair with Monica Lewinsky because, he said, he had never slept with her—they "only" had oral sex, no intercourse. Imagine how much fuzzier the definition of fidelity is today when some two billion people[1] regularly click on to the virtual playground of the Internet, often connecting graphically and pornographically with others they'll not only never touch, they'll never meet. Cyberspace has become the new singles bar—a fantasy world for hooking up with the hottie tottie or soulmate of your dreams, without ever leaving home.

So what constitutes an affair in cyberspace? Is it primarily sexual? Emotional? Secretive? Is the key issue whether the violation is discovered or disclosed?[2] Whether it goes from virtual to real life? Are you being unfaithful when you:

- friend an old high school flame on Facebook without telling your partner?
- send a flirtatious instant message to a newfound friend in a chat room?
- talk sex with your online partner?
- sext a crotch shot of yourself to an anonymous admirer?
- masturbate to a YouTube video of your pregnant neighbor?
- send a flurry of e-mails to your newly divorced tennis instructor about personal matters that have nothing to do with your game?
- move the cyber-conversation from general ("What type of breast implant feels most natural?") to personal ("Would you like to feel my breasts?")?
- get more excited receiving e-mails from an online person than from your spouse?
- discuss your personal life with your online partner ("My husband spends more time on the golf course than with me")?
- move from keyboard to face-to-face encounters?
- fantasize about your virtual mate while you're having sex with your partner?
- prefer virtual sex to sex with your partner?
- get aroused watching your virtual partner dance naked on Skype, though you live a continent apart and have no intention of meeting?

In pre-Internet days, an affair was usually defined as a violation of sexual exclusivity, in which one heterosexual partner had intercourse with someone other than his or her marriage partner, without the spouse's knowledge or consent. Today, we need to broaden this definition to apply not only to same-sex and unmarried couples, but to a whole host of secretive and sexual transactions, including digital affairs.

As I say in the Introduction to this book, your definition of an affair depends on what you and your partner agree to. What's critical for the health of your relationship is that the two of you have a clearly articulated agreement, whatever that may be. Some couples abide by an "if you don't ask, I won't tell" policy. Others want a relationship ruled by complete honesty and disclosure, one in which both partners admit when they feel emotionally or physically drawn to someone else—*before* they act on that impulse. Unfortunately, in real life, most committed couples don't spell out the rules of fidelity until one partner learns that the other has broken them, and by then their relationship is shattered.

Here's a definition that may help you and your partner plan for the future: *Affairs, at their core, are about secrets and the violation of trust.* This means that if the two of you agree to allow each other multiple or polyamorous relationships, on- or offline, there is no affair because there is no betrayal. Often, however, one person knows his partner would object, and unilaterally grants himself permission to connect with a third party. This often leads to chaos. Committed partners who want to create and sustain a healthy, respectful bond must come to a consensus on the rules of their relationship.

Let's clarify a few terms. *Cybersex* refers to a sexual encounter in which two or more persons send each other sexually explicit messages via the computer. A *cyber-affair* can be emotional, sexual, or both. *Sexting* is the sending of explicit sexual messages or images primarily between mobile phones. *IMing* is instant messaging—text-based online chat in real time.

Throughout this chapter, for simplicity's sake, I refer to the hurt partner as a *she* and the online partner as a *he*, even though the reality is more complex. Men are more likely to go online for visual stimulation and solitary sexual activities, such as watching porn, but women are more likely to go online for erotic chats and other interpersonal exchanges.[3] Cyber-relationships have a special appeal to women. On the Internet, they have equal access to partners, as well as equal power and control, without having to risk disease, pregnancy, abuse, or societal condemnation.[4]

This chapter is meant to help you begin an informed conversation with yourself and your partner on what spells trouble in cyberspace. Your assumptions about sex, secrets, affairs, and addiction will significantly shape both the choices you make and your partner's response to your behavior. To the extent that you, the hurt partner, are overreacting, this section may help reassure you. To the extent that you, the unfaithful partner, are minimizing, this section may help you grasp the seriousness of your actions. Let's look at what each of you may believe when it comes to the Internet.

Assumptions about Sex, Secrets, Affairs, and Addiction in Cyberspace

Hurt partners typically assume:

1. "If you're on the Internet secretly relating to someone sexually or emotionally, we're in trouble. This person is a serious threat to our relationship."
2. "I've called up images of people you chat with and fantasize about online. I'm so not like them. You must want someone completely different from me."

Online users typically assume:

1. "I know it's easy to be drawn to someone in cyberspace, but I won't get hooked. My cyber-relationships aren't a threat to us."
2. "Internet sexual addiction affects a small number of people who lack control and have serious psychological problems. That's not me. I'm no cybersex addict."

3. "Having the freedom to explore relationships online makes me feel closer to you and actually strengthens our bond."

Let's take a deeper look at each of these assumptions and how they may wreak havoc on you and your committed relationship.

HURT PARTNER'S ASSUMPTIONS
Assumption #1: "If you're on the Internet secretly relating to someone sexually or emotionally, we're in trouble. This person is a serious threat to our relationship."
Discovering that your partner has hooked up with someone in cyberspace can be as devastating as finding them naked in your bed. But watch what conclusions you draw. Your assumptions may be accurate and useful, or they may leave you feeling far more threatened than necessary. People use the Internet and develop cyber-bonds for a variety of reasons, some of them meant to preserve or enhance their committed relationship.

Here's a case in point: When a patient named John went to CVS one night, his wife, Robin, turned on his computer and found a folder of downloaded sex videos. When he got home, she demanded, "What's xhamster.com? And who the hell is Barbie?" John admitted that for the past four months he had been casing out chat rooms, watching videos of couples having sex, and IMing a woman named Barbie. Robin assumed the marriage was over. But in couples counseling a more complex story evolved.

"I've always felt shy and inadequate," John explained. "About four months ago, when I turned forty, I watched a program about traumatized, obese kids who used food to soothe themselves. I began to put the pieces of my life together. When my older sister died—I was just born—my mother fell into a depression and never recovered. She had nothing to give me, and I took it personally." John began to heave with tears. "I found comfort in food, and I've been stuffing my face ever since," he said, turning to his wife. "My lack of self-confidence has been a problem for both of us. And it comes out in our sexual relationship. I don't know if I've ever turned you on. I want to please you, but I worry I'm too small, I lack technique. I know I lack confidence. I went on the Internet to educate myself. This may sound like bullshit, but it's true. Online, I watched people make love. I watched how they touched each other and themselves. I started studying how other couples do it, in the same way I tackled my Ph.D. in engineering. Yes, I was turned on. Yes, I masturbated. And, yes, I went to chat rooms and talked to strangers the way I never talked to you. This Barbie woman became a mentor and a kind of friend. I don't want to date her. I don't want to marry her. I don't even want to meet her. What kept me from being open with you is not my wish to cover my tracks or replace you, but my shame. I only want to be with you, but in a different way than we've been before."

What Robin didn't realize was that John and people like him turn to the Internet for information and education to bolster their self-esteem and to make themselves more desirable as partners. Others simply want to satisfy their curiosity: "How do different men and women look in the buff?" "What's it like to watch someone get off by themselves?" The viewer's interest in cybersex has nothing to do with replacing his partner or exiting the marriage.

Still others use the Internet to normalize themselves. "I sometimes get aroused thinking about other women when I'm having sex with my husband," a patient named Mary told me. "Am I perverted? Bisexual? What do my fantasies say about me?" The beauty of the Internet, Mary discovered, is that you can go to virtual communities and "meet" vast numbers of people who do just what you do. Chatting with them can make you feel normal about almost anything you dream up. Without fear of judgment or condemnation, without releasing information that might derail or transform your life, you, like Mary, can ask questions and find like-minded souls who offer support and a sense of belonging.

People also use the Internet to act out hidden or repressed sexual fantasies or fetishes—being whipped, wearing diapers or army boots, you name it. Often, what one partner finds thrilling, the other finds shocking and disgusting, creating a schism that blocks them from sharing and unlocking the meaning of their fantasies. Online communities can provide you with what sex therapist Tammy Nelson calls "sexual empathy"—a state of safety and connection that allows you to explore erotic images and activities that arouse you.[5]

Some turn to the Internet to help them live with partners who have different sexual preferences or different levels of sexual desire. If they want sex when their partner isn't interested or available, or in a way that would offend or alienate their partner, they turn on the Internet to turn themselves on. They don't go online to replace their partner but to satisfy needs their partner can't or won't satisfy for them.

Sometimes people use the Internet to take the place of a partner who isn't available for sex because of health problems or geographical considerations. One woman's spouse developed Peyronie's disease, which curved his penis and made intercourse painful. She masturbated to images of erect penises or used these images in fantasy when she was having oral sex with her husband. To her, it was a healthy adaptation that kept her marriage bond strong. A man whose wife had herpes used fantasy in a similar way. They couldn't have oral sex when she was viral, but he could use fantasy drummed up on the Internet.

Your partner may love making love to you but still masturbate to cyber-images as an occasional diversion from, let's say, the exigencies of life. Many men would agree with author and blogger Ian Kerner (Goodinbed.com), who writes, "What women don't understand is that for many guys, porn is more like a grilled cheese sandwich than a gourmet meal . . . more like a thirty-second rub-down than a weekend at a spa—complete with happy ending. It feels good, relieves stress, and functions as a quick little treat . . . no big deal."[6]

One of the challenges you and your partner face is learning where to draw the line between an innocent sexual release—a momentary high—and an obsession that poisons your relationship. There are other dangers to guard against. Your partner's online sex may lead to offline sex and deep emotional attachments that compromise your love life at home.[7] Masturbating may deplete his sexual energy, leaving none for you. Accustomed to the pressure of his grip, he may not be able to climax through sexual intercourse. Zeroing in on intensely arousing images on a screen and reaching a quick climax, he may lose interest in the intimate but often challenging give-and-take of real lovemaking and find himself preferring his hand to yours. Woody Allen was on to something when he quipped, "Hey, don't knock masturbation. It's sex with someone I love."

Assumption #2: "I've called up images of people you chat with and fantasize about online. I'm so not like them. You must want someone completely different from me."

Before the Internet, your partner may have secretly and routinely conjured up sexual images of other people to arouse him, with little or no impact on you or your relationship. Now, confronted with the raw truth on his computer screen, you may feel stunned or stung, and question both your desirability and his sanity. But watch out for the conclusions you draw.

Many people use fantasy adaptively and creatively to add variety and spice to their lives without compromising or sacrificing their primary relationship. You shouldn't assume that if your partner masturbates to images of, say, your cousin or best friend he wants to have sex with them or spend his life with them, not you.

What often makes sexual fantasy hot and juicy are experiences that seem novel, naughty, forbidden, and transgressive, like being seduced by your very respectable family doctor during a pregnancy exam or being tied down, blindfolded, and passionately taken by the gardener. These fantasies are likely to be far outside your own or your partner's comfort zone. The beauty and richness of fantasy in cybersex is that it allows you to transcend your ordinary, everyday self; engage in the weird, wild, and wicked; and weave the rush and flush of arousal into the fabric of your committed relationship—with no necessary cost or consequence.

Your distress may come from taking your partner's fantasies (or your own) too literally, at face value. Often fantasies have deep roots, emanating from childhood deprivations, traumas, or longings. Decoding the meaning of a fantasy can be as revelatory and intimate as any sexual experience you and your partner share. Bernice's story illustrates this. When her husband, Don, learned that she was sleeping with an old college classmate, he secretly went on Facebook and masturbated to fantasies of Bernice making love to other men in their class. When he confessed this, she felt confused, insulted, and threatened. Was Don gay? Was he trying to rub her affair in her face? Hold on to his grudge? What she failed to understand was the personal significance these fantasies had for Don. Throughout his life, he had been a caregiver—to his disabled twin brother, his cancer patients, his aging parents. His voyeuristic fantasies allowed him to be a spectator, selfish and self-involved, without catering to the needs of others. What excited Don was the way he experienced *himself* in these fantasies: totally alive in a way that asked nothing of him. Focusing too closely on the images on the screen, Bernice missed the big picture and failed to realize that often it's not the fantasy but the *meaning* of the fantasy that turns people on and allows them to enjoy and express themselves erotically.

At what point should you be worried about the fantasies that arouse your partner? This is a question both of you need to address, individually and as a couple. Certainly, if your partner pressures you to play out fantasies that insult or frighten you, or wants to act out scenarios that make you feel unloved or unsafe, you should draw a line and honor what feels comfortable to you. That's what a divorce attorney named Judy did. Though she was disturbed to catch her husband on the Internet masturbating to images of group sex, she agreed to watch them with him and even found herself getting turned on. But their relationship quickly derailed when he began to pressure her to invite a friend to join them in a ménage à trois. She could tolerate his fantasies, explore the reasons they excited him, and even enjoy them herself, so long as they remained in the realm of imagination. But for Judy, as perhaps for you, there are certain experiences that must remain in a virtual landscape and not cross over into real life.

Let's turn now to what you, the online partner, might believe about your Internet use and how your assumptions might deceive you and drive a wedge between you and your partner.

ONLINE PARTNER'S ASSUMPTIONS
Assumption #1: "I know it's easy to be drawn to someone in cyberspace, but I won't get hooked. My cyber-relationships aren't a threat to us."

Most people don't browse the Web intending to have an affair.[8] Cyber-interactions usually begin innocently in a chat room or user group (for chess, say, or an environmental cause). But be forewarned: Attractions can heat up with a click of a mouse. You say you won't be fooled, but don't be foolish. The blinding, erotic charge of a real-life, face-to-face romance makes it hard enough to see yourself or the object of your affection objectively. The Internet has its own seductions. Here are three.

1. On the Internet, You Can Be Anyone You Want to Be
There's a famous *New Yorker* cartoon in which two dogs are sitting in front of a computer screen together. One happily says to the other, "On the Internet, nobody knows you're a dog."[9]

How freeing is that? How fabulous? In cyberspace, you control the way you present yourself, the impression you convey, and the way you experience yourself. You've had a stammer your whole life? Online, you can be a fast and smooth talker. You're short, fat, bald, and broke? On the Internet, you're the new Brad Pitt. Your acne or flat chest has always made you shy?

Online, you can be as smooth and sexy as Lady Gaga. You can pretend you're black when you're white, or gay when you're straight. Given "the almost universal wish to be found interesting and desirable,"[10] it's no wonder that so many people are drawn to cyber-flirting, which allows them to be anyone they dream of being.

The anonymity of the Internet creates a safe haven where you can try on new personas. And that experience of transcending the limitations of your old, familiar self can be thrilling, even magical. You may experience an intimacy, a connection, an aliveness that puts you over the moon. But be careful. You risk attributing this expansive feeling to your new friend, this person you've never met, when your attraction may stem more from the way you experience yourself on the Internet than from someone on the other side of the screen.

2. On the Internet, Cyber-Partners Can Be Anyone They Want to Be

Of course, cyber-partners get to invent themselves, too. They're free to manipulate the impression they make on you, showing you the person they want to be or the person they think you want them to be. Without lifting a finger. Or simply by lifting a finger.

One patient told me she was chatting nightly with a "priest," confiding in him while he counseled her about her marital dissatisfaction. Was this man really a priest? A sex counselor? Or was he a sex addict? Was this man even a man?

3. On the Internet, You Can Project onto the Cyber-Partner Your Fantasy of Who They Are

The Internet is the perfect place to project onto someone you don't know all that's missing in yourself and your life. Suddenly, your new cyber-mate seems custom-made for you. Flawless. She complements and completes you. She's the antidote to your childhood traumas, marital deprivations, and everyday complaints. An unintentional splitting takes place in which you romanticize the cyber-mate and trash your marriage partner. This happens easily enough in real-life affairs; in cyberspace, fantasy rules and is even more ripe for projection. The less you know about this other person, the freer you are to fill in the blanks and endow her with characteristics you crave.

"She's exceptional!" exclaimed a fifty-eight-year-old investment banker, married thirty years, referring to a woman he had met on the Internet two weeks earlier. "In fact, she's exceptional in every way!" It takes knowing someone only two weeks (not to mention, only online) to make that sort of sweeping proclamation with such conviction.

But here's the rub: No one can compete with a fantasy. Not only can't the real-life partner compete with the fantasy of the online partner, the *online partner* can't compete with the fantasy of the online partner. If the two of you set up shop together, I promise you'll have to struggle to rise above the creeping disillusionment that takes place in any enduring relationship. That doesn't mean this person is bad or wrong for you. It just means that right now you have no idea what you're bargaining for. Your thoughts and emotions are likely to be playing tricks on you, leading you toward someone who is bigger and better than life can deliver.

It may help to know there's a neurobiological explanation for this. We're wired for sex to survive, so when a fiery, new cyber-friend pops up on the screen, our hearts and minds get hijacked. Areas of the brain tied to desire get activated in the blink of an eye—less than two hundred milliseconds[11] or 20 percent faster than any other form of stimulation.[12]

And so, people find themselves sleeping with their cell phones, incessantly tweeting and text messaging someone they've never met in real life. Who is that interesting that you'd want to exchange thirty, forty e-mails a day with her? This is a form of insanity. More accurately, it's a form of "cybercoke"[13]— thoroughly exhilarating and potentially addictive.

Assumption #2: "Internet sexual addiction affects a small number of people who lack control and have serious psychological problems. That's not me. I'm no cybersex addict."

Cybersex addicts are often saddled with serious mood or impulse disorders and early childhood traumas,[14] but no one is immune to the addictive draw of the Internet. Once online, you bombard your brain with multiple sexual images, cherry-pick your fantasy du jour, and zoom straight to the most intense point of sexual arousal, all with complete anonymity and abandon. And, you convince yourself, with no apparent risk.

As you surf for pornography or cyber-relationships, masturbate, and reach orgasm, you release powerful, intoxicating chemicals such as dopamine, adrenaline, serotonin, and endorphins[15] that trigger the need for more. There's a huge body of literature documenting the addictive nature of brain stimulation rewards. In one study, rats hit a lever some twenty-nine times a minute over twenty days to stimulate the pleasure centers of their brains while ignoring other levers that would deliver essential supplies of food or water. If the experiment continued, the rats would have died.[16]

What you can take away from this research is that Internet sexual addiction isn't about enjoying sex or feeling so intimately drawn to a cyber-partner that you can't keep your hands off the keyboard. It's primarily an addiction to the brain chemicals released as you search for and experience intense, erotic, often forbidden stimulation seldom replicable in the real world. A sense of danger, risk, or fear also releases chemicals such as PEA and testosterone that heighten your arousal and activate the reward centers of your brain. Your high comes not from taking an external substance (such as alcohol or cocaine) but from engaging in fantasies and actions that stimulate the release of your own internal brain substances.

These endogenous, self-produced mood-altering drugs may distract you from whatever is missing in your life and create an artificial high. But only temporarily. Once the spell is broken (you reach orgasm, you get caught), reality sets in, and so do anxiety, shame, despair, and a sense of emptiness—emotions that make you dependent on another fix. As you build a tolerance for these chemicals, your brain craves more, until the cycle is broken again. No wonder Internet sex addicts usually prefer the hunt to the kill.

What lies at the core of the addict's behavior is its *compulsive* nature, characterized by a loss of self-control and a destructive disregard for personal values, family, finances, and career.[17] The addictive cycle stops when you stop denying you have a problem and become curious and seriously concerned about your behavior. Here are nine questions you could ask yourself to help you determine whether your Internet use qualifies as a cybersex addiction.[18]

1. Do you routinely spend significant amounts of time sending intimate online messages to someone other than your partner, downloading pornographic images, or communicating in chat rooms?
2. Do you stay online longer than you intended, or longer than you think is good for you?
3. Are you preoccupied with finding online sexual partners, even when you're not online?
4. Do you spend an inordinate amount of time anticipating online sexual arousal or gratification?
5. Do you hide your online interactions from your significant other?
6. Do you find yourself less invested in your real-life sexual partner?
7. Do you prefer cybersex as your primary form of sexual gratification?
8. Have your cybersex activities forced you to compromise your values?
9. Have your online activities jeopardized a significant relationship? A job? An educational or career opportunity? Your financial security?

According to Stephanie and Patrick Carnes, sustained recovery from sexual addiction, on or off the Internet, can take up to four or five years or longer.[19] A description of the key steps you must take is beyond the scope of this book but includes such measures as (1) abstaining from all sexual activity for at least three months; (2) becoming more conscious of the thoughts, emotions, and behaviors that support your online activities; (3) reporting them to an accountability partner (a friend, a therapist) with rigorous honesty; and (4) implementing soothing self-care measures to manage toxic mood shifts and life challenges. In the Notes section, I've included a list of books[20] and organizations[21] that should provide further guidance.

Assumption #3: "Having the freedom to explore relationships online makes me feel closer to you and actually strengthens our bond."

Your partner's willingness to allow you to explore online relationships and even to become sexually aroused by virtual images may fuel your desire for her—emotionally and physically. Freedom may breed intimacy. Having several degrees of separation from your partner may, paradoxically, allow you to feel closer and more physically attracted to her. Conversely, being under her watchful eye and hemmed in by prohibitions may push you away and leave you feeling resentful, micromanaged, and caged.

Your partner's willingness to allow a more open relationship may also draw *her* closer to *you*. In recognizing and respecting your otherness, and tasting the possibility of losing you, she may have the experience of wanting you but not "owning" you.[22] Seeing you through the eyes of others, she may realize you have countless options, and feel more appreciative and sexual toward you.

There's some recent support for this idea. Couples and family therapist Esther Perel notes that "fire needs air."[23] She maintains that intimacy in America has been defined by a tell-all, know-all, share-everything mentality that has led to a suffocating closeness often accompanied by a decrease in sexual desire and vitality. In essence, a dead bed. Arousal, certainly in affairs, is often fueled by mystery, novelty, uncertainty, curiosity, the forbidden, the magic of the unknown, the excitement of the chase. Intimacy and desire may not go hand in hand. The more transparent we are with our partners and the tighter our embrace, the more we may want to flee.

There's no question that the online world provides all of us with an extraordinary opportunity to taste freedom and to individuate ourselves within the confines of a committed relationship. The problem is that one person's heaven may be another's hell. What makes you desire your committed partner may be a complete turn-off to her, forcing her to shrink back from you emotionally and sexually.

As marriage and family therapist Susan Johnson and sex therapist Dino Zuccarini point out, when committed partners, women in particular, feel threatened and competitive—as they're likely to when they catch their partners trolling for relationships online—the alarm centers of their brains (the amygdala and hippocampus) start ringing, and they're less likely to relax, enjoy sex, or reach orgasm. What keeps committed relationships healthy and hot, Johnson and Zuccarini maintain, is the level of emotional attunement between partners—the extent to which they feel understood, secure, and valued.[24] If your forays into the online world strip your partner of her trust in you and destroy her sense of safety and connection, the two of you can say goodbye to passionate, exploratory sex—at least with each other.

Here's a story that illustrates how partners can negotiate their different attitudes toward extramarital relations without sacrificing their integrity or self-respect.

Evan got an e-mail from his former high school girlfriend Sarah announcing plans for a forty-fifth reunion. They began a daily correspondence online. He hid nothing from his wife, Emma, but she grew agitated, watching him check his Black-

Berry and lighting up with delight as he fired off daily messages to his newfound friend. As Emma grew more insecure, she became increasingly angry and critical. Evan, in turn, became more defensive, annoyed, and withdrawn. The couple began to fight and stopped having sex. "I don't have many friends," Evan argued. "Sarah and I go way back. I'm not doing anything wrong. Why do you need to control me?"

Emma fought back. "Don't make me justify my concern," she argued. "You slept with this woman when you were dating her. You screwed around in your first marriage. My first husband had an affair. Don't make me feel like I'm crazy to feel threatened. I see danger here, and I'm fighting for you and our marriage. I need you to care about how you're making me feel—or simply how *I* feel—and help me through this."

After much heated debate, Evan asked Emma what she wanted and what she thought would help her feel more comfortable.

"Have you told Sarah about us?" Emma asked.

"No," Evan said. "She knows I'm married."

"But do you talk about me? Does Sarah ask about me?"

"No, of course not."

"That makes me feel threatened," Emma blurted out. "When I get together with my best friends, they always ask about you. It's scary that the two of you don't even mention my name."

Evan and Emma both had a point they needed the other to hear. Evan wanted the freedom to have online relationships and real-time, nonsexual relationships with other women. He wanted Emma to control and take responsibility for her insecurity. Emma wanted Evan to see the reasonableness of her concern and to make her feel safe and special.

Eventually, they reached an agreement. Evan would mention Emma affectionately in some of his e-mails to Sarah, and let Sarah know he was happily married (which he believed he was). He also agreed to let Emma know when he heard from Sarah and to show his wife Sarah's e-mails. (Emma told him this wasn't necessary, but for several weeks she secretly checked his e-mails while he slept.) Emma agreed to address her life-long insecurities with the help of a therapist.

When Sarah asked to meet Evan for lunch, Emma said okay. She appreciated his openness. But when Sarah invited him to an opera at the Met, he proposed they get together as couples: Sarah could invite someone she was dating, and he'd bring Emma.

This is a work in progress with no easy answers. Evan continues to be transparent and accountable to Emma in ways that make her feel loved without sacrificing his sense of self. Emma works to allow Evan a degree of autonomy and privacy—enough to give him space to breathe and be himself. They have carved out an imperfect but good enough compromise, which is no small achievement.

A similar dialogue is taking place across the country as committed couples struggle to negotiate a reasonable and workable fidelity agreement that, given the miracles of modern medicine, could last five decades or more.

In a controversial front-page article in the *New York Times Magazine* titled "Infidelity Keeps Us Together: Reconsidering What Makes a Healthy Marriage," the Catholic-raised, sex-advice columnist Dan Savage describes his marriage to his male partner as *monogamish*. "Men were never expected to be monogamous," he explains. "A more realistic sexual ethic would prize honesty, a little flexibility and, when necessary, forgiveness over absolute monogamy."

Unless you're always "good, giving and game," Savage argues—in other words, unless you're always willing to meet your partner's sexual preferences and needs—you should allow him to go outside the bounds of marriage if that's what it takes to make the marriage work.[25] New York University sociologist Judith Stacey writes, "Monogamy is not natural, nonmonogamy is not natural. Variation is what's natural."[26]

Savage and his partner came up with a flexible policy that works for them. You may take a more orthodox line, one that doesn't allow fantasies or friendships that threaten you, on—

or offline. There's no right or wrong, one-size-fits-all solution. What matters is that you spell out together in explicit detail the terms of your agreement—call it your Online Fidelity Contract if you'd like—and are clear about the points on which you disagree. For example, you may agree to masturbate only to photos or videos but not to live persons you can interact with in chat rooms. As I said before, if you disagree, disagree openly, with honesty and integrity. Don't keep your reservations or objections to yourself. You'll still have to deactivate any minefields you uncover, but at least you'll know where they are.

Staying Connected in an Electronic World

You and your partner may be able to cut an affair-person out of your lives, but you're not going to cut out your use of computers and apps. In a digital universe, the challenge for the online partner becomes, "How can I make my hurt partner feel secure in our relationship?"; and for the hurt partner, "How can I give my online partner the freedom he needs to be himself?"

The following trust-building exercise is similar to the one we discussed in Chapter 6, except that the behaviors here pertain to cyberspace. Each of you writes down and shares a list of specific behaviors you'd like from your partner that will reestablish trust and draw you closer together. It may help to think of these behaviors as "love buttons." Push them, and your partner is likely to feel more secure, cared for, and understood. Ignore them, and the gulf between you will widen.

Trust-Building Behaviors Requested by the Hurt Partner

Here is a list of trust-building behaviors that hurt partners might request. It's a starting point only. You'll need to adapt it to your own needs.

- With an open heart (without hesitancy, without attitude, without my having to ask), give me the passwords to your computer, e-mail, BlackBerry, or other electronic devices and online accounts, and make it easy for me to check them.

- If I enter the room when you're on the computer, leave the screen on.
- Install blocking software to porn sites.
- Provide me with your phone records without my having to ask.
- Provide me with your credit card records without my having to ask.
- Cancel subscriptions to porn sites or other sites I object to.
- Watch porn or certain specified online sites only with me.
- Agree to time limits on your use of the computer and stick to them.
- When you're traveling, don't use the Internet when you're drinking alcohol or using other drugs.
- Change your e-mail address so online contacts I consider threatening can't reach you.
- Throw away all of your cell phones except the ones I agree to (so I know you're not speaking on secret lines).
- When I call or text you, respond as soon as possible.
- Tell me if you hear from someone I'd consider a threat. Forward me, that same day, any e-mails, text messages, or pictures you receive, and don't respond to that person until we've talked it over.
- If our online rules leave you feeling resentful or controlled, tell me and let's discuss it in a calm, respectful tone.
- Take a fair share of responsibility for any anger you feel when I ask you about your Internet use.
- If you're thinking of masturbating to porn, invite me to make love with you instead.
- Watch sex videos with me and tell me what arouses you and how you like to be touched.
- Tell me if you *haven't* heard from the online affair-person— without my having to ask. Don't leave me wondering and worrying.

- When you're away from home, stay in touch by phone, e-mail, or text message. Let me know I'm on your mind and we're okay.
- If you masturbate online, look only at photos or videos. Don't contact, exchange e-mails, IM, or otherwise interact with people you've met online.
- Tell me when you feel attracted to someone (you see an old friend on Facebook, for example) and let me know how you're managing your feelings.
- Send me an e-mail or text message on a "sensitive" day (for example, the day I learned of your affair). Let me know you feel sorry for the damage you caused. Help me feel less alone.
- Try to identify those negative feelings that trigger your inappropriate online activity. Notice when you're feeling bored, depressed, lonely, critical, angry, offended, caged, or entitled, and work with a therapist to manage these emotions more responsibly. Share what you're learning about yourself with me.
- Spell out with me what constitutes an affair in cyberspace. If we disagree, use my definition. Define a threat through my eyes, not yours.
- If my definition of a cyberspace affair conflicts with yours, disagree with me openly and get into couples therapy with me to work out our differences.
- If someone sends you an e-mail, photo, or text message, be guided by what *I* would consider inappropriate.
- Respect that we may not always want to be aroused in the same way. Work with me to discover ways we can please each other that feel comfortable to both of us.
- Invite me into your online world. Share your favorite porn sites, online sexual fantasies, and chat rooms with me. Let me watch with you.
- Tell me if the limits I set for your cyberspace behavior make you feel caged or resentful. Let's talk about your feelings and try to find some common ground.

- Try to understand how your cyberspace activity makes me feel insecure and unloved. Even if you don't agree, show me you understand by mirroring me (capturing my point in your own words).
- Explore with a therapist or with me those personal issues that predate our marriage that contribute to your cyberspace behavior. For example, take responsibility for your self-esteem issues; your drug use; your tendency to feel bossed, controlled, demeaned, entitled; your family-of-origin issues; your wounds from past relationships.
- Let me know what it is about me and our marriage that influences your online use.
- Attend a sexual addiction group or read a book on sexual addiction and tell me if and how you see any relevance to you.
- Tell me what you fantasize to online and why these fantasies might be powerful to you, given your background, vulnerabilities, and longings.

Trust-Building Behaviors Requested by the Online Partner
Here is a list of trust-building behaviors that online partners might request—behaviors meant to help him feel valued, understood, respected, and forgiven.

- Notice and tell me what I'm doing to help you feel more safe and loved. Be specific. For example, you might say, "When I came into the room, I noticed you left your computer screen on. I appreciate that."
- Read a book or attend a workshop or retreat with me on how we can become more intimate and sexual offline.
- Talk to me about my online activities in a tone that's calm and respectful. Don't push me away.
- Mirror my feelings even if you don't agree with them. Let me know you understand what I'm trying to say.
- Tell me if my feelings make sense to you and if you agree with them.

- Let me know what online rules and restrictions I can relax as I earn your trust.
- Let me know what I do or say that makes you fear my use of the Internet.
- Let me go online without being monitored. If I want to violate our agreement, I'll tell you first. I won't do it secretly.
- Work with me to incorporate my online fantasies into our sex life.
- Explore with me or with a therapist those past relationship wounds that make you insecure about my online use—wounds that leave you afraid of being abandoned, replaced, not good enough to love.
- Explore with me how we might handle those times when I want to have sex and you don't.
- Take interest in my loneliness and reach out to me to warm the space between us.
- Join me in couples therapy to discuss what it is about your behavior that made me want to go online for sex or companionship (for example, your alcohol abuse, your unwillingness to address your weight problem, your lack of interest in sex, your anger, your withdrawal from me and overinvolvement with our children or your job).
- Work toward lowering your guard as I work to earn your trust. I understand your suspicion is your protection, and you may be afraid to let it go.
- Give me a chance to make good.

Honoring each other's concrete, trust-building requests will help you grow as individuals and partners. Relationships thrive on cooperation, not coercion. No one wants to be another person's warden or prisoner. And no one wants a partner who grudgingly obeys a list of "shoulds." Attitude matters.

In any relationship, there's a need to balance autonomy against security and connection. The Me with the We. The problem is, you and your partner aren't one—that's the grand illusion of romantic love. You're two. You're bound to see things differently and want different things. What makes one of you soar may make the other crash, no matter how compatible you once appeared to each other.

Committed relationships in a cyber-world face extraordinary challenges. There are so many temptations today, so many opportunities for misunderstanding and betrayal. For couples to flourish, or just survive, they need a generous dose of flexibility and sensitivity to each other's otherness. It may help to remember that, in or out of cyberspace, your attachment to your partner will grow as much by how you *extend* yourself to them as by what you *receive* from them. As you reach out with compassion, in ways that ground and delight your partner, you may come to embrace the wisdom of Antoine de Saint-Exupéry's Little Prince: "It's the time you spent on your rose that makes your rose so important."[27]

EPILOGUE

Revealing the Secret:
Truth and Consequences

This section is written to help you, the unfaithful partner, decide whether to reveal your affair or not. Most of this book is predicated on the assumption that your partner knows the truth, and that the two of you are struggling to rebuild your lives in the face of it. But what if your affair is still a secret? Does your partner ever need to know? If you want to strengthen your relationship, does it make sense to confess?

There are some compelling reasons for keeping the affair to yourself. You may want to hold on to both your lover and your spouse, and know that you'll be forced to choose between them once the truth is out. You may have trouble coping with conflict and want to avoid the emotional avalanche you're likely to set off when the affair is revealed. You may feel that you lack the strength and commitment to endure your partner's vicious accusations, or worse, perhaps, your partner's sobs of grief.

There are some equally strong reasons for confessing. If you want to escape an unhappy marriage, you can use the truth as an exit visa. If you want to hurt your partner for ignoring or mistreating you, you can use your revelation as a weapon of revenge. If your relationship is faltering or simply standing still, you can speak out to shake it from its lethargy.

Whatever you choose to do, it's important to do it deliberately, after exploring your motives and thinking through the long-term implications. Once your secret is out, you can't get it back, and the two of you will have to live with the repercussions for the rest of your lives. If you decide not to tell, you'll have to live with the effects of your silence, which will take a toll of their own.

Most of you, I assume, are motivated by a desire to work things out with your partner, or at least to find out whether reconciliation is possible. The rest of this section is to help you explore your alternatives, weigh the advantages and disadvantages of each, and make a decision that's right for you.

Keep in mind that even if you're determined to rebuild your relationship, there's no correct response: *It's not always better to confess or to conceal.* You may decide to tell in order to get close again, and you may decide *not* to tell in order to get close again.

Therapists and writers on infidelity are quick with opinions on which option is best, but there's no definitive research on how a couple's healing process is helped or crippled by the truth. Remember, we're talking only about whether to reveal the affair, not about whether to give it up. That's discussed in Chapters 3 and 4.

DISADVANTAGES OF TELLING

From my clinical experience with couples, I've identified four situations in which it may work against you to disclose your affair:

1. You believe the revelation will crush your partner's spirit irremediably.

2. You believe the revelation will create an obsessional focus on the affair, and keep the two of you from examining the problems that caused it.
3. Your partner is physically disabled and unable to provide sexual companionship, and you choose to stay together to provide medical and emotional support to someone you care about.
4. You believe your partner will physically harm you.

The last two scenarios are outside the scope of this book. Let's turn to the first two, which have broader application, and see how they apply to you.

Disadvantage #1: You believe the revelation will crush your partner's spirit irremediably.
You may not want to tell the truth if you think your partner is too fragile or vulnerable to make constructive use of it. You'll want to be particularly careful with partners who have been devastated by past betrayals or losses, and who may accept the news as punishment for their failings or as proof of their own unworthiness. There's no way to predict with certainty how your partner will react, today or over time, but if your knowledge of your partner's character and personal history leads you to suspect that your secret will shatter his or her sense of self, it's probably wiser to keep the truth to yourself.

Tim told his wife, Tina, about his former lover so he could wipe the slate clean, but his confession did more damage than good. Had he considered her childhood experiences, he might have anticipated her response.

Tina had been sexually abused by her stepfather when she was a teenager. A former fiancé had cheated on her. Her husband's revelation ravaged her again, and reinforced her belief that men were cruel and sordid. "I'll never allow myself to trust a man or be intimate with one again," she told him. Tim spent the next two years struggling to win her back. The couple managed to stay together, but Tina remained immersed in obsessive thoughts about the world's unfairness and her own basic unde-sirability. Today, the two of them are as far apart emotionally as they were when Tim confessed.

Jeremy, a forty-three-year-old advertising executive, looked more closely at his wife Anne's vulnerabilities, and took an-other, more productive tact. She was raised by a mother who convinced her she was too plain to attract a man, and she grew up hating her body. "I've been married seventeen years," Anne told me, "and I still feel repulsed every time I get undressed and see my sagging breasts and thick legs in the mirror."

Her husband, Jeremy, had assumed all those years that he was sexually incompetent, and that his penis was too small to please her—why else would she be so unresponsive in bed? He had slept with one of his clients mainly to prove to him-self that he was a good lover, and had succeeded. Now, armed with this corrective feedback, he came to see that his sexual problems with Anne were more a result of their insecurities than her looks or his organ size. Less obsessed with his virility, he worked to convince her that she was physically attractive to him, and helped her overcome her shyness. He kept his affair to himself, however, realizing how the truth would only under-mine her confidence. Today, four years later, he still believes his decision was the right one.

Remaining silent may be right for you, too. If you have reason to believe that your revelation will harm the relation-ship as much as the affair itself; if you fear that the news will permanently scar your partner and lead to a separation; if you want to contain the damage and keep your relationship intact, it may make sense to keep the secret secret.

Disadvantage #2: You believe the revelation will create an obsessional focus on the affair, and keep the two of you from examining the problems that caused it.

Another reason to hide the affair is so that you and your part-ner won't spend all your time picking through its lurid details when you should be working to improve your relationship.

There's always a danger, when the affair is known, that your partner will be swallowed up in bitterness and resentment and not allow the two of you to piece together what it was about your relationship that made room for a third person. To keep your sights where they need to be—on the two of you—you may have to keep your secret tucked away.

Several well-known therapists and researchers have supported this idea that the truth can cause more harm than good. Frederick Humphrey, Professor Emeritus of Family Studies at the University of Connecticut, believes that revealing the affair permanently alters, sometimes even destroys, a relationship, and that couples have a better chance of pulling together when unfaithful partners first try to work through their own ambivalences and dissatisfactions, preferably in individual or couples therapy. Humphrey blasts therapists who push their patients to spill their secrets. "Verbal exhibitionists," he calls them—people with an inflated sense of authority and a rigid, unquestioned sense of right and wrong, who substitute principles for research.[1] Humphrey traces their tell-it-all mentality both to the let-it-all-hang-out sensibilities of the 1960s and to the Judeo-Christian concept that confession is good for the soul. Corroborating Humphrey's position is statistical evidence that when husbands learn their wives' secrets, their marriages are likely to worsen or end in divorce.[2]

My friend and colleague Bert Diament has reached a similar conclusion. He recommends that "if you want to do your partner a favor, if you want to feel less guilty and prove your love, get out of the extramarital relationship, keep it to yourself, and work to develop an intimate partnership with your spouse. Find out what's wrong and work to make it right."[3]

ADVANTAGES OF TELLING
There are equally compelling reasons for owning up. Here are four common ones. Some may strike a chord with you:

1. Telling the truth is usually better than having your partner stumble on it.

2. Telling may increase your chances of staying faithful.
3. Telling may waken your partner to the need to address what's upsetting you before it's too late.
4. Telling reestablishes the primacy of your relationship with your partner.

Advantage #1: Telling the truth is usually better than having your partner stumble on it.

If you end the affair and reveal it, your honesty may earn you a modicum of trust—certainly more than if you're caught in a lie. When your partner has to deal with a double deception— the affair and the cover-up—recovery becomes twice as hard.

Gail and Chris are a case in point. Chris was spending an excessive amount of time on business trips with his office manager, Sandy; he was hardly ever home anymore. Gail confronted him more than once, but he adamantly denied any wrongdoing and tried to make her feel ridiculous for fabricating "such nonsense." She tried to trap him with a lie of her own: that she had hired a detective who had seen him entering Sandy's apartment. He admitted going there, but insisted that he was merely picking her up for a company lunch. It was only when Gail got his mother to make him swear his fidelity on the Bible (he was a devout Catholic) that he admitted the truth.

Gail was angry about the affair, but what really infuriated her was the way Chris had continued to lie about it and make a fool of her. She still loved him and wanted to keep the family together, but she felt too insulted, too betrayed to rededicate herself to him. Her pride told her to get out, and she did.

Recovering from an affair is hard enough, but if you leave the discovery to chance—a suspicious bill, an undeleted text message, or some other incontrovertible evidence (one of my patients learned about her husband's adulterous life when she contracted gonorrhea)—you may set up a barrier of distrust that can't ever be dismantled. Even if the two of you decide to stay together, you can expect your partner to adopt a seek-and-ye-shall-find mentality, forever on the lookout for signs of infidelity. Your double deception will have taught your partner to look for lies behind your every word and promise. Your pledge to remain faithful is more likely to fall on receptive ears if you confess of your own free will than if you're trapped into a confession by a suspicious partner.

Advantage #2: Telling may increase your chances of staying faithful.

By telling the truth you're more likely to confront its meaning and avoid a repeat performance. Without this kind of bold self-examination, you may dismiss the affair too lightly and maintain the fiction that everything is fine and back on track.

Telling also puts your partner on guard, and makes it harder for you to cheat. Denver-based psychologist Len Loudis suggests that when you reveal the affair, you should fill in all the details, not about your sexual escapades, but about your modus operandi—the excuses, the lies, the maneuvers you used to orchestrate your rendezvous—as a kind of insurance against using these methods again. By surrendering your battle plans, you keep yourself in check and let your partner know you're serious about staying honest and committed.[4]

Advantage #3: Telling may waken your partner to the need to address what's upsetting you before it's too late.

Revealing your secret may sound an alarm that you're unhappy, and give your partner a chance to address your grievances.

Tom, a thirty-nine-year-old teacher, never disclosed his affair to his wife, even after they entered couples therapy. She knew they had problems—they hadn't made love for more than four months—but she assumed he would always be there for her and their baby, and never took his complaints seriously. It was only when he announced that he was seeing another woman that she realized how furious, how discounted he had felt, and how fragile their marriage had become. "I don't know how many times he told me he was miserable," she acknowledged after he left her, "but somehow it never registered until it was too late." Had Tom told her he was interested in someone else, it might have awakened her in time to the fullness of his distress.

Sometimes it takes a confession for your partner to hear your cry for help. Divulging your secret may hurt, but it may also be an act of kindness that your partner will come to appreciate if the alternative is to lose you, or to drift through life with someone who is only half there.

Advantage #4: Telling reestablishes the primacy of your relationship with your partner.

When only you and the affair-person know the truth, you create a conspiracy of silence between you, even when the affair is over. As infidelity expert Frank Pittman notes, secrecy can damage a relationship as much as sex; the problem is not just whom you're lying with, but whom you're lying to.[5] The person who knows the truth becomes the person you're closer to. The person in the dark becomes the outsider. When you tell your partner your secret, you give this relationship the primacy it deserves.

Knowledge is power, and when you share your secret, you give your partner both. Your confession says, in effect, "I don't have the right to control critical information about our relationship that I know would matter to you greatly. I don't have the right to decide what's best for you. You should be able to decide whether to stay with me, knowing everything I know, with equal access to the truth." By revealing your secret, you put the two of you back on an equal footing and allow yourselves to reconnect in an authentic way.

In Barbara Kingsolver's novel *Pigs in Heaven*, Jax sleeps with his girlfriend Taylor's landlady, and wrestles over whether to confess it. When the landlady asks him, "Who does it hurt if you don't tell her?" Jax replies:

Then I know something she doesn't. I've got this robin's egg in my hand. Do I give it to her or do I not? Maybe she'll cook it, maybe she will throw it at me, who knows? So I keep it in my hand, right here. And every day when I talk to Taylor, and when I lie in bed with Taylor, it's here in my hand and I'm thinking, if I forget for one minute then we'll roll over in this thing, uh-oh, big mess. Until that happens, I'm holding it and I can feel the shell of it as thin as the shell on your teeth. I'm choosing what Taylor knows and what she doesn't. I have the power. I will be the nervous yet powerful guy in the know, and she will be the fool . . . and if she's the fool, then how can I worship the ground she walks on? I'm being a bad boy. But bad boys can still confess and beg for penance.[6]

Jax's secret created a palpable distance between him and his girlfriend. A patient named Jane set up a similar barrier when she kept her affair from her husband, Larry. When his business began to fail, he took to drinking and retreated into himself. She had given up a high-powered job to take care of their baby and felt isolated, overwhelmed, and unattractive. When her gynecologist made a play for her, she was flattered.

Jane kept her secret to herself, and let her husband think he was the only one letting the family down. But eventually she realized how unfair she was being. "We were both running away from stresses in our lives," she told me, "so who was I to feel so holier-than-thou? I sat him down and told him about my affair. At first I thought he'd get up and leave, but he just sat there staring into space. Then he began to cry. Neither of us had any idea what the other had been struggling with and how lonely we both felt. Knowing that we were both hurting made us less ashamed, and taught us to look to each other for support, rather than to something outside ourselves, like alcohol and lovers."

When you, like Jane, divulge your secret, you allow your partner to know you. You also allow yourself to experience your partner's acceptance of you. Without this acceptance, your guilt and your deception may sit between you, never allowing you to feel as close to your partner as you did to the affair-person.

DECIDING WHAT'S BEST FOR YOU

Several infidelity specialists maintain that confessing the secret is a nonnegotiable first step toward restoring trust. "Any effort to disorient your partner is a power play that will eventually hurt the relationship," says Frank Pittman in *Private Lies*. "People who are lied to become dependent, anxious, delicate, and overreactive. . . . Dishonesty is the enemy of intimacy, and is not likely to be good for marriage. Dishonesty creates distance."[7]

To Emily Brown, author of *Patterns of Infidelity and Their Treatment,* secrecy is "crazy-making."[8] Telling the truth, she points out, serves the critical function of precipitating a domestic crisis and creating an opportunity for honest dialogue and self-examination.

My own view is that no two situations are alike and that what is good for one couple may be bad for another. Even if you're committed to rebuilding the relationship, there's no one clear way to proceed.

For some couples, the truth can have adverse, even destructive, consequences. For others, it's essential for restoring a damaged relationship. Managing the truth of your affair is not unlike managing the truth about cancer—some people recover better when they know everything; others do worse. In grappling for the best strategy, therefore, it may help to ask, "Best for whom?" What may be good for you may prove disastrous for your partner and your relationship, and vice versa.

If you decide to confess, keep in mind that your partner's reaction will be influenced by the way he or she reads your motives. If you're perceived as trying to respect your partner's right to be as informed as you, your admission is likely to elicit a more positive response. If you come across as someone who merely wants to be absolved of guilt, your partner won't be as receptive or forgiving. Your intentions can be misinterpreted, of course, so it's a good idea to make them clear.

Some of you may want to remain silent about affairs that were one-night stands or that happened long ago, on the assumption that they no longer pose a threat to your relationship. Others may argue the opposite: If the affair were so innocuous, so deeply buried in the past, then why *not* reveal it? By keeping it a secret, you may be imbuing it with an importance it doesn't deserve.

Should you disclose the affair and fail to process what it says about you and your partner, your relationship will probably not hold together over time—or will merely hold together. Restoring intimacy takes more than a confession of infidelity. Should you neither disclose the affair nor process what it says about you and your partner, you may be lulled by the apparent lack of conflict between you and think that all is well again. But nothing will have changed.

Many unfaithful partners decide to hold on to their secret while they address what's bothering them in the relationship. That's a solution worth considering; you can certainly confront your partner with your unhappiness without revealing the affair or making your partner go through the arduous and delicate task of learning to trust and forgive you.

However you decide to handle your secret, the idea that one solution is always better than another is, I believe, an illusion. When you do *X*, *Y* doesn't always follow; the human heart doesn't run by these kinds of laws. All you can do is try to make a thoughtful and judicious decision, taking into account both your motives and the impact your behavior is likely to have on your partner. In the final analysis, if an intimate reconnection is what you hope to achieve, what matters most is not that you reveal or hide your affair, but that you use its lessons to strengthen your relationship.

NOTES

INTRODUCTION
CAN A COUPLE SURVIVE INFIDELITY?
1. In 1992, the National Opinion Research Center at the University of Chicago conducted a nationwide study (Laumann, Gagnon, Michael, and Michaels, 1994, pp. 215–216) in which it asked 3,432 men and women, ages eighteen to fifty-nine, "Have you ever had sex with someone other than your husband or wife while you were married?" The number of men who answered yes ranged from 7.1 percent (ages eighteen to twenty-nine) to 37 percent (ages fifty to fifty-nine). The number of women who answered yes ranged from 11.7 percent (ages eighteen to twenty-nine) to 19.9 percent (ages forty to forty-nine). Only 12 percent of women in the fifty to fifty-nine age group reported having extramarital affairs. The results were averaged together, so that those who were youngest, with fewer years of marriage, were averaged in with those who were older, with more years of marriage. The researchers didn't draw any conclusions; they simply indicated on a chart that some 25 percent of married men and 15 percent of married women in their study reported having at least one extramarital affair sometime during their married life. This statistic, most often quoted by the media, misrepresents the data. The figure of 37 percent is likely to be more accurate for men, for it represents the number who were unfaithful *over the course of their lives.* As for women, the figure of 20 percent is likely to be more accurate. That women over age fifty had a lower rate may reflect the fact that they missed the sexual revolution. Approximately 20 percent of the designated study participants refused to be interviewed or couldn't be located. This leaves open the question of how many were unwilling to divulge their affairs.

In 2010, NORC, a research center at the University of Chicago, found

303

that, among those who had been married at least once, 14 percent of women and 20 percent of men *admitted* to affairs. Statistics vary considerably from study to study, depending on who participates, who tells the truth, and how an affair is defined.

2. According to a March 2007 poll conducted by the U.S. Census Bureau, there were 58,945,000 married couples in the United States.

3. In Annette Lawson's British study (1988, p. 37), more than 40 percent of the participants reported a relationship that they considered "adulterous," even though it didn't involve sexual intercourse.

4. In a recent survey, a random sample of practicing couples therapists (all members of the American Psychological Association or the Association for Marriage and Family Therapy) rated extramarital affairs as the third most difficult problem to treat, and the second most damaging problem that couples face. They also reported that infidelity was an issue for nearly 30 percent of the couples they treated (Whisman, Dixon, and Johnson, unpublished manuscript).

5. Herman (1992), p. 158. The exact quote is: "No longer imprisoned in the wordlessness of the trauma, she discovers that there is a language for her experience. She discovers that she is not alone; others have suffered in similar ways. She discovers further that she is not crazy; the traumatic syndromes are normal human responses to extreme circumstances. And she discovers, finally, that she is not doomed to suffer this condition indefinitely; she can expect to recover, as others have recovered."

CHAPTER ONE
THE HURT PARTNER'S RESPONSE:
BURIED IN AN AVALANCHE OF LOSSES

1. A hurt partner who learns of a mate's infidelity often exhibits psychological and physiological symptoms that are similar to those of people diagnosed with post-traumatic stress disorder. In the past, this diagnosis could be given only to individuals who had had a life-threatening experience (*Quick Reference to the Diagnostic Criteria from DSM-IV,* 1994, p. 209). There is much debate about whether to allow the proposed, new *Diagnostic and Statistical Manual* (*DSM-V*) to include "subthreshold" events that don't involve actual threat to a person's life (McNamara, 2007).

2. Abram Kardiner, quoted in Herman (1992), p. 35.

3. Franck (1993), p. 126.

4. Jack (1991), p. 32.

5. Kushner (2004), p. 2.

6. Nadler and Dotan (1992), pp. 308–309.

7. Jack (1991), pp. 128–182.

8. Brown and Gilligan (1992), p. 4.

9. Ibid., p. 37.

10. In February 1986, Yale sociologist Neil Bennett first reported in a phone interview with the *Stamford Advocate* that college-educated women

who postpone marriage for the sake of their education and career have a harder time finding a husband. In Faludi (1991), pp. 9–14.

11. Ibid., p. 14.
12. Richardson, "Dreaming Someone Else's Dreams," *New York Times Magazine,* Jan. 28, 1990, p. 14, quoted in Faludi (1991), p. 103.
13. England and McClintock (2009, p. 814) reported that women who are over forty and want to marry or remarry find that older men often choose younger brides. Men over age sixty typically "marry down" about ten years.
14. Fitzpatrick (2010) noted that women are far more likely to take time off to start a family or to work part-time while rearing one, often going through a full calendar year earning nothing at all.
15. Hewlett, *A Lesser Life,* 1989, p. 63; Deborah L. Rhode, "Rhode on Research," *Institute for Research on Women and Gender Newsletter,* Stanford University, 13, no. 4 (Summer 1989): 4; quoted in Faludi (1991), p. 24.
16. Fitzpatrick (2010).
17. Mayo Clinic Staff, 2010.
18. Jack (1991), p. 21.
19. Reinisch with Beasley (1990), p. 74.
20. DePaula, Epstein, and Wyer (1993), p. 133.
21. Nolen-Hoeksema (1987, pp. 259–282) found that women tend to dwell on depressive episodes, thereby amplifying and prolonging their depressive symptoms. Men, in contrast, tend to distract themselves from depressive episodes by thinking about other things, ignoring their problems, or engaging in physical activity.

CHAPTER TWO
THE UNFAITHFUL PARTNER'S RESPONSE: LOST IN A LABYRINTH OF CHOICES

1. Carder with Jaenicke (1992), p. 115.
2. Beattie (1994), Introduction. The exact quote is: "It's not the passage of time that heals, he whispered. It's the passage through experiences."
3. Person (1988), p. 322.
4. Allen and Baucon (2004).
5. Glass and Wright (1988), p. 318.
6. Glass and Wright (1992), p. 379.
7. Botwin (1994), p. 62.
8. Gregory (2003).
9. Harley (1986), pp. 72–85.
10. Glass and Wright (1985, p. 1115) found that 56 percent of the men in their study who had extramarital sex reported happy marriages, as compared to 34 percent of the women in their study.
11. Wright (1988), p. 29.
12. Brown (1991), p. 7.
13. Janus and Janus (1993), p. 332.

14. Researchers Etxebarria, Ortiz, Conejero, and Pascual (2009) found that women are more likely than men to experience guilt when they cause others to suffer. Women, particularly between the ages of twenty-five and thirty-three, score higher than men on tests of interpersonal sensitivity.
15. Botwin (1994), pp. 39, 62, 120.
16. Jack (1991), p. 87.
17. McAdams and Constantian (1983), p. 856.
18. Ross and Holmberg (1990); found in DePaulo, Epstein, and Wyer (1993), p. 127.
19. Glass and Wright (1985), p. 1114.
20. Michael, Gagnon, Laumann, and Kolata (1994), p. 156.
21. Botwin (1994).
22. Heyn (1992).
23. Botwin (1994), pp. 44–53.

CHAPTER THREE
EXPLORING YOUR IDEAS ABOUT LOVE

1. Otto Kernberg, interviewed by Linda Wolfe (1978), p. 56.
2. *Quick Reference to the Diagnostic and Statistical Manual IV-TR* (2000), pp. 291–292.
3. Barreca (1993), p. 198.
4. Beck, Freeman, and Davis (2007).
5. Person (1988), p. 322.
6. Winterson (1989), p. 13.
7. Toufexis (1993), p. 50.
8. Person (1988), p. 48.
9. Walsh (1991), p. 188.
10. Mercer (1988), p. 177.
11. Fisher (1992), p. 171.
12. Dyn and Glenn (1993), pp. 54–57, 78–86.
13. Stuart and Jacobson (1985), p. 57.
14. Gottman, personal e-mail correspondence (Sept. 2, 2011).
15. Gottman (1993).
16. Estés (1992), p. 140. Ballantine Books: Excerpts from *Women Who Run with the Wolves* by Clarissa Pinkola Estés, Ph.D. Copyright © 1992, 1995 by Clarissa Pinkola Estés, Ph.D. All performance, derivative, adaptation, musical, audio and recording, illustrative, theatrical, film, pictorial, electronic, and all other rights reserved. Reprinted by kind permission of the author, Dr. Estés, and Ballantine Books, a division of Random House, Inc.
17. Money (1988).
18. I'm indebted to Dr. Reuben Baron (1970) for his development of the theory of social reinforcement, and Dr. Harville Hendrix (1988) for his imago theory.

CHAPTER FOUR
CONFRONTING YOUR DOUBTS AND FEARS
1. Stanley and Markman (1992), p. 595.
2. Baumeister (1991), pp. 182–206.
3. Shaver and Hazen (1988), p. 491; see Stanley (1986).
4. Cherlin, Furstenberg, et al. (1991), p. 252.
5. Amato and Keith (1991, p. 30) add, however, that the differences between divorced and intact families are not as strong and pervasive as often presented.
6. Eldar-Avidan, Haj-Yahia, and Greenbaum (2009).
7. Ahrons (1994), p. 14; also Ahrons (2004).
8. Kelly (1993), p. 45.
9. Ahrons (1994), p. 2.
10. Kelly (1993), p. 35.
11. Franck (1993), p. 76.

CHAPTER FIVE
LEARNING FROM THE AFFAIR
1. I'm indebted to Dr. Jeffrey Young for his development of schema-based life traps. See Young and Klosko (1993) for help in understanding and healing them.
2. Hendrix (1988).
3. Anaïs Nin, quoted in Efran (1994), p. 221.
4. Efran (1994), p. 221.
5. Baron (1970).
6. Person (1988), p. 233.
7. Ibid., p. 232.
8. You might want to refer to Maggie Scarf's *Intimate Partners* (2008) or Jeffrey Young and Janet Klosko's *Reinventing Your Life* (1993) to help you identify how you and your partner may be interacting in ways that evoke the worst from both of you.
9. Gerson (1989), found in Brown (1991), p. 15.
10. Brown (1991), p. 15.
11. Abrahms and Spring (1989).
12. Scarf (2008), p. 93.
13. Hammen, Ellicott, and Gitlin (1985).
14. Abrahms and Spring (1990).

CHAPTER SIX
RESTORING TRUST
1. Stuart (1980), p. 200. Adapted from his "Caring-days List" exercise, which he developed to help couples enhance feelings of marital satisfaction.
2. Abrahms (1990).
3. Hibbs and Getzen (2010).
4. Burns (2008).

5. Hendrix (2001).
6. Bly (1990), p. xi.

CHAPTER SEVEN
HOW TO TALK ABOUT WHAT HAPPENED
1. See Brown and Gilligan (1992), p. 4.
2. Thomas (1993), pp. 26, 46–47.
3. Burns (1980), pp. 128–131.
4. For a more complete discussion of the different ways in which men and women express and listen to conflict, I recommend *Men Are from Mars, Women Are from Venus* (Gray, 2004) and *You Just Don't Understand: Men and Women in Conversation* (Tannen, 2001).
5. Gottman (1994), p. 95.
6. Jack (1991), p. 42.
7. Lerner (2012).
8. Gottman, Gottman, and DeClaire (2007).

CHAPTER EIGHT
SEX AGAIN
1. Glass and Wright (1985), p. 1113.
2. Michael, Gagnon, Laumann, and Kolata (1994), p. 124.
3. Nelson (2008).
4. Barbach (1983).
5. Williams (1988), p. 172.
6. Masters and Johnson (1970), pp. 71–75.
7. Reinisch with Beasley (1990), p. 98.
8. These statistics pertain to men and women ages twenty-five to twenty-nine. The Kinsey Institute, National Survey of Sexual Health and Behavior, 2010. For more information, visit NationalSexStudy.indiana.edu/.
9. Reinisch with Beasley (1990), p. 91.
10. Michael, Gagnon, Laumann, and Kolata (1994), p. 165.
11. Ibid., p. 158.
12. Ibid., p. 165.
13. Winterson (1994), p. 21.
14. Kinsey, Pomeroy, Martin, and Gebhard (1953) discuss the anatomical reasons that many women do not have vaginal orgasms. "The relative unimportance of the vagina as the center of erotic stimulation is further attested by the fact that relatively few females masturbate by making deep vaginal insertions" (p. 580). For further discussion of the myth of the vaginal orgasm, see Cass, *The Elusive Orgasm* (2004).
15. Michael, Gagnon, Laumann, and Kolata (1994), p. 123.
16. Goodrich (1994), p. 88.
17. Williams (1988), p. 15.
18. Heiman, LoPiccolo, and LoPiccolo (1976), p. 80.
19. Friday (1998).
20. Friday (2008).

21. Avery (1989), p. 27.
22. Borden (1932), p. 300.
23. Gunn (1992), p. 3.

CHAPTER NINE
LEARNING TO FORGIVE

1. *Random House Dictionary of the English Language,* 2nd ed. unabridged (1987), s.v. "forgive."
2. Thrall (1995), p. 3.
3. Spring (2005), p. 123.
4. Herman (1992), p. 211.
5. Hunter (1978), p. 171.
6. Simon and Simon (1990).
7. Thompson (1992), p. 19.
8. Flanigan (1992), p. 122.
9. Ibid., p. 107.
10. Nietzsche (1887).
11. Herman (1992), p. 190.
12. Lovinger (1990), pp. 177–178.
13. Estés (1992), p. 371.
14. Smedes (1984), p. 133.
15. McCullough and Worthington (1994), p. 8.
16. Murphy (1982), p. 505.
17. Horney (1950), pp. 239–258.
18. McCullough and Worthington (1994), p. 4.
19. Thrall (1995), p. 9.
20. Bugen (1990), p. 344.
21. Erikson (1950), pp. 247–274.
22. Jung (1959), p. 535.

CHAPTER TEN
SEX, SECRETS, AND AFFAIRS IN CYBERSPACE

1. Internet World Stats. Internet Usage Statistics. Internet usage information comes from data published by Nielsen Online, by the International Telecommunications Union, by GFK, local regulators, and other reliable sources. Copyright © Miniwatts Marketing Group.
2. In an online survey, infidelity expert Peggy Vaughan found that hurt parties are often more traumatized when the affair is discovered rather than disclosed. Personal e-mail correspondence, July 7, 2011.
3. Ferree (2003), pp. 385–393. Also, Smith (2011), p. 48.
4. Daneback, Cooper, and Mansson (2005), p. 326.
5. Nelson (2008).
6. Kerner (2010).
7. Hertlein and Webster (2008) documented many negative effects of online sex, including less interest in sex in the committed relationship and neglect of work and time with children.

A study of married men's online sexual behavior revealed approximately 78 percent of participants reported having one face-to-face sexual encounter with someone they met online over the past year. Dew, Brubaker, and Hays (2006), pp. 195–207.

8. Atwood and Schwartz (2002), pp. 37–56.

9. Steiner (1993), p. 61.

10. Atwood and Schwartz (2002), pp. 37–56.

11. Stephanie Ortigue, an assistant professor at the psychology department at the University of Geneva in Switzerland, and Francesca Bianchi-Demicheli, quoted in the *New York Times* by Rosenbloom (2011).

12. Anokhin, Golosheykin, Sirevaag, Kristjansson, Rohrbaugh, and Heath (2006), pp. 167–177.

13. Wylie (2010), p. 30.

14. Carnes and Carnes (2010), p. 13.

15. Presentation by Robert R. Johnson, Medical Director, Sierra Tucson (2011).

16. Wise (1996), pp. 319–340; Valenstein and Beer (1964), pp. 183–184.

17. Weiss and Schneider (2006), p. 35.

18. Adapted with permission from Dr. Kimberly Young's Cybersex Self Test and Internet Addiction Test, www.netaddiction.com. Also, see Griffiths (2004), p. 200.

19. Carnes and Carnes (2010), p. 15.

20. Recommended books about cybersex addiction:
    In the Shadows of the Net: Breaking Free of Compulsive Online Sexual Behavior (Carnes, Delmonico, Griffin, and Moriarty, 2004).
    Untangling the Web: Sex, Porn, and Fantasy Obsession in the Internet Age (Weiss and Schneider, 2006).
    Tangled in the Web: Understanding Cybersex from Fantasy to Addiction (Young, 2001).
    Getting Web Sober: Help for Cybersex Addicts and Their Families (Young, 2000) ebooklet.

21. Recommended organizations for the treatment of cybersex addiction: Sex and Love Addicts Anonymous, www.slaafws.org; Sex Addicts Anonymous, www.sexaa.org; Sexual Compulsives Anonymous, www.sca-recovery.org; Sexaholics Anonymous, www.sa.org; SMART Recovery, www.smartrecovery.org; Codependents of Sex Addicts, www.cosa-recovery.org.

22. Perel (2007).

23. Ibid.

24. Johnson and Zuccarini (2010), p. 434.

25. Oppenheimer (2011), p. 24.

26. Ibid., p. 27.

27. Saint-Exupéry (2000), p. 64.

EPILOGUE
REVEALING THE SECRET: TRUTH AND CONSEQUENCES

1. Dr. Frederick Humphrey, personal communication, September 1993.
2. Blumstein and Schwartz (1983, p. 313) found that the nonmonogamous woman, whether lesbian or heterosexual, is more likely than the nonmonogamous man to end the relationship with her partner, in part because she's likely to fall in love with someone else and "cannot treat the new person as someone auxiliary to her existing relationship." Other explanations they offer are that (1) the male hurt partner is less forgiving than the female hurt partner and therefore less likely to take his partner back; and (2) the male hurt partner is (or feels) less economically and emotionally dependent than the female hurt partner and therefore is more likely to end the relationship.
3. Dr. Bert Diament, personal communication, August 1995.
4. Dr. Len Loudis, personal communication, August 1995.
5. Pittman (1989), p. 53. For more discussion about the negative impact of undisclosed affairs, see Butler, Harper, and Seedall (2009).
6. Kingsolver (1993), pp. 162–163.
7. Pittman (1989), p. 66, 70.
8. Brown (1991), p. 53.

BIBLIOGRAPHY

Abrahms, Janis Lieff. (1990). The restoration of trust following an extramarital affair: A cognitive-behavioral approach. *ICTN* 3(1), 2, 4.

Abrahms, Janis Lieff, and Spring, Michael. (1989). The flip-flop factor. *ICTN* 5(10), 1, 7–8.

Abrahms, Janis Lieff, and Spring, Michael. (1990). Responsibility sharing: A cognitive-behavioral intervention for distressed couples. *Behavior Therapist* 13(8), 176–178.

Ahrons, Constance. (1994). *The Good Divorce: Keeping Your Family Together When Your Marriage Comes Apart.* New York: HarperCollins.

Ahrons, Constance. (2004). *We're Still Family: What Grown Children Have to Say About Their Parents' Divorce.* New York: HarperCollins.

Allen, E. S., and Baucom, D. H. (2004). Adult attachment and patterns of extradyadic involvement. *Family Process* 43(4), 467–488.

Amato, Paul R., and Keith, Bruce. (1991). Parental divorce and the well-being of children: A meta-analysis. *Psychological Bulletin* 110(1), 26–46.

Amodeo, John. (1994). *Love and Betrayal: Broken Trust in Intimate Relationships.* New York: Ballantine.

Anokhin, A. P.; Golosheykin, S.; Sirevaag, E.; Kristjansson, S.; Rohrbaugh, J. W.; and Heath, A. C. (2006, June 6). Rapid discrimination of visual scene content in the human brain. *Brain Research* 1093(1), 167–177.

Atwood, Joan D., and Schwartz, Limor. (2002). Cyber-sex: The new affair treatment considerations. *Journal of Couple and Relationship Therapy* 1(3), 37–56.

Avery, Carl S. (1989, May). How do you build intimacy in an age of divorce? *Psychology Today,* 27–31.

Barbach, Lonnie Garfield. (1983). *For Each Other: Sharing Sexual Intimacy.* New York: Anchor.

Baron, Reuben M. (1970). The SRS model as a predictor of Negro responsiveness to reinforcement. *Journal of Social Issues* 26(2), 61–81.

Bibliography

Barreca, Regina. (1993). *Perfect Husbands (& Other Fairy Tales): Demystifying Marriage, Men, and Romance.* New York: Harmony.

Baucom, Donald, and Epstein, Norman. (1990). *Cognitive-Behavioral Marital Therapy.* New York: Brunner/Mazel.

Baumeister, Roy F. (1991). *Meanings of Life.* New York: Guilford, 182–206.

Beattie, Melody. (1994). *The Lessons of Love.* San Francisco: Harper.

Beck, Aaron T. (1976). *Cognitive Therapy and the Emotional Disorders.* New York: International Universities Press.

Beck, Aaron T. (1988). *Love Is Never Enough.* New York: Harper & Row.

Beck, Aaron T. (1993). Cognitive therapy: Past, present and future. *Journal of Consulting and Clinical Psychology* 61, 194–198.

Beck, Aaron T.; Freeman, Arthur; and Doris, Denise D. (2007). *Cognitive Therapy of Personality Disorders,* 2nd ed. New York: Guilford.

Beck, Aaron T.; Rush, A. John; Shaw, Brian R.; and Emery, Gary. (1979). *Cognitive Therapy of Depression.* New York: Guilford.

Black, Aaron E., and Pedro-Carroll, Joanne. (1993). Role of parent-child relationships in mediating the effects of marital disruption. *Journal of the American Academy of Child and Adolescent Psychiatry* 32(5), 1019–1027.

Blumstein, Philip, and Schwartz, Pepper. (1983). *American Couples: Money, Work, Sex.* New York: William Morrow.

Bly, Robert. (1990). *Iron John: A Book. About Men.* New York: Vintage.

Borden, Mary. (1932). *The Technique of Marriage.* Garden City, N.Y.: Doubleday, Doran.

Botwin, Carol. (1994). *Tempted Women: The Passions, Perils, and Agonies of Female Infidelity.* New York: William Morrow.

Brown, Emily. (1991). *Patterns of Infidelity and Their Treatment.* New York: Brunner/Mazel.

Brown, Lyn Mikel, and Gilligan, Carol. (1992). *Meeting at the Crossroads.* New York: Ballantine.

Bugen, Larry A. (1990). *Love and Renewal: How to Get Past Disenchantment, the Impasse Between Romance and Lasting Love.* Oakland, Calif.: New Harbinger.

Burns, David D. (1980). *Feeling Good.* New York: William Morrow.

Burns, David D. (2008). *Feeling Good Together: The Secret of Making Troubled Relationships Work.* New York: Broadway Books.

Burns, David D. (1985). *Intimate Connections.* New York: William Morrow.

Butler, Mark H.; Harper, James M.; and Seedall, Ryan B. (2009, January). Facilitated disclosure versus clinical accommodation of infidelity secrets: An early pivot point in couple therapy. *Journal of Marital and Family Therapy* 35(1), 125–143.

Carder, David, with Jaenicke, Duncan. (1992). *Torn Asunder: Recovering From Extramarital Affairs.* Chicago: Moody.

Carnes, Patrick; Delmonico, David L.; Griffin, Elizabeth; and Moriarty, Joseph M. (2007). *In the Shadows of the Net: Breaking Free of Compulsive Online Sexual Behavior,* 2nd ed. Center City, Minn.: Hazelden.

Bibliography

Carnes, Stefanie, and Carnes, Patrick J. (2010, January/February). Understanding cybersex in 2010. *Family Therapy Magazine,* 10–17.

Cass, Vivienne. (2007). *The Elusive Orgasm: A Woman's Guide to Why She Can't and How She Can Orgasm.* New York: Marlowe and Co.

Cherlin, Andrew J.; Furstenberg, Frank F., Jr.; Chase-Lansdale, Lindsay; Kiernan, Kathleen E.; Robins, Philip K.; Morrison, Donna R.; and Teitler, Julien O. (1991, June 7). Longitudinal studies of effects of divorce on children in Great Britain and the United States. *Science* 252, 1386–1389.

Daneback, Kristian; Cooper, Al; and Mansson, Sven-Axel. (2005). An Internet study of cybersex participants. *Archives of Sexual Behavior* 34(3), 321–328.

Dattilio, Frank M., and Padesky, Christine A. (1990). *Cognitive Therapy with Couples.* Sarasota, Fla.: Professional Resource Exchange.

DePaula, Bella M.; Epstein, Jennifer A.; and Wyer, Melissa M. (1993). Sex differences in lying: How women and men deal with the dilemma of deceit. In *Lying and Deception in Everyday Life.* Edited by Michael Lewis and Carolyn Saarni. New York: Guilford, 126–147.

Dew, Brian; Brubaker, Michael; and Hays, Danica. (2006). From the altar to the Internet: Married men and their online sexual behavior. *Sexual Addiction and Compulsivity* 13(2), 195–207.

Dobson, Keith. (1989). A meta-analysis of the efficacy of cognitive therapy for depression. *Journal of Consulting and Clinical Psychology* 57, 414–419.

Dyn, Barry, and Glenn, Michael. (1993, July/August). Forecast for couples. *Psychology Today,* 54–56, 78–86.

Edell, Ronnie. (1983). *How to Save Your Marriage from an Affair: Seven Steps to Rebuilding a Broken Trust.* New York: Kensington.

Efran, Jay S. (1994). Mystery, abstraction, and narrative psychotherapy. *Journal of Constructivist Psychology* 7, 219–227.

Eldar-Avidan, Dorit; Haj-Yahia, Muhammad M.; and Greenbaum, Charles W. (2009, January). Divorce is a part of my life . . . resilience, survival, and vulnerability. *Journal of Marital and Family Therapy* 35(1), 30–46.

Eliot, George. (1965). *Middlemarch.* New York: Penguin.

England, Paula, and McClintock, Elizabeth Aura. (2009, December). The gendered double standard of aging in US marriage markets. *Population and Development Review* 35(4), 797–816.

Erikson, Erik H. (1950). *Childhood and Society,* 2nd ed. New York: Norton.

Estés, Clarissa Pinkola. (1992). *Women Who Run with the Wolves: Myths and Stories of the Wild Woman Archetype.* New York: Ballantine.

Etxebarria, I., Ortiz, M. J., Conjero, S. and Pascual, A. (2009, November). Intensity of habitual guilt in men and women: Differences in interpersonal sensitivity and the tendency towards anxious-aggressive guilt. *Spanish Journal of Psychology* 12(2), 540–554.

Faludi, Susan. (1991). *Backlash: The Undeclared War Against American Women.* New York: Crown.

Ferree, Marnie. (2003). Women and the web: cybersex activity and implications. *Sexual and Relationship Therapy* 18(3), 385–393.

Fisher, Helen E. (1992). *Anatomy of Love: The Natural History of Monogamy, Adultery, and Divorce.* New York: Norton.

Fitzpatrick, Laura. (2010, April 20). Why do women still earn less than men? *Time.*

Flanigan, Beverly. (1992). *Forgiving the Unforgivable: Overcoming the Bitter Legacy of Intimate Wounds.* New York: Macmillan.

Franck, Dan. (1993). *Separation.* New York: Knopf.

Friday, Nancy. (1998). *Men in Love: Men's Sexual Fantasies: The Triumph of Love Over Rage.* New York: Delacorte.

Friday, Nancy. (2008). *My Secret Garden: Women's Sexual Fantasies.* New York: Pocket.

Friedman, Sonya, with Sondra Forsyth. (1994). *Secret Loves: Women With Two Lives.* New York: Crown.

Gerson, Randy. (1989, October 27). Genograms, family patterns, and computer graphics. Presentation at the American Association for Marriage and Family Therapy Conference. San Francisco.

Glass, Shirley P., and Wright, Thomas L. (1988). Clinical implications of research on extramarital involvement. In *Treatment of Sexual Problems in Individual and Couples Therapy.* Edited by Robert A. Brown and Joan Roberts Field. New York: PMA.

Glass, Shirley P., and Wright, Thomas L. (1992, August). Justifications for extramarital relationships: The association between attitudes, behaviors, and gender. *Journal of Sex Research* 29(3), 361–387.

Goodrich, Thelma Jean. (1994, September/October). Turning down the temperature. *Family Therapy Networker,* 86–89.

Gorer, Geoffrey. (1971). *Sex and Marriage in England Today.* London: Nelson.

Gottman, John Mordechai. (1993). *What Predicts Divorce?: The Relationship Between Marital Processes and Marital Outcomes.* UK: Psychology Press.

Gottman, John Mordechai; Gottman, Julie S.; and De Claire, Joan. (2007). *10 Lessons to Transform Your Marriage: America's Love Lab Experts Share Their Strategies for Strengthening Your Relationship.* New York: Three Rivers Press.

Gottman, John Mordechai, and Silver, Nan. (1994). *Why Marriages Succeed or Fail.* New York: Simon & Schuster.

Gray, John (2004). *Men Are from Mars, Women Are from Venus.* New York: HarperCollins.

Gregory, Alex. (2003, August 4). "Male Prostitute." *The New Yorker.*

Griffiths, Mark. (2004). Sex addiction on the Internet. *Janus Head* 7(1), 188–217.

Gunn, Thom. (1992). The hug. *The Man with Night Sweats.* New York: Farrar, Straus, & Giroux.

Hammen, C.; Ellicott, A.; and Gitlin, M. (1989). Vulnerability to specific life events and prediction of course of disorder in unipolar depressed patients. *Canadian Journal of Behavioral Science* 21, 377–388.

Harley, Willard F., Jr. (1986). *His Needs, Her Needs: Building an Affair-Proof Marriage.* Old Tappan, N.J.: Fleming H. Powell.

Bibliography

Heiman, Julia; LoPiccolo, Leslie; and LoPiccolo, Joseph. (1976). *Becoming Orgasmic.* Englewood Cliffs, N.J.: Prentice-Hall.

Hendrix, Harville. (2001). *Getting the Love You Want: A Guide for Couples.* New York: Holt.

Herman, Judith Lewis. (1992). *Trauma and Recovery.* New York: Basic.

Hertlein, Katherine M., and Webster, Megan (2008). Technology, relationships, and problems: A research synthesis. *Journal of Marital and Family Therapy* 34(4), 445–460.

Hetherington, E. Mavis. (1989). Coping with family transitions: Winners, losers, and survivors. *Child Development* 60, 1–14.

Hetherington, E. Mavis. (1992). Coping with marital transitions. *Monographs of the Society for Research in Child Development* Serial No. 227, 57(2–3).

Heyn, Dalma. (1992). *The Erotic Silence of the American Wife.* New York: Turtle Bay.

Hibbs, B. Janet, and Getzen Karen J. (2010). *Try to See It My Way: Being Fair in Love and Marriage.* New York: Avery.

Hite, Shere. (1987). *Women and Love.* New York: Knopf.

Horney, Karen. (1950). *Neurosis and Human Growth: The Struggle Toward Self-Realization.* New York: Norton.

Hunter, R. C. A. (1978, April). Forgiveness, retaliation, and paranoid reactions. *Journal of Canadian Psychiatric Association* 23, 167–173.

Jack, Dana Crowley. (1991). *Silencing the Self: Women and Depression.* Cambridge, Mass.: Harvard University Press.

Janus, Samuel S., and Cynthia L. (1993). *The Janus Report on Sexual Behavior.* New York: Wiley.

Johnson, Robert R. (2011). The neurobiology of misbehavior: Understanding and treating addiction, thrill-seeking, and dry-drunk behavior. Presentation in Westport, Conn.

Johnson, Susan, and Zuccarini, Dino. (2010, October). Integrating sex and attachment in emotionally focused couple therapy. *Journal of Marital and Family Therapy* 36(4), 431–445.

Jung, Carl G. (1959). *Basic Writings.* Edited by Violet de Laszlo. New York: Modern Library.

Kaplan, Bruce Eric. (1993, March 29). *New Yorker Magazine.*

Kelly, Joan B. (1993). Current research on children's postdivorce adjustment: No simple answers. *Family and Conciliation Courts Review* 31(1), 29–49.

Kelly, Joan B. (2000, August). Children's adjustment in conflicted marriage and divorce: A decade review of research. *Journal of the American Academy of Child and Adolescent Psychiatry* 39(8), 963–973.

Kernberg, Otto, interviewed by Linda Wolfe. (1978, June). Why some people can't love. *Psychology Today,* 55–59.

Kerner, Ian (2010, August 5). Does too much porn mess with a guy's sex skills? http://www.goodinbed.com/sex_on_the_brain/2010/08/does-too-much-porn-mess-with-a-guys-sex-skills/.

Bibliography

Kingsolver, Barbara. (1993). *Pigs in Heaven*. New York: HarperCollins.

Kinsey, Alfred C.; Pomeroy, Wardell B.; Martin, Clyde E.; and Gebhard, Paul H. (1953). *Sexual Behavior in the Human Female*. Philadelphia: Saunders.

Koss, Mary; Goodman, Lisa; Fitzgerald, Louise; Russo, Nancy; Keita, Gwendolyn; and Browne, Angela Browne. (1994). *No Safe Haven*. Washington, D.C.: American Psychological Association.

Kushner, Harold S. (2004). *When Bad Things Happen to Good People*. New York: Anchor Books.

Laumann, Edward O.; Gagnon, John H.; Michael, Robert T.; and Michaels, Stuart. (1994). *The Social Organization of Sexuality*. Chicago: University of Chicago Press.

Lawson, Annette. (1988). *Adultery: An Analysis of Love and Betrayal*. New York: Basic.

Lerner, Harriet Goldhor. (1989). *The Dance of Intimacy: A Woman's Guide to Courageous Acts of Change in Key Relationships*. New York: HarperCollins.

Lerner, Harriet Goldhor. (1993). *The Dance of Deception: Pretending and Truth-Telling in Women's Lives*. New York: HarperCollins.

Lerner, Harriet Goldhor. (2012). *Marriage Rules: A Manual for the Married and the Coupled Up*. New York: Gotham Books.

Lovinger, Robert J. (1990). *Religion and Counseling: The Psychological Impact of Religious Belief*. New York: Continuum.

Masters, William H., and Johnson, Virginia E. (1970). *Human Sexual Inadequacy*. London: J. & A. Churchill.

Mayo Clinic Staff. (2010, September 1). Depression in women: Understanding the gender gap. MayoClinic.com/health/depression/MH00035.

McAdams, Dan P., and Constantian, Carol A. (1983). Intimacy and affiliation motives in daily living: An experience sampling analysis. *Journal of Personality and Social Psychology* 45, 851–861.

McCullough, Michael E., and Worthington, Everett L., Jr. (1994). Encouraging clients to forgive people who have hurt them: Review, critique, and research prospectus. *Journal of Psychology and Theology* 22(1), 3–20.

McNamara, Damian. (2007, November). Latest evidence on PTSD may bring changes in DSM-V: Subthreshold events can lead to disorder. *Clinical Psychiatry News* 35(11).

Mercer, Cheryl. (1988). *Grown-ups*. New York: Putnam.

Michael, Robert T.; Gagnon, John H.; Laumann, Edward O.; and Kolata, Gina. (1994). *Sex in America: A Definitive Survey*. Boston: Little, Brown.

Money, John. (1980). *Love and Lovesickness: The Science of Sex, Gender Difference, and Pair Bonding*. Baltimore: Johns Hopkins University Press.

Money, John. (1988). *Love Maps: Clinical Concepts of Sexual/Erotic Health and Pathology, Paraphilia, and Gender Transposition in Childhood, Adolescence, and Maturity*. Buffalo, N.Y.: Prometheus.

Murphy, Jeffrie G. (1982). Forgiveness and resentment. *Midwest Studies in Philosophy* 7, 503–516.

Bibliography

Nadler, Arie and Dotan, Iris. (1992). Commitment and rival attractiveness: Their effects on male and female reactions to jealousy-arousing situations. *Sex Roles* 26(7/8), 293–310.

National Task Force. (1990). "Women and Depression: Risk Factors and Treatment Issues." Edited by Ellen McGrath, Gwendolyn Puryear Keita, Bonnie R. Strickland, and Nancy Felipe Russo. Washington, D.C.: American Psychological Association.

Nelson, Tammy. (2008). *Getting the Sex You Want: Shed Your Inhibitions and Reach New Heights of Passion Together.* Beverly, Ma.: Quiver.

Nietzsche, F. W. (1887). *The Genealogy of Morals* (trans. by P. Watson). London: S.P.C.K.

Nolen-Hoeksema, Susan. (1987). Sex differences in unipolar depression: Evidence and theory. *Psychological Bulletin* 101(2), 259–282.

Norton, Arthur J., and Miller, Louisa F. (1992). Marriage, divorce, and remarriage in the 1990's. *Current Population Reports,* 23–180. Washington, D.C.: U.S. Government Printing Office.

Oppenheimer, Mark. (2011, June 30). Married, with infidelities. *New York Times Magazine,* 24.

Parker-Pope, Tara. (2010, January 26). Marriage and women over 40. *New York Times,* well.blogs.nytimes.com/2010/01/26/marriage-and-women-over-40.

Perel, Esther. (2007). *Mating in Captivity: Unlocking Erotic Intelligence.* New York: Harper.

Person, Ethel Spector. (1988). *Dreams of Love and Fateful Encounters: The Power of Romantic Passion.* New York: Norton.

Pittman, Frank. (1989). *Private Lies.* New York: Norton.

Quick Reference to the Diagnostic and Statistical Manual IV-TR. (2000). Washington, D.C.: American Psychiatric Association.

Random House Dictionary of the English Language, 2nd ed. unabridged. (1987). Edited by Stuart Berg Flexner and Leonore Crary Hauck. New York: Random House.

Reibstein, Janet, and Richards, Martin. (1993). *Sexual Arrangements: Marriage and the Temptation of Infidelity.* New York: Scribner's.

Reinisch, June M., with Beasley, Ruth. (1990). *The Kinsey Institute New Report on Sex.* New York: St. Martin's.

Rosenbloom, Stephanie. (2011, June 19). Ambition + desire = trouble. *New York Times.*

Ross, M., and Holmberg, D. (1990). Recounting the past: Gender differences in the recall of events in the history of a close relationship. In *Self-Inference Processes: The Ontario Symposium, Volume 6.* Edited by J. M. Olson and M. P. Zanna. Hillsdale, N.J.: Erlbaum, 135–152.

Saint-Exupéry, Antoine de. (2000). *The Little Prince.* New York: Harcourt Inc.

Scarf, Maggie. (1986, November). Intimate partners. *Atlantic Monthly,* 49–54, 91–93.

Bibliography

Scarf, Maggie. (2008). *Intimate Partners: Patterns in Love and Marriage.* New York: Ballantine Books.

Shaver, Phillip R., and Hazen, Cindy. (1988). A biased overview of the study of love. *Journal of Social and Personal Relationships* 5, 473–501.

Simon, Sidney B., and Simon, Suzanne. (1990). *Forgiveness: How to Make Peace With Your Past and Get on with Your Life.* New York: Warner.

Smedes, Lewis B. (1984). *Forgive and Forget: Healing the Hurts We Don't Deserve.* San Francisco: Harper & Row.

Smith, Brendan L. (2011, March). Are Internet affairs different? *American Psychological Association* 42(3), 48.

Spring, Janis Abrahms. (2005). *How Can I Forgive You?: The Courage to Forgive, the Freedom Not To.* New York: HarperCollins.

Stanley, Scott M. (1986). *Commitment and the Maintenance and Enhancement of Relationships.* Unpublished doctoral dissertation. University of Denver.

Stanley, Scott M., and Markman, Howard. (1992, August). Assessing commitment in personal relationships. *Journal of Marriage and the Family* 54, 595–608.

Steiner, Peter. (1993, July 5). On the Internet, nobody knows you're a dog. *The New Yorker* 69 (20), 61.

Sternberg, Robert J., and Barnes, Michael L. (eds.). (1988). *The Psychology of Love.* New Haven, Conn.: Yale University Press.

Stuart, Richard. (1980). *Helping Couples Change: A Social Learning Approach to Marital Therapy.* New York: Guilford.

Stuart, Richard B., and Jacobson, Barbara. (1985). *Second Marriage: Make It Happy! Make It Last!* New York: Norton.

Tannen, Deborah. (2001). *You Just Don't Understand: Men and Women in Conversation.* New York: Quill.

Thomas, Sandra P. (1993). *Women and Anger.* New York: Springer.

Thompson, Marjorie J. (1992, March/April). Moving toward forgiveness. *Weavings: A Journal of the Christian Spiritual Life* VII(2), 16–26.

Thrall, Grace. (1995, April). *Forgiveness: At the Interface of Psychiatry and Spirituality.* Paper presented at the Institute of Living, Hartford, Conn.

Toufexis, Anastasia. (1993, February 15). The right chemistry. *Time Magazine,* 49–51.

Valenstein, E. S., and Beer, B. (1964, March). Continuous opportunity for reinforcing brain stimulation. *Journal of the Experimental Analysis of Behavior* 7, 183–184.

Viorst, Judith. (1984). *Necessary Losses.* New York: Simon & Schuster.

Walsh, Anthony. (1991). *The Science of Love: Understanding Love and Its Effects on Mind and Body.* Buffalo, N.Y.: Prometheus.

Weiner, Marcella Bakur, and Starr, Bernard D. (1991). *Stalemates: The Truth About Extra-Marital Affairs.* Far Hills, N.J.: New Horizon.

Weiss, Robert, and Schneider, Jennifer P. (2006). *Untangling the Web: Sex, Porn, and Fantasy Obsession in the Internet Age.* New York: Alyson Books.

Bibliography

Whisman, Mark A.; Dixon, Amy E.; and Johnson, Benjamin. *Therapists' Perspectives of Couple Problems and Treatment Issues in the Practice of Couple Therapy.* Unpublished manuscript.

Williams, Warwick. (1988). *Rekindling Desire: Bringing Your Sexual Relationship Back to Life.* Oakland, Calif.: New Harbinger.

Winterson, Jeanette. (1989). *The Passion.* New York: Vintage.

Winterson, Jeanette. (1994). *Written on the Body.* New York: First Vintage International Edition.

Wise, R. A. (1996). Addictive drugs and brain stimulation reward. *Annual Review of Neuroscience* (19), 319–340.

Wright, Robert. (1988, July 11). Why men are still beasts. *New Republic,* 27–32.

Wylie, Mary Sykes. (2010). The www.Addiction. *Psychotherapy Networker* 34(5), 30.

Young, Jeffrey E., and Klosko, Janet S. (1993). *Reinventing Your Life.* New York: Dutton.

Young, Kimberly S. (2000). *Getting Web Sober: Help for Cybersex Addicts and Their Families.* Ebooklet.

Young, Kimberly S. (2001). *Tangled in the Web: Understanding Cybersex from Fantasy to Addiction.* Indiana: 1stBooks.

INDEX

Abandonment: effects of childhood experience of, 118, 119–21, 133–34; feeling of, 9–11

Abuse: childhood experience of, 119–21; expression of rage and possibility of, 187

Accidents; and effects on a relationship, 147

Addiction: and effects on a relationship, 149; online sexual, 280–82, 289

Adequacy, feelings of: childhood experience of, 125; hurt partner and, 118, 125–26; unfaithful partner and, 118, 125–26

Adultery: number of partners involved in, 1, 303–4n1; reactions of others to, 29–30, 31; transgenerational injuries from parental, 132–39. *See also* Affairs

Affair-person: saying goodbye to, 191; sexual fantasies about, 208, 242–45; use of term, 3

Affairs: advantages of revealing, 296–301; assumptions about, 46–47, 271; behavior constituting, 1–2; in cyberspace, 268–91, 309n2, 310n7; definition of, 269–70, 288; disadvantages of revealing, 293–96; discovery versus disclosure of, 309n2; effects of ongoing, 68; justification of, 46–47; learning from, 115–56; number of partners involved in, 1, 303–4n1;

reactions of others to, 29–30, 31; reasons for having, 60–61; responses to. *See* Response of the hurt partner; Response of the unfaithful partner; stages of healing after, 4–5; suspicions about, 19–20, 69–70, 121, 211–14; use of terms in, 3

Affection; and deciding to recommit, 87, 107–9

Ahrons, Connie, 104

AIDS testing, 245–46

Albee, Edward, 60

Alcoholism: as compulsive behavior, 23; effects on a relationship of, 149

Allen, Woody, 275

Ambivalence: deciding whether to recommit or quit and, 107–9; paralysis in decision-making and, 55–56

Anger: cathartic expression of, 185; as a man's response to the affair, 33, 35–36; trust-building techniques and, 171, 172–73, 176–77; of the unfaithful partner, 41, 44, 45. *See also* Rage

Antisocial personality disorder, 72

Anxiety: compulsive behavior as a response to, 23–25; as a response of the unfaithful partner, 41, 43–44

Assumptions: ability to change after the affair and, 87, 94–98; ability to speak up and not be silent and, 181–84; about cyberspace activities, 271–86;

Index

Index

Dyn, Barry, 79
Dysfunctional Thought Form, 213, 219, 221, 230, 241

Eating; as compulsive behavior, 23–24
Economic factors; and divorce, 34–35, 101–2
Efran, Jay S., 119
Emotional abuse; childhood experience of, 119–21
Emotional component of change, 152, 153, 155
Emotional intimacy; and sexual intimacy, 251
Emotions: attitudes about relationships learned in childhood and, 118; cathartic expression of, 185; deciding whether to recommit or quit and, 110; physiological impact of the affair and, 11–13; psychological impact of the affair and, 13–33; romantic love and changes in, 75. *See also specific emotion*
Empty-nest syndrome, 149
Endorphins, 76
Erikson, Erik, 265
Estés, Clarissa Pinkola, 67, 82, 258
Euripides, 37
Exercise; as compulsive behavior, 23–24
Exercises: challenging assumptions using a Dysfunctional Thought Form, 213–14, 219–21, 230, 240–41; covenant of promises, 263–65; on critical growth experiences in childhood, 130–32; on effects of parental infidelities, 137–39; on Flip-Flop Factor regarding personality traits, 139–46; on responsibility sharing, 151–56; sensate focus, 225; thought stopping in, 213; trust-building, 286. *See also* Suggestions
Expectations about love and marriage, 77–79
Extramarital affairs. *See* Affairs

Failure; and effects on a relationship, 149
Faith; loss of, as an impact of the affair, 14, 27–28
Faludi, Susan, 35
Families. *See* Childhood of partners; Children of partners

Fantasies: cyberspace activities and, 269, 271, 274, 275–77, 278–79, 280, 288, 289, 290; sexual, 242–45, 269, 271, 274, 275–77, 278–79, 280, 288, 289, 290
Fears: of loneliness, 101. *See also* Doubts
Feeling Good Together (Burns), 161
Feelings: attitudes about relationships learned in childhood and, 118; loss and. *See* Loss; normalizing. *See* Normalizing feelings; physiological impact of the affair and, 11–13; psychological impact of the affair and, 13–33; unfaithful partner and identification of, 40–41. *See also specific feeling*
Flanigan, Beverly, 256
Flip-Flop Factor regarding personality traits: description of, 139–45; exercise on, 145–46
For Each Other (Barbach), 216
Forgiveness, 252–67; assumptions about, 252–58; being a good person and, 258–60; conflict in the relationship after, 260; covenant of promises in, 263–65; definitions of, 253, 256; disappearance of negative feelings related to, 254–55; forgetting the injury and, 257–58; forgiving too easily in, 258–60; hope and renewal after, 265–67; impatience of unfaithful partner seeking, 42; listening and, 198, 199; restitution and, 256–57; of self, 58–59, 261–63
Forgiving the Unforgivable (Flanigan), 256
Franck, Dan, 13
Freud, Sigmund, 206
Friday, Nancy, 243
Friends: feeling of isolation and, 52–53; feeling of loss of connection and, 30, 31; reactions to adultery by, 30, 31
Fun: childhood experience of, 118, 127; hurt partner and letting go and, 118, 127, 128; unfaithful partner and letting go and, 118, 127, 128

Gender-specific patterns of response, 35–38. *See also* Sex differences
Getting the Love You Want (Hendrix), 161

Index

Index

Index

Order; loss of sense of, as an impact of the affair, 13, 25–26

Orgasm; emphasis on, 235–37, 308n14

Parents (of partners): abandonment and abuse by, 119–21; attitudes about relationships learned from, 116, 117–39; communication skills influenced by, 187–88; damage from infidelities of, 132–39; feeling of isolation by unfaithful partner and, 52; feeling of loss of connection by hurt partner and, 29, 31; functioning independently and, 122; ideas about love and experience of, 70, 83–84; listening skills influenced by, 199–200

Partners: compulsive behavior in checking up on, 22–23; critical growth experiences in childhood and later choice of, 118–19; effects of ongoing affairs on, 68; Flip-Flop Factor regarding personality traits of, 139–46; illusion of romantic love and, 82; responsibility sharing exercise for, 151–56. *See also* Hurt partners; Unfaithful partners

Perel, Esther, 282–83

Person, Ethel Spector, 48, 74, 76

Personality disorders; and unrequited love, 72–73

Personality traits; and Flip-Flop Factor, 139–46

Physical abuse: childhood experience of, 119–21; expression of rage and possibility of, 187

Physiological impacts: of the affair, 11–13; of emotional confrontations, 201

Pittman, Frank, 299, 301

Pledge; in rebuilding a relationship, 111

Pornography; Internet and, 270, 274, 280, 281, 287, 288

Positive attributes of partners; and Flip-Flop Factor, 139–45

Positive feelings: childhood experience of, 118; forgiveness and, 236–37

Post-Traumatic Stress Disorder, 11, 304n1

Pregnancy; and effects on a relationship, 149

Private Lies (Pittman), 301

Psychological impact of the affair, 13–33. *See also* Loss

Purpose; loss of sense of, as an impact of the affair, 14, 32–33

Rabbi; and loss of faith, 27–28

Rage: betrayal and expression of, 37, 42; cathartic expression of, 185; listening and, 198; possibility of physical abuse and, 187. *See also* Anger

Rationalizations justifying the infidelity, 46–47

Reacting to the affair, 7–64; hurt partner's response in, 9–38; as a stage of healing, 4–5; unfaithful partner's response in, 39–64

Rebuilding a relationship, 113–267; making a pledge for, 111; nonreactive listening and, 111–12; as a stage of healing, 5; suggestions for getting started in, 109–12; time projection for, 111. *See also* Affairs: learning from; Communication skills; Forgiveness; Sex: after the affair; Trust

Reciprocity; and personality disorders, 72

Relationships: assumptions about working of, 25–26; compromise in, 285; confronting expectations about, 77–79; critical life events affecting, 146–49; cyberspace as threat to, 271, 272–75, 277–79; definition of affair and, 270; early life experiences of partners and undermining of, 117–32; effects of parental infidelities on adult, 132–39; emotional attunement in, 283–85; emotional connections with others and, 118, 123–25; feeling safe or secure and, 118, 119–21; Flip-Flop Factor regarding personality traits and, 139–46; functioning independently and, 118, 122–23; impact of cyberspace activities on, 268–91; mistrust of a partner's motives for returning to, 87, 99–101; mistrust of a partner's motives for staying in, 87, 101–3; online partnerships as means for strengthening, 282–86; rebuilding. *See* Rebuilding a relationship; rules of, 270; secrecy about the affair and,

Index

Index

Walsh, Anthony, 76

Weight gain or loss; and loss of self-respect, 17

Will to live; loss of, as an impact of the affair, 14, 32–33

Williams, Warwick, 223

Winterson, Jeanette, 75

Wives. *See* Hurt partners; Marriage; Partners; Unfaithful partners; Women

Women: anguishing over an affair by, 62–63; attempts to preserve the relationship by, 33, 34–35; cyberspace activities and, 270–71; depression of, as a response to the affair, 33, 35–36; economic consequences of divorce for, 34–35, 101–2; feeling of inadequacy as companions held by, 36–37; involvement in extramarital affairs by, 1, 303–4n1; love as justification for an affair and, 61; reasons for having affairs given by, 60–61. *See also* Sex differences

Woolf, Leonard, 237

Wright, Robert, 60

Yeats, William Butler, 157

Zuccarini, Dino, 283

About the Authors

JANIS ABRAHMS SPRING, Ph.D., ABPP, is a board certi-
fied clinical psychologist and a nationally acclaimed expert on
issues of trust, intimacy, and forgiveness. She is the author of
the award–winning books, *How Can I Forgive You?: The Courage to Forgive, the Freedom Not To,* which presents a radically
new approach to healing interpersonal wounds, and *Life with
Pop: Lessons on Caring for an Aging Parent.* A recipient of the
Connecticut Psychological Association's Award for Distin-
guished Contribution to the Practice of Psychology, Dr. Spring
trains thousands of therapists each year and is known for the
richness and originality of her clinical skills.

Dr. Spring received her B.A., magna cum laude, from
Brandeis University, her Ph.D. in clinical psychology from the
University of Connecticut, and her postgraduate training from
Aaron T. Beck, M.D., at the Center for Cognitive Therapy at the
University of Pennsylvania. A former clinical supervisor in the
department of psychology at Yale University, she often serves as
a guest expert in the national media (*Good Morning America,
NPR,* the *New York Times,* the Huffington Post, and others). In
private practice for thirty-five years, Dr. Spring resides in West-

port, Connecticut, and can be reached at www.janisaspring .com. She and her husband, Michael Spring, have four sons and five grandchildren.

MICHAEL SPRING is a former publisher of the *Frommer's Travel Guides* at John Wiley & Sons. He has a B.A. from Haverford College and an M.A. in English literature from Columbia University.

BOOKS BY
JANIS ABRAHMS SPRING

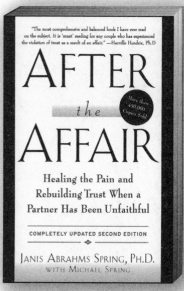

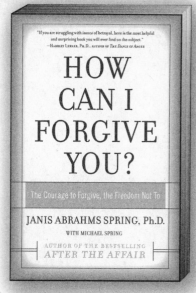

AFTER THE AFFAIR
Healing the Pain and Rebuilding Trust When a Partner Has Been Unfaithful

Completely Revised and Updated, With a New Chapter on Affairs in Cyberspace

ISBN 978-0-06-212270-4 (paperback)

Infidelity is often the deathblow to a relationship. But it can also be a wake-up call, challenging couples to grow from the experience. Offering concrete, practical strategies, this award-winning book can help partners cope with raging emotions, make a thoughtful decision about their future, and, if they choose to recommit, reclaim a life together.

"The most comprehensive and balanced book I have ever read on the subject."
—Dr. Harville Hendrix

HOW CAN I FORGIVE YOU?
The Courage to Forgive, the Freedom Not To

ISBN 978-0-06-000931-1 (paperback)

Drawing from 35 years of clinical experience, Dr. Spring offers a radical, new approach to healing that helps hurt parties overcome the corrosive effects of hate and get on with life—*with or without forgiving*. She also teaches offenders how they can earn forgiveness. Beautifully written and compelling, *How Can I Forgive You?* is bound to change forever the way we recover from interpersonal wounds.

"If you are struggling with issues of betrayal…here is the most helpful and surprising book you will ever find on the subject."
—Harriet Lerner, Ph.D., author of *The Dance of Anger*

Visit www.janisaspring.com for more information.

Available wherever books are sold, or call 1-800-331-3761 to order.